SUNDAY GOSPELS OF KIAHK, TUBAH AND AMSHIR

TREASURES OF THE FATHERS OF THE CHURCH SERIES

Our paramount objective in this series is to introduce the believers to the trialogue of faith—the harmony among the Holy Scriptures, the Church Fathers, and the rites of the Coptic Orthodox Church. Throughout this symphony of discourse, the believer not only reads the Holy Scriptures, but understands it through the homilies, exegeses, and commentaries of the Church Fathers. This is a brief and simple companion to the Coptic Orthodox lectionary. We hope and pray that through this series, the Holy Scriptures, the Church Fathers, and the Church rites are not only introduced to each believer, but are experienced by the believer as a deep source of blessing, wisdom, and faith.

His Grace Bishop Serapion
Editor-in-Chief

Father Ishak Azmy Yacoub
Father John Paul Abdelsayed
Series Editors

Volumes Currently in Print

VOLUME *Ia*
Sunday Gospels of Tute, Babeh and Hatour

VOLUME *Ib*
Sunday Gospels of Kiahk, Tubah and Amshir

VOLUME II
Sunday Gospels of the Great Lent

VOLUME III
The Holy Pascha

VOLUME IV
Sunday Gospels of the Holy Fifty Days

Ⲥⲩⲛ Ⲑⲉⲱ Ⲓⲥⲭⲩⲣⲟⲥ

TREASURES OF THE FATHERS OF THE CHURCH

VOLUME IB

Sunday Gospels of Kiahk, Tubah and Amshir

PATRISTIC MEDITATIONS ON THE SUNDAY GOSPELS OF THE COPTIC LECTIONARY

Saint Paul Brotherhood Press

Coptic Orthodox Diocese of Los Angeles, Southern California and Hawaii

SUNDAY GOSPELS OF KIAHK, TUBAH AND AMSHIR

SAINT PAUL BROTHERHOOD PRESS

Coptic Orthodox Diocese of Los Angeles, Southern California, and Hawaii
Saint Paul Brotherhood
38740 Avenida La Cresta
Murrieta, California 92562
www.SaintPaulBrotherhood.org

ISBN 978-0-9800065-8-2
LCCN 2001012345

PRINTED IN THE UNITED STATES OF AMERICA

"The Faith which I was taught by the Holy Fathers, which I taught at all times: without adjusting according to the times, this Faith I will never stop teaching. I was born with it and I live by it."

—St. Gregory the Theologian

His Holiness Pope Tawadros II
118th Pope of Alexandria and
Patriarch of the Great See of Saint Mark

His Eminence Metropolitan Serapion
Metropolitan of Los Angeles
Southern California, and Hawaii

CONTENTS

PREFACE

As a mother feeds her child—with the proper food, at the proper time, and with the proper utensils—the Church feeds us the Word of God in manageable portions, at different times of the liturgical year, and using the golden spoon of the Church Fathers. In all wisdom, tender care and love, our Mother Church yearns to feed her children the Holy Scriptures and nourish them with the Bread of Life.

With great joy and enthusiasm, we present to you Sunday Gospels of Kiyahk, Tubah, Amshir, Volume *Ib* of the *Treasures of the Fathers of the Church* series. This book contains excerpts from patristic writings on the Sunday Gospels of these three blessed months of the Coptic Church year.

In addition, the book features several commentaries and notes on the Coptic lectionary to enhance the believer's understanding and appreciation of depth of the rites of the Church. Our paramount objective in this series is to introduce the believers to the trialogue of faith—the harmony among the Holy Scriptures, the Church Fathers, and the rites of the Coptic Orthodox Church. Throughout this symphony of discourse, the believer not only reads the Holy Scriptures, but understands it through the homilies, exegeses, and commentaries of the Church Fathers. This is a brief and simple companion to the Coptic Orthodox lectionary. We hope and pray that through this series, the Holy Scriptures, the Church Fathers, and the Church rites are not only introduced to each believer, but are experienced by the believer as a deep source of blessing, wisdom, and faith.

With the Grace of God and His mighty Hand, the St. Paul Brotherhood Press has published Volumes Ia, II, III and IV of this series on the Great Lent, Holy Pascha and the Holy Fifty Days. This is the fifth work published in the series, which, like the others, includes many excerpts from the patristic writings of St. Athanasius, St. Cyril of Alexandria, St. John Chrysostom, St. Gregory of Nazianzus, St. Basil the Great, the Scholar Origen, and many others. God willing, we hope to also publish Volume V for the last months of the Coptic Year.

This book is also published on the occasions of the one-year anniversary of the enthronement of our beloved, His Holiness Pope Tawadros II. On this blessed occasion, God also granted us the opportunity to ordain two blessed deacons to the presbyterate for the Brotherhood, Deacon Theophilus Paul and Deacon Antony Paul who both labored in the production of this book. May the Lord continue to bless their priestly service throughout our beloved Diocese to yield fruit a hundredfold.

May our Lord Jesus Christ, the Good One and Lover of Mankind, shower us continually with His love, bless us with every spiritual blessing, shepherd us with His Mighty Hand, and raise us up forever. Through the never-ending intercessions of the Holy Theotokos St. Mary, St. Paul the Apostle, and the prayers of all His angels, apostles, martyrs, and saints who pleased Him from the beginning, we pray that this work will be a source of blessing for the glory of His Name and the spread of His Kingdom.

Glory be to the Holy Trinity, our God, unto the Ages of all ages, Amen.

Bishop Serapion

The Commemoration of the First Ecumenical Council at Nicaea (325 A.D.) and the Anniversary of the Ordination of His Holiness Pope Tawadros II (2012 A.D.)
9 Hatour 1730
18 November 2013

ABBREVIATIONS

ANF	Ante-Nicene Fathers Series
ACW	Ancient Christian Writers Series
FCS	Fathers of the Church Series
NPNF	Nicene and Post-Nicene Fathers
PG	*Patrologia Graeca*
PL	*Patrologia Latina*
PLS	*Patrologia Latina, Supplementum*
SC	*Sources Chretiennes*
SSGF	Sunday Sermons of the Great Fathers

INTRODUCTION

The Holy Scriptures enjoy a special prominence in the Coptic Orthodox Church, not only in Her liturgical life, but also in the lives of the believers, because they constitute the manifestation of God's plan for our salvation. For this reason, the Fathers of the Church considered the importance of arranging specific readings from the Holy Scriptures in the Church's lectionary to satisfy believers' needs through their prayers in the Divine Liturgy.

Tile Church readings that are read through the Coptic year come from five main books or volumes, called *Katameros,* which is a Greek word meaning "according to the days." It consists of two syllables: *kata,* which means "according to" and *meros,* or "the days." The volumes of the *Katameros* are 1) annual cycle for the Sunday Gospels, 2) the Great Lent, 3) the Holy Pascha, 4) the Holy Fifty Days, and 5) daily readings in the annual season.

Accordingly, Saint Paul Brotherhood has published this Treasures of the Fathers series as a patristic guide to these Church Readings, one volume for each collection of readings. Thus, far the Brotherhood has published four major volumes in this series: The Holy Pascha (2006); The Holy Fifty Days (2007), The Great Lent (2009), and Sundays Readings of Tute, Babeh, and Hatour (2011). Now, dear reader, we present Sunday Readings of Kiahk, Tubah, and Amshir.

The Sunday Readings differ from those of the weekdays. The latter, based on the Synaxarium, are arranged according to the commemorations of the saints, such as the Holy Virgin Mary, the angels, the apostolic fathers and our fathers, the martyrs. However, the Sundays Readings are selected on an entirely distinct bases.

By the guidance of the Holy Spirit, the Church conceived that all the Sundays Readings throughout the year should share a common theme: "the work of the Holy Trinity in the Church" and its impact on the management, sacrifice, salvation, guidance, and leadership of the Church. These readings feature the sayings and deeds of our Lord Jesus Christ, organized in thirteen topics according to the months of the year to suit the starting and the ending of the Coptic year and the work of our Lord Jesus Christ in the salvation of man. In this arrangement, the agricultural year was also considered. Thus, for example, two of the Sundays of the month of Hatour concern the parable of the Sower, since this time of year corresponds to the period of sowing.

Now, let us briefly examine the themes of the Sunday gospels of the second three months of the Coptic year, covered in this volume.

The Month of Kiahk comes with its hymns and praises to prepare the faithful of the Church to receive the Savior. These readings all concern the first chapter of the gospel of our teacher, St. Luke, as follows: The First Sunday contains (Lk. 1:1-25) the joyful announcement of the birth of St. John the Baptist as a forerunner who will pave the way for the coming Savior. In the Second Sunday we read of the cheerful announcement of the birth of the Savior, in Luke 1:26-38. The Third Sunday concentrates on Luke 1:39-56, which declares the visit of St. Mary to Elizabeth and the praise of St. Mary which highlights His fairness and mercy. The Fourth Sunday involves the birth of St. John the Baptist and Zacharias starts talking and the infertility of Elisabeth. It ends with the announcement of the Savior coming to the world (Lk. 1:57-80).

The month of Tubah announces the salvation of Jesus Christ to all the nations. In the First Sunday we read Matt. 2:13-23, the visit of the Holy Family to Egypt the land of pagans. The psalm of the Liturgy says, "The Lord has made known His salvation; His righteousness He has revealed in the sight of the nations. He has remembered His mercy and His faithfulness to the house of Israel; all the ends of the earth have seen the salvation of our God" (Ps. 98:2, 3). In the Second Sunday, we read Luke 11:27-36, which shows us the blessings of salvation if we light our lamps and put it on the lampstand, thereby converting the darkness in us into light, and enlightening the way for others. For that reason the readings of the Third Sunday concern the life of salvation and the everlasting life with Jesus Christ which the believers enjoy. "He who believes in the Son has everlasting life." (Jn. 3:36) The Fourth Sunday presents the lighting of our insight for salvation through the miracle of opening the eyes of the man who was blind from birth (Jn. 9:1-38).

Whereas during the blessed month of Kiahk our Lord Jesus Christ appears as the Incarnate Logos; and during the blessed month of Tubah He is manifested as the Living Water and the Light of the World; in the blessed month of Amshir, He is presented as the Bread of Life. The four main Sunday gospels of Amshir are read from the sixth chapter of the Gospel according to Saint John. The First Sunday focuses on the eternal food that does not perish, the Second Sunday on the Five Loaves and two fish, and the third on the Bread of Life. After concluding the passage of John 6 in these first two sundays, the Church proceeds with the message from Luke 6 and the Story of Zacchaeus.

For this reason, I ask you, my dear reader, to read this book and to follow the homilies and the sayings of our fathers on each Sunday, so that you may discover how the Church utilizes the Holy Scriptures.

Asking you to remember us in your prayers so that our Lord Jesus may grant us the blessings of those treasures hidden in the Holy Scriptures through the prayers of our beloved father His Holiness Pope Tawadros II, and his partner in the apostolic service, our beloved father, His Grace Bishop Serapion, who has helped and supported us so much to publish this series. May God grant us every heavenly blessing through their prayers.

For this reason, I ask you, my dear reader, to read this book and to follow the homilies and the sayings of our fathers on each Sunday, so that you may discover how the Church uses the Holy Scriptures.

Asking you to remember us in your prayers so that our Lord Jesus may grant us the blessings of those treasures hidden in the Holy Scriptures through the prayers of our beloved father His Holiness Pope Tawadros II and his partner in the apostolic service, our beloved father, His Grace Bishop Serapion, who has helped and supported us so much to publish this series. May God grant us every heavenly blessing through his prayers.

Father Ishak Boules Azmy

9 Hatour 1730
18 November 2013

THE COPTIC READINGS

St. Paul Brotherhood

Since the ancient days of Judaism before the birth of our Lord, the Jews read daily selections in the Jewish daily prayers of the synagogue, especially on Saturdays.[1] These included one reading from the Pentateuch (five books of Moses) and one reading from the prophesies.

The Christians of the Early Church inherited the importance of such daily readings during the celebrations of worship. By the second century, the Church set selected readings and apostolic writings for many days, especially for the Feasts of Resurrection and Pentecost.[2] Afterwards, additional readings were placed for the feasts of the martyrs and Sundays. By the time of the Ecumenical Council at Nicaea, the Church had at least one lectionary.[3]

For each day of any given Coptic month, the Church assigned nine separate scriptural readings which are compiled in the Coptic *Katameros:*

- Three psalms and three gospel readings (one of each is read during Vespers, Matins, and the Divine Liturgy);
- One selection from Saint Paul's epistles (Pauline);
- •One from the Catholic or general epistles *(Katholikon);* and
- One reading from the Book of Acts *(Praxis).*

---

[1] John Gordon Davies, *A Dictionary of Liturgy and Worship* (SCM Press, 1978), p. 211. This introduction is based on the extended discussion of the readings of the Coptic year, found in Fr. Tadros Malaty's *Introduction to the Coptic Church*

[2] Dom Gregory Dix, *The Shape of Liturgy* (London: A&C Black Publishers, 1975), p. 39.

[3] Ibid., pp. 39, 370.

These readings comprise one common theme for each day of the Coptic year. These themes for each day progress, until the divine readings reach a climax during the gospel reading of each Sunday's Liturgy. Patriarch Cyril II (67th patriarch of Alexandria, 1078 AD) wrote a canon which requires the readings of these five books with their prayers and incense within the church.

Moreover, the Church selects from three additional types of readings throughout the year: the Synaxarium (biographies of saints), the *Difnar* (an additional biography and praise of the saints read during Midnight Psalmody before the Commemoration of the Concluding praise, "Your mercies O my God"), and homilies or sermons of the fathers (like St. Athanasius, St. Cyril, St. John Chrysostom, St. Shenouda the Archimandrite, and others which are read during Holy Pascha week and other occasions).

The Coptic year consists of various seasons (e.g., Great Lent, Holy Fifty Days, Nativity, etc.), each with its own set of readings, called "lectionaries." Through the great wisdom and guidance of the Holy Spirit, the Church arranged the readings of each day and season according to various spiritual themes. A brief summary of these seasons and their themes are as follows:

From the Nayrouz Feast to the Feast of the Cross (Tute 1-19)

The Coptic year starts with the spiritual joy in the Lord together with the desire of the continual renewal as a basis for our spiritual life. The first verse read in the Coptic New Year echoes the theme of this season: "Sing to the Lord a new song." These first two feasts are chanted in the festal and Hosanna tunes as an expression of Christian joy throughout times of suffering in bearing the Cross and martyrdom. Thus, during this time the Church joyfully bears the Cross together with her Heavenly Groom.

Advent Fast (Preparation for the Feast of Nativity)

The Church fasts for 43 days before the Feast of the Nativity and arranges readings that concentrate on God's friendship with man which is realized by the Divine Incarnation.

The Feasts of Nativity, Circumcision and Epiphany

These readings focus on our Lord as our Friend, Who became like us, submitted Himself to the Law and was circumcised. He also entered with us into the Jordan River and was baptized to lift us up to the spiritual circumcision, changing our friendship with Him into true adoption to God (Rom. 8:15; Gal. 4:5; Eph. 1:5) that we might become "members of the household of God" (Eph. 2:19). In other words, the "Divine Friendship" (Nativity) can be realized through two integral actions: the descent of the Word of God unto us (His circumcision like us), and lifting us up to Him by His Holy Spirit (our spiritual circumcision or baptism). He became like us and subjected Himself to the Law which He issued that we might become like Him, children of His Holy Father!

The Fast of the Ninevites ("Pasch of Jonah")

Our adoption to God is realized through the "pass-over" (pasch), for we must die with our Lord Christ, be buried with Him (as though we were in the belly of the great fish), so that we might reign with Him and enjoy the new life. The readings of the "Pasch" of Jonah represent a call to believers that they might read the books of the Old Testament in a new concept, through the events of the Christian Pasch, i.e., the Crucifixion and Resurrection of Christ.

The Readings of the Great Lent

These readings are taken from the Old and New Testaments and they urge us to accept the true and practical communion with Christ, our Pasch, who was slain for our sake. Each of these Sunday gospels focus on our relationship with the Lord, as this period was a special time to prepare catechumens for their upcoming baptism.

The Readings of Holy Pascha Week

The readings from Lazarus Saturday until the Feast of Resurrection are considered the center of all Church readings, for through them the Church follows all the events of salvation, hour by hour, to declare the mystery of the redeeming divine love from the Old and New Testaments. Thus, the believers may live in these events with all their hearts and senses until we may enjoy the Lord's Resurrection.

The Days of Pentecost

This joyful period is full of readings that reveal the mysteries of the Kingdom of Heaven, which in its essence is the enjoyment of communion with the Risen Christ, Who is in the heavens.

The Fast and Feast of the Apostles (5 Abib - 12 July)

The readings of this period are full of preaching, unceasing service, and the acceptance of the apostolic life.

The Fast and Feast of the Holy Virgin Mary (16 Mesra - 22 August)

This period declares the glories that a believer might attain by his unity with the Lord Christ which is revealed through the Holy Virgin Mary as the excellent member among the believers. It also assures us of the communion of saints.

The Preparation for El-Nayrouz

In the last two weeks of the Coptic year, church readings attract our sight and mind towards the events of the end of the world and Christ's last Advent. Church readings prepare the believers to sing: "Come, Lord Jesus." Thus, through this yearly cycle of readings, the Coptic Church presents to us God's love and His redeeming work together with our spiritual struggle, meditation on the heavenly glories, and joyful suffering.

The Coptic Calendar and Its History

The Coptic calendar is among the oldest in history. Some believe it is more than 6000 years old—although the exact date of its origin is unknown. Initially, Egyptians devised a lunar calendar and marked its beginning by the annual Nile flood season, and named its first month after Tute (or Thoth) the moon god. After observing the rising of a bright star (later identified as Sirius Canis Major, or the Dog Star), which appeared before the annual Nile flood, the Egyptians realized that the lunar calendar was inadequate.

Therefore, the ancient Egyptians devised a solar calendar, which is believed to date as far back as 4236 BC.[4] To resolve the incompatibilities between the two calendars, they devised a civil calendar of 365 days. This year had three seasons, each consisting of four months. These seasons were based on the regular flood of the Nile and the agricultural activities in Egypt: Akhit, the inundation season; Perit, the season for planting crops; and Shemu, the season for harvesting. To complete the year a short month of intercalary days were added at its end, called *El Nasie* in Coptic.

The year starts on September 11 in the Gregorian Calendar (September 12 in a leap year). The leap year in the Coptic calendar follows the same rules as the Gregorian so that the extra month always has six days in the year before a Gregorian Leap Year.

---

[4] Ed Rizkalla, "Celebrating the Coptic New Year and Honoring the Martyrs: The Origin and History of the Coptic Calendar," *Watani Magazine,* September, 2003, p. 2.

The Blessed Month of Kiahk

INTRODUCTION TO THE SUNDAY READINGS OF KIAHK

"The promise of the Virgin birth brought by the angel from the Holy Spirit, the guiding star of the Magi, the reverence paid Him in His cradle, the majesty attested by the Baptist, of Him Who condescended to be baptized...and the Father Himself speaks from heaven (to testify to His glory so that)...we might recognize as the Son of God, Him Who was visible as Man, to accomplish the mystery of our salvation."

— *St. Hilary of Poitiers*[5]

Truly our Church has benefited from the sayings of the Fathers of the Church. Their words, sayings, and thoughts are at the very heart of Orthodox theology.

This book is a collection of commentaries of the Church Fathers on the Sunday readings of Kiahk, as well as the Paramon and Feast of the Nativity of our Lord. The majority of these texts are taken from the Ante-Nicene Fathers (Ante Nicene Fathers) and Nicene and Post Nicene Fathers (Nicene and Post Nicene Fathers) collection. The text has been edited for the modern reader.

---

[5] St. Hilary of Poitiers, *On the Trinity,* NPNF S. 2, v. 9, p. 350. Although a great father, St. Hilary is often an obscure and unknown figure among the fathers. As a disciple of Origen, he has natural ties with the Alexandrian fathers. Very little is known about his life, since he rarely spoke of himself in his writings. Neither he nor his writings are mentioned by St. Athanasius nor by the historians of the Church.

The fourth month of the Coptic year is known as *Kiahk* in Arabic (*Koiak* in Bohairic; *Koiahk* in Sahidic). Its name is derived from a ritual vase that was probably used for measuring incense and was very important in the celebration of the funerary feast originally known as the Union of the Ka.[6]

During this month, the great Osirian festivals were held, events of considerable importance to the ancient Egyptians.

Sunday Readings

The Sunday readings of Kiahk are all taken from the Gospel according to St. Luke in such a way that the entire story of the Incarnation in the gospel is read chronologically with 10-20 verses read each Sunday.

SUNDAY	TITLE	PASSAGE
First Sunday	Annunciation of St. John's Birth	Luke 1:1-25
Second Sunday	Holy Annunciation of our Lord	Luke 1:26-38
Third Sunday	St. Mary Visits St. Elizabeth	Luke 1:39-56
Fourth Sunday	Nativity of St. John the Baptist	Luke 1:57-80
Paramon of the Nativity	Preparation for the Holy Nativity of our Lord	Luke 2:1-20
Feast of the Nativity	Holy Nativity of our Lord	Matthew 2:1-12

During this month, the Sunday gospel readings are taken from the first two chapters of the Gospel according to Saint Luke. The selected readings for the Holy Annunciation in the second Sunday is abbreviated here, as

[6] Ceres Wissa Wassef, "Calendar, Months of Coptic," in *Coptic Encyclopedia*, v. 2, p. 438.

there are many homilies on this subject and as this feast is a recurring feast.[7]

We also read from the first two chapters of St. Luke on two occasions: on the Entry of the Holy Theotokos into the temple when she was three years old (3 Kiyhak), in which we read about the visitation of St. Mary to St. Elizabeth in Luke 1:39-56, and on the commemoration of Archangel Gabriel (22 Kiahk), in which we read from Luke 1:26-38.

[7] St. Jerome used the Annunciation often in his letters to nuns. St. Gregory the Wonder-Worker also composed four homilies on this subject. ANF v. 6, pp. 136-164.

First Sunday

THE ANNUNCIATION OF THE BIRTH OF ST. JOHN THE BAPTIST

Meditations on the First Sunday of the Blessed Month of Kiahk

GOSPEL READING OF THE FIRST SUNDAY

LUKE 1:1-25

"Inasmuch as many have taken in hand to set in order a narrative of those things which have been fulfilled among us, just as those who from the beginning were eyewitnesses and ministers of the word delivered them to us, it seemed good to me also, having had perfect understanding of all things from the very first, to write to you an orderly account, most excellent Theophilus, that you may know the certainty of those things in which you were instructed.

There was in the days of Herod, the king of Judea, a certain priest named Zacharias, of the division of Abijah. His wife was of the daughters of Aaron, and her name was Elizabeth. And they were both righteous before God, walking in all the commandments and ordinances of the Lord blameless. But they had no child, because Elizabeth was barren, and they were both well advanced in years. So it was, that while he was serving as priest before God in the order of his division, according to the custom of the priesthood, his lot fell to burn incense when he went into the temple of the Lord. And the whole multitude of the people was praying outside at the hour of incense. Then an angel of the Lord appeared to him, standing on the right side of the altar of incense. And when Zacharias saw him, he was troubled, and fear fell upon him. But the angel said to him, "Do not be afraid, Zacharias, for your prayer is heard; and your wife Elizabeth will bear you a son, and you shall call his name John. And you will have joy and gladness, and many will rejoice at his birth. For he will be great in the sight of the Lord, and shall drink neither wine nor strong drink. He will also be filled with the Holy Spirit, even from his mother's womb. And he will turn many of the children of Israel to the Lord their God. He will also go before Him in the spirit and power of Elijah, 'to turn the hearts of the fathers to the children,' and the disobedient to the wisdom of the just, to make ready a people prepared for the Lord." And Zacharias said to the angel, "How shall I know this? For I am an old man, and my wife is well advanced in years." And the angel answered and said to him, "I am Gabriel, who stands in the presence of God, and was sent to speak to you and bring you these glad tidings. But behold, you will be mute and not able to speak until the day these things take place, because you did not believe my words which will be fulfilled in their own time." And the people waited for Zacharias, and marveled that he lingered so long in the temple. But when he came out, he could not speak to them; and they perceived that he had seen a vision in the temple, for he beckoned to them and remained speechless. And so it was, as soon as the days of his service were completed, that he departed to his own house. Now after those days his wife Elizabeth conceived; and she hid herself five months, saying, "Thus the Lord has dealt with me, in the days when He looked on me, to take away my reproach among people."

"Zacharias and Elizabeth"

St. Irenaeus of Lyons[8]

And they were both righteous before God, walking in all the commandments and ordinances of the Lord blameless." And again, speaking of Zacharias: "And it came to pass, that while he executed the priest's office before God in the order of his course, according to the custom of the priest's office, his lot was to burn incense"; and he came to sacrifice, "entering into the temple of the Lord."

Angel Gabriel, also, stands prominently in the presence of the Lord, simply, absolutely, and decidedly confessed in his own person as God and Lord, Him Who had chosen Jerusalem, and had instituted the sacerdotal office. For he knew of none other above Him; since, if he had been in possession of the knowledge of any other more perfect God and Lord besides Him, he surely would never—as I have already shown—have confessed Him, whom he knew to be the fruit of a defect, as absolutely and altogether God and Lord. And then, speaking of John, he thus says: "For he shall be great in the sight of the Lord, and many of the children of Israel shall he turn to the Lord their God. And he shall go before Him in

[8] St. Irenaeus of Lyons, *Against the Heresies*, 3.10, *ANF*, v. 1.

the spirit and power of Elijah, to make ready a people prepared for the Lord."

For whom, then, did he prepare the people, and in the sight of what Lord was he made great? Truly of Him Who said that John was something even "more than a prophet," and that "among those born of women none is greater than John the Baptist"; who did also make the people ready for the Lord's advent, warning his fellow-servants, and preaching to them repentance, that they might receive remission from the Lord when He should be present, having been convened to Him, from Whom they had been alienated because of sins and transgressions. As also David says, "The alienated are sinners from the womb: they go astray as soon as they are born" (Psa. 57:3). And it was on account of this that he, turning them to their Lord, prepared, in the spirit and power of Elijah, a perfect people for the Lord.

And again, speaking in reference to the angel, [St. Luke] says: "But at that time the angel Gabriel was sent from God, who did also say to the virgin, 'Do not be afraid, Mary; for you have found favor with God'" (Lk. 1:26). And he says concerning the Lord: "He shall be great, and shall be called the Son of the Highest; and the Lord God shall give to Him the throne of His father David; and He shall reign over the house of Jacob for ever; and of His kingdom there shall be no end" (Lk. 1:32).

Who else is there who can reign uninterruptedly over the house of Jacob forever, except Jesus Christ our Lord, the Son of the Most High God, Who promised by the law and the prophets that He would make His salvation visible to all flesh, so that He would become the Son of Man for this purpose, that man also might become the son of God?

Mary, rejoicing because of this, cried out, prophesying on behalf of the Church, "My soul magnifies the Lord, and my spirit has rejoiced in God my Savior...For He has helped His servant Israel, in remembrance of His mercy, as He spoke to our fathers, to Abraham, and to his seed forever" (Lk. 1:46, 47, 54, 55). By these and similar passages the gospel points out that it was God Who spoke to the fathers; that it was He Who, by Moses, instituted the legal dispensation, by which giving of the law we know that He spoke to the fathers.

This same God, after His great goodness, poured His compassion upon us, through which compassion "the Dayspring from on high has visited upon us; to give light to those who sit in darkness and the shadow of death, to guide our feet into the way of peace" (Lk. 1:78, 79).

Zacharias, recovering from the state of speechlessness, which he had suffered because of his unbelief, having been filled with a new spirit, did bless God in a new manner. For all things had entered upon a new phase, the Logos arranging after a new manner His advent in the flesh, that He might win back that human nature which had departed from God. Therefore, men were taught to worship God after a new fashion, but not another god, because in truth "since, there is one God who will justify the circumcised by faith and the uncircumcised through faith" (Rom. 3:30).

But Zacharias prophesying, exclaimed, "Blessed be the Lord God of Israel; for He has visited and redeemed His people, and has raised up a horn of salvation for us in the house of His servant David; as He spoke by the mouth of His holy prophets, which have been since the world began; that we should be saved from our enemies, and from the hand of all who hate us; to perform the mercy promised to our fathers, and to remember His holy covenant, the oath which He swore to our father Abraham: to grant us that we, being delivered from the hand of our enemies, might serve Him without fear, in holiness and righteousness before Him, all the days of our life" (Lk.1:68-75).

Then he says to John, "And you, child, will be called the prophet of the Highest; for you will go before the face of the Lord to prepare His ways; to give knowledge of salvation to His people, by the remission of their sins" (Lk.1:76-79). For this is the knowledge of salvation which they desired, that of the Son of God, which John made known, saying, "Behold the Lamb of God, Who takes away the sin of the world! This is He of whom I said, 'After me comes a Man Who is preferred before me, for He was before me.' This is He of Whom I said, 'After me comes a Man Who was before me; for He was before me'; and of His fullness we have all received" (Jn. 1:29-30, 15-16).

This, therefore, was the knowledge of salvation, but [it did not consist in] another god, nor another father...but the knowledge of salvation was the knowledge of the Son of God, Who is both called and actually is, salvation, Savior, and salutary. Salvation, indeed, as follows: "I have waited for Your salvation, O Lord" (Gen. 49:18). And then, again, Savior: "Behold my God, my Savior, I will put my trust in Him" (Isa. 12:2). But as bringing salvation, thus: “God has made known His salvation in the sight of the nations” (Psa. 98:2). For He is indeed Savior, as being the Son and Word of God. He is salutary, since [He is] Spirit, for he says: “The Spirit of our countenance, Christ the Lord” (Lam. 4:20). But salvation, as being flesh, for “the Word became flesh and dwelt among us” (Jn. 1:14). This knowledge of salvation, therefore, John imparted to those repenting and believing in the Lamb of God, Who takes away the sin of the world.

And the angel of the Lord, [St. Luke] says, appeared to the shepherds, proclaiming joy to them: “‘For there is born in the house of David, a Savior, which is Christ the Lord.’ And suddenly there was with the angles a multitude of the heavenly host, praising God, and saying, ‘Glory in the highest to God, and on earth peace, goodwill toward men.” The falsely called Gnostics say that these angels came from the Ogdoad[9] and made manifest the descent of the superior Christ. But they are again in error, when saying that the Christ and Savior from above was not born, but that also, after the baptism of the dispensational Jesus, He, [the Christ of the Pleroma][10] descended upon Him as a dove.

Therefore, according to these men, the angels of the Ogdoad lied, when they said, “For unto you is born this day a Savior, who is Christ the Lord, in the city of David.” For neither was Christ, nor the Savior born at that time, by their account. But (they claim) that this dispensational Jesus, was the framer of the world, the (Demiurge), and upon whom, after his baptism, that is, after (the lapse of) thirty years, they maintain the savior from above descended.

---

[9] The Ogdoad (Greek ογδοάς, the eightfold) were eight deities worshipped in Hermopolis during the Old Kingdom period in Ancient Egypt between 2686 and 2134 BC. This concept reappears in Gnostic systems in the Early Church, and was especially developed by the famous Gnostic theologian, Valentinus (ca. 160 AD).

[10] *Pleroma* generally refers to the totality of divine powers, coming from the Greek word for “fullness,” πλήρωμα. This word is used over 10 times throughout the Pauline epistles. However, Gnostics used the term to refer to the light that existed above our world which contained spiritual beings called “aeons.” These Gnostics asserted that Jesus was an intermediary aeon sent with Sophia (Wisdom) from the Pleroma to restore unity between that world and the human world. St Irenaeus here refutes this belief.

But why did [the angels] add, "in the city of David" (Lk. 2:11), if they did not proclaim the glad tidings of the fulfillment of God's promise made to David, that from the fruit of his body there should be an eternal King?

However, the Framer (Demiurge) of the entire universe made a promise to David, as David himself declares: "Our help is from God, Who made heaven and earth" (Psa. 124:8). And again: "In His hand are the ends of the earth, and the heights of the mountains are His. For the sea is His, and He did Himself make it; and His hands founded the dry land. Come, let us worship and fall down before Him, and weep in the presence of the Lord Who made us; for He is the Lord our God" (Psa. 94:6, 7).

The Holy Spirit evidently thus declares by David to those hearing him that there shall be those who despise Him Who formed us and Who is God alone. Therefore he also uttered the foregoing words, meaning to say, "Make no mistake—there is no other god besides or above Him, to Whom you should rather stretch out [your hands], thus rendering us pious and grateful towards Him Who made, established, and [still] nourishes us." What, then, shall happen to those who have been the authors of so much blasphemy against their Creator?

This identical truth was also what the angels [proclaimed]. For when they exclaim, "Glory to God in the highest, and in earth peace" (Lk. 2:14), they have glorified with these words Him Who is the Creator of the highest, that is, of super-celestial things, and the Founder of everything on earth: Who has sent to His own handiwork, that is, to men, the blessing of His salvation from heaven. Thus, he adds, "The shepherds returned, glorifying God for all which they had heard and seen, as it was told to them" (Lk. 2:20).

For the shepherds of Israel did not glorify another god, but Him Who had been announced by the law and the prophets, the Maker of all things, Whom also the angels glorified. But if the angels who were from the Ogdoad were accustomed to glorify any other, different from Him whom the shepherds [adored], these angels from the Ogdoad brought to them error and not truth.

And still further Luke says in reference to the Lord: "Now when the days of her purification were completed, they brought Him up to Jerusalem to present Him to the Lord, as it is written in the law of the Lord, 'Every male who opens the womb shall be called holy to the Lord'; and to offer a sacrifice according to what is said in the law of the Lord, 'A pair of turtledoves or two young pigeons'": in his own person most clearly calling Him Lord, who appointed the legal dispensation. But Simeon, [St. Luke] says, "Blessed God, and said, 'Lord, now You are letting Your servant depart in peace; for my eyes have seen Your salvation, which You have prepared before the face of all people; a light to bring revelation of the Gentiles, and the glory of Your people Israel.'"

Also, he says that Anna the prophetess similarly glorified God when she saw Christ "and spoke of Him to all them who were looking for the redemption of Jerusalem." Now by all these one God is shown forth, revealing to men the new dispensation of liberty, the covenant, through the new advent of His Son.

For this reason also, Mark, the interpreter and follower of Peter, does thus commence his gospel narrative: "The beginning of the gospel of Jesus Christ, the Son of God. As it is written in the Prophets: 'Behold, I send My messenger before Your face, Who will prepare Your way before You. The voice of one crying in the wilderness: "Prepare the way of the LORD; Make His paths straight" '" (Mk. 1:1-3).

Plainly the commencement of the gospel quotes the words of the holy prophets, and point Him out at once, Whom they confessed as God and Lord; Him, the Father of our Lord Jesus Christ, Who had also made promise to Him, that He would send His messenger before His face, who was John, crying in the wilderness, in "the spirit and power of Elijah": "Prepare the way of me Lord, make His paths straight." For the prophets did not announce one and another God, but one and the same; under various aspects, however, and many titles. For varied and rich in attribute is the Father, as I have already shown in the book preceding this; and I shall show [the same truth] from the prophets themselves in the further course of this work.

Also, towards the conclusion of his gospel, Mark says: "So then, after the Lord Jesus had spoken to them, He was received up into heaven, and sits on the right hand of God" (Mk. 16:19), confirming what had been spoken by the prophet: "The Lord said to my Lord, 'Sit on My right hand, until I make Your enemies Your footstool'" (Psa. 110:1; cf. Matt. 22:44, Mk. 12:36, Lk. 20:42, Acts 2:34, and Heb. 1:13). Thus God and the Father are truly one and the same, He who was announced by the prophets, and handed down by the true gospel, Whom we Christians worship and love with the whole heart as the Maker of heaven and earth, and of all things therein.

Second Sunday

THE ANNUNCIATION OF THE BIRTH OF OUR LORD JESUS CHRIST

Meditations on the Second Sunday of the Blessed Month of Kiahk

GOSPEL READING OF THE SECOND SUNDAY

LUKE 1:26-38[11]

Now in the sixth month the angel Gabriel was sent by God to a city of Galilee named Nazareth, to a virgin betrothed to a man whose name was Joseph, of the house of David. The virgin's name was Mary. And having come in, the angel said to her, "Rejoice, highly favored one, the Lord is with you; blessed are you among women!" But when she saw him, she was troubled at his saying, and considered what manner of greeting this was. Then the angel said to her, "Do not be afraid, Mary, for you have found favor with God. And behold, you will conceive in your womb and bring forth a Son, and shall call His name Jesus. He will be great, and will be called the Son of the Highest; and the Lord God will give Him the throne of His father David. And He will reign over the house of Jacob forever, and of His kingdom there will be no end." Then Mary said to the angel, "How can this be, since I do not know a man?" And the angel answered and said to her, "The Holy Spirit will come upon you, and the power of the Highest will overshadow you; therefore, also, that Holy One who is to be born will be called the Son of God. Now indeed, Elizabeth your relative has also conceived a son in her old age; and this is now the sixth month for her who was called barren. For with God

[11] The selected readings for the Holy Annunciation in the Second Sunday is abbreviated here, as there are many homilies on this subject and as this feast is a recurring feast. St. Jerome used the Annunciation often in his letters to nuns. St. Gregory Thaumaturgus wrote three homilies on this subject alone. ANF V. 6, pp. 136-164.

> *nothing will be impossible." Then Mary said, "Behold the maidservant of the Lord! Let it be to me according to your word.." And the angel departed from her.*

"The Sealed Book"

St. Gregory Thaumaturgus[12]

"Hear what the prophet says about this man (Joseph) and the Virgin: A "This book that is sealed shall be delivered to a man that is learned."[13] What is meant by this sealed book other than the undefiled virgin? From whom is this to be given? From the priests evidently. And to whom? To the carpenter Joseph. As, then, the priests espoused Mary to Joseph as to a prudent husband and committed her to his care in expectation of the time of marriage, and as it behooved him, then on obtaining her to keep the virgin untouched, this was announced by the prophet long before, when he said:

This book that is sealed shall be delivered to a man that is learned." And that man will say, I cannot read it. "But why can't you read it, O Joseph?" "I cannot read it," he says, "because the book is sealed." "For whom, then, is it preserved?" "It is preserved as a place of sojourn for the Maker of the universe.

"Rejoice, O Highly Favored One"

St. Jerome[14]

Set before you the blessed Mary, whose surpassing purity made her worthy to be the mother of the Lord. When the angel Gabriel came down to her in the form of a man and said, "Rejoice, highly favored one; the Lord is with you" (Lk. 1:28), she was terror-stricken and unable to reply, for she had never been saluted by a man before.

But, on learning who he was, she spoke, and the one who had been afraid of a man, conversed fearlessly with an angel. Now you too may be the Lord's mother. "Take you a great roll and write in it with a man's pen

---

[12] St. Gregory Thaumaturgus, *Homily 3 on the Annunciation, ANF,* v. 6, p. 153.

[13] Although uncertain, it seems St. Gregory refers here to Isa. 29:11.

[14] St. Jerome, *Letter 22* (to Lady Eustochium), *NPNF,* s. 2, v. 6, p. 141.

Maher-shalal-hash-baz." And when you have gone to the prophetess, and have conceived in the womb, and have brought forth a son, say: "Lord, we have been with child by Your fear, we have been in pain, we have brought forth the spirit of Your salvation, which we have wrought upon the earth." Then shall your Son reply: "Behold my mother and my brethren." And He Whose name you have so recently inscribed upon the tablet of your heart, and have written with a pen upon its renewed surface—He, after He has recovered the spoil from the enemy, and has spoiled principalities and powers, nailing them to His Cross— having been miraculously conceived, grows up to manhood; and, as He becomes older, regards you no longer as His mother, but as His bride. To be as the martyrs, or as the apostles, or as Christ, involves a hard struggle, but brings with it a great reward.

"The Holy Annunciation and Psalm 87"

St. Athanasius the Apostolic[15]

So that no one would think that His coming was in appearance only, Psalm 87 shows that He Who was to come should both come as man and at the same time be the One by Whom all things were made. For it says, "'Mother Zion' a man will say; and a man was living in her: and the Most High Himself has founded her" (Psa. 87:5). This is the equivalent of saying, "The Logos was God and all things were made by Him, and the Logos became flesh." Neither is the Psalmist silent about the fact that He should be born of a virgin. He underlines it clearly in Psalm 45 when he says, "Listen, O daughter, see and incline your ear; forget your own people and your father's house. So the King has desired your beauty because He is your Lord" (Psa. 45:10). Is this not like what Gabriel said, "Hail to You, O Full of Grace, the Lord is with you?" For the Psalmist, having called Him the Anointed One— that is Messiah or Christ—with this declares His human birth by saying, "Listen, O daughter and see." The only difference is that Gabriel addresses Mary with an epithet because he is of a different race than her while David properly calls her his own daughter because it was from him that she should spring.

[15] St. Athanasius, *Letter to Marcellinus on the Interpretation of the Psalms.*

"Listen, O Daughter!"

St. Gregory Thaumaturgu[16]

Today, melodies of praise are sung joyfully by the choir of angels, and the light of the advent of Christ shines brightly upon the faithful.

Today is the glad springtime to us, and christ the Sun of righteousness has beamed with clear light around us, and has illumined the minds of the faithful.

Today Adam is made anew, and moves in the choir of angels, having winged his way to heaven.

Today the whole circle of the earth is filled with joy, since the sojourn of the Holy Spirit has been realized to men.

Today the Grace of God and the hope of the unseen shine through all wonders transcending imagination, and make the mystery that was kept hid from eternity plainly discernible to us.

Today are woven the chaplets of never-fading virtue.

Today, God, willing to crown the sacred heads of those whose pleasure is to hearken to Him, and who delight in His festivals, invites the lovers of unswerving faith as His called and His heirs; and the heavenly kingdom is urgent to summon those who mind celestial things to join the divine service of the incorporeal choirs.

Today the word of David is fulfilled, "Let the heavens rejoice, and let the earth be glad. The fields shall be joyful, and all the trees of the wood before the Lord, because He comes" (Psa. 96:11-13). David thus made mention of the trees; and the Lord's forerunner also spoke of them as trees that should "bear fruits worthy of repentance" (Mt. 3:8), or rather for the coming of the Lord. But our Lord Jesus Christ promises perpetual gladness to all those who believe on Him. For He says, "I will see you, and your heart shall rejoice, and your joy no one will take from you" (Jn. 16:22).

Today is the illustrious and ineffable mystery of Christians, who have willingly set their hope like a seal upon Christ, plainly declared to us.

---

[16] St. Gregory Thaumaturgus, *First Homily on the Annunciation,* ANF v. 6, pp. 136-141.

Today did Gabriel, who stands by God, come to the pure Virgin, bearing to her the glad annunciation, "Hail, you who are highly favored! And she cast in her mind what manner of salutation this might be. And the angel immediately proceeded to say, "'The Lord is with you: fear not, Mary; for you have found favor with God. Behold, you shalt conceive in your womb, and bring forth a Son, and shalt call His name Jesus. He will be great, and will be called the Son of the Highest; and the Lord God will give to Him the throne of His father David. And He shall reign over the house of Jacob forever, and of His kingdom there shall be no end.'

"Then Mary said to the angel, 'How shall this be, since I do not know a man?'" She pondered, thinking, "Shall I still remain a virgin? Will I then lose the honor of virginity?"...But while the holy one pondered these things in perplexity with herself, she also says to the angel, "Where have you brought this blessing from? Out of what treasure-stores is the pearl of the word dispatched to us? From where has the gift acquired its purpose toward us? You have come from heaven, yet you walk upon earth! You exhibit the form of man, yet you are glorious with dazzling light."

These things the holy one considered within herself and the archangel solved the difficulty expressed in such reasonings by saying to her: "'The Holy Spirit will come upon you, and the power of the Most High will overshadow you. Therefore, also, that Holy One Who is to be born of you will be called the Son of God.' And fear not, O Mary, for I am not come to overpower you with fear, but to repel the subject of fear. Fear not, Mary, for you have found favor with God. Do not question grace by the standard of nature. For grace does not endure to pass under the laws of nature.

"You know, O Mary, things that were hidden from the patriarchs and prophets. You have learned, O Virgin, things which were kept concealed till now from the angels. You have heard, O purest one, things of which even the choir of inspired men was never deemed worthy. Moses, and David, and Isaiah, and Daniel, and all the prophets, prophesied of Him, but they did not know Him in this way.

"Yet You alone, O purest Virgin, have now received things of which all these were ignorant of, and you know the origin of them. For where the Holy Spirit is, there are all things readily ordered. Where Divine Grace is present, all things are found possible with God. The Holy Spirit shall come upon you, and the power of the Most shall overshadow you.

Therefore, also, that Holy One Who is to be born of you will be called the Son of God."

And if He is the Son of God, then is He also God, of One essence with the Father, and co-eternal; in Him the Father possesses all manifestation; He is His Image in the Person, and through His reflection the (Father's) glory shines forth. And as from the ever-flowing fountain the streams proceed, so also from this ever-flowing and ever-living fountain does the light of the world proceed, the perennial and the true, namely Christ our God.

For it is of this that the prophets have preached: "The streams of the river make glad the city of God" (Psa. 45:5). And not one city only, but all cities; for even as it makes glad one city, so does it also the whole world.

Appropriately, therefore, did the angel say to Mary the Holy Virgin first of all, "Hail to you O Full of Grace, the Lord is with you," inasmuch as with her was laid up the full treasure of grace. For of all generations she alone has risen as a virgin pure in body and in spirit; and she alone bears Him who bears all things on His word. Nor is it only the beauty of this holy one in body that calls forth our admiration, but also the innate virtue of her soul. Wherefore also the angels addressed her first with the salutation, "Hail to you, O Full of Grace! The Lord is with you, and no spouse of earth;" He Himself is with you Who is the Lord of sanctification, the Father of purity, the Author of incorruption, and the Bestower of liberty, the Curator of salvation, and the Steward and Provider of the true peace, Who out of the virgin earth made man, and out of man's side formed Eve in addition. Even this Lord is with you, and on the other hand also is of you.

Come, therefore, beloved brethren, and let us take up the angelic strain, and to the utmost of our ability return the due reward of praise, saying: "Hail to you, O Full of Grace, the Lord is with you!" For it is yours truly to rejoice, seeing that the Grace of God, as He knows, has chosen to dwell with you—the Lord of Glory dwelling with the handmaiden; "He Who is more beautiful than the sons of men" (Psa. 44:3), with the fair virgin, He Who sanctifies all things with the undefiled. God is with you, and with you also is the perfect Man in Whom dwells the whole fullness of the Godhead (Col. 2:9).

"Hail to you, O Full of Grace, the fountain of the light that lightens all who believe in Him! Hail to you, O Full of Grace, the rising of the rational Sun, and the undefiled flower of Life! Hail to you, O Full of Grace, the reward of sweet savor! Hail to you, O Full of Grace, the ever-blooming vine, that makes glad the souls of those who honor you?

"Hail to you, O Full of Grace—the soil that, all untilled, bears bounteous fruit: for you have brought forth in accordance with the law of nature indeed, as it goes with us, and by the set time of practice, and yet in a way beyond nature, or rather above nature, by reason that God the Word from above took His abode in you, and formed the new Adam in your holy womb, and inasmuch as the Holy Spirit gave the power of conception to the holy virgin; and the reality of His body was assumed from her body. And just as the pearl comes of the two natures, namely lightning and water, the occult signs of the sea; so also our Lord Jesus Christ proceeds, without fusion and without mutation, from the pure, and chaste, and undefiled, and Holy Virgin Mary; perfect in divinity and perfect in humanity, in all things equal to the Father, and in all things consubstantial with us, apart from sin."

Most of the holy fathers, and patriarchs, and prophets desired to see Him, and to be eyewitnesses of Him, but were not able to. Some of them beheld Him in visions, but darkly and in type. Others were privileged to hear the divine voice through the medium of the cloud and were favored with sights of holy angels. But to Mary the pure virgin alone did the Archangel Gabriel manifest himself luminously, bringing her the glad address, "Hail to you, O highly favored one!" And thus she received the Word, and in the due time of the fulfillment according to the body's course she brought forth the priceless Pearl.

Come, then, you too, dearly beloved, and let us chant the melody which has been taught us by the inspired harp of David, and say, "Arise, O Lord, into Your rest; You, and the Ark of Your sanctuary" (Psa. 131:8). For the Holy Virgin is in truth an ark, wrought with gold both within and without, that has received the whole treasury of the sanctuary. "Arise, O Lord, into Your rest." Arise, O Lord, out of the Bosom of the Father, in order that You may raise up the fallen race of the first-formed man. Setting these things forth, David in prophecy said to the rod that was to spring from himself, and to sprout into the flower of that beauteous fruit: "Listen, O daughter, see and incline your ear; forget your own people and your father's house. So the King has desired your beauty because He is your Lord" (Psa. 45:10). Listen, O daughter, to the things which were prophesied beforetime of you, in order that you may also behold the things themselves with the eyes of understanding. Listen to me while I announce things beforehand to you, and listen to the archangel who declares expressly to you the perfect mysteries."

Come then, dearly beloved, and let us fall back on the memory of what has gone before us; and let us glorify, and celebrate, and laud, and bless that rod that has sprung so marvelously from Jesse (cf. Isa. 11:1). For Luke, in the inspired gospel narratives, delivers a testimony not to Joseph only, but also to Mary the Theotokos, and gives this account with reference to the very family and house of David: "Joseph also went up," he says, "from Galilee, out of the city of Nazareth, into Judea, to the city of David, which is called Bethlehem, because he was of the house and lineage of David, to be registered with Mary, his betrothed wife, who was with Child. So it was, that while they were there, the days were completed for her to be delivered. And she brought forth her firstborn Son, and wrapped Him in swaddling cloths, and laid Him in a manger, because there was no room for them in the inn" (Lk. 2:4-7).

She wrapped in swaddling-clothes Him Who is covered with light as with a garment (cf. Psa. 103:2). She wrapped in swaddling-clothes Him Who made every creature. She laid in a manger Him Who sits above the Cherubim, and is praised by myriads of angels. In the manger set apart for ignorant brutes did the Word of God repose, in order that He might impart to men, who are really irrational by free choice, the perceptions of true reason.

In the board from which cattle eat was laid the heavenly Bread, in order that He might provide participation in spiritual sustenance for men who live like the beasts of the earth.

Nor was there even room for Him in the inn. He found no place, Who by His word established heaven and earth; "for though He was rich, for our sakes He became poor" (2 Cor. 8:9), and showed extreme humiliation on behalf of the salvation of our nature, in His inherent goodness toward us.

He Who fulfilled the whole administration of unutterable mysteries of the economy in heaven in the bosom of the Father, and in the cave in the arms of the mother, reposed in the manger. Angelic choirs encircled Him, singing of glory in heaven and of peace on earth. In heaven He was seated at the right hand of the Father; and in the manger He rested, as it were, upon the cherubim. Even there was in truth His cherubic throne; there was His royal seat. Holy of the holy, and alone glorious upon the earth, and holier than the holy, was that in which Christ our God rested.

To Him be glory, honor, and power, together with the Father undefiled, and the altogether Holy and Life-Giving Spirit, now and ever, and unto ages of ages. Amen.

"Hail to You, O Mary!"

St. Gregory Thaumaturgus[17]

It is our duty to present to God, like sacrifices, all the festivals and hymnal celebrations; and first of all, the annunciation to the holy mother of God, to wit, the salutation made to her by the angel, "Hail to You O Full of Grace!" For first of all wisdom and saving doctrine in the New Testament was this salutation, "Hail to You, O Full of Grace!" conveyed to us from the Father of lights. And this address, "full of grace," embraced the whole nature of men. "Hail to You, O Full of Grace!" in the holy conception and in the glorious pregnancy, "I bring you good tidings of great joy, which shall be to all people."

And again the Lord, who came for the purpose of accomplishing a saving passion, said, "I will see you again and your heart will rejoice, and your joy no one will take from you" (Jn. 16:22). And after His Resurrection again, by the hand of the holy women, He gave us first of all the salutation "Hail!" And again, the Apostle made the announcement in similar terms, saying, "Rejoice always, pray without ceasing, in everything give thanks" (1 Thess. 5:16-18).

See, then, dearly beloved, how the Lord has conferred upon us everywhere, and indivisibly, the joy that is beyond conception, and perennial. For since the Holy Virgin, in the life of the flesh, was in possession of the incorruptible citizenship, and walked as such in all manner of virtues, and lived a life more excellent than man's common

[17] St. Gregory Thaumaturgus *The Second Homily on the Annunciation*, ANF v. 6, p. 143.

standard. Therefore the Word that comes from God the Father thought it meet to assume the flesh, and endue the perfect man from her, in order that in the same flesh in which sin entered into the world, and death by sin, sin might be condemned in the flesh, and that the tempter of sin might be overcome in the burying of the Holy Body, and that therewith also the beginning of the resurrection might be exhibited, and life eternal instituted in the world, and fellowship established for men with God the Father.

And what shall we state, or what shall we pass by here? Or who shall explain what is incomprehensible in the mystery? But for the present let us fall back upon our subject.

Gabriel was sent to the Holy Virgin; the incorporeal was dispatched to her who in the body pursued the incorruptible conversation, and lived in purity and in virtues. And when he came to her, he first addressed her with the salutation: "Hail to You, O Full of Grace! The Lord is with you. Hail to You, O Full of Grace! For you do what is worthy of joy indeed, since you have put on the garment of purity, and are clothed with the sash of prudence. Hail to You, O Full of Grace! For to your lot it has fallen to be the vehicle of celestial joy. Hail to You, O Full of Grace! For through you joy is decreed for the whole creation, and the human race receives again by you its pristine dignity. Hail to You, O Full of Grace! For in your arms the Creator of all things will be carried."

And she was perplexed by this word, for she was inexperienced in all the addresses of men, and welcomed quiet, as the mother of prudence and purity. Yet being a pure image herself, she did not hide in terror from the angelic apparition, like most of the prophets—for true virginity has a kind of affinity and equality with the angels. The holy Virgin carefully guarded the torch of virginity, and gave diligent care that it should not be extinguished or defiled.

And as one who is clad in a brilliant robe deems it a matter of great moment that no impurity or filth be allowed to touch it anywhere, so did the holy Mary consider with herself, and said, "Does this act of attention imply any deep design or seductive purpose? Shall this word 'Hail' prove the cause of trouble to me, as of old the fair promise of being made like God, which was given to our first mother Eve by the serpent-devil? Has the Devil, who is the author of all evil, become transformed again into an angel of light; and bearing a grudge against my espoused husband for his admirable temperance, and having assailed him with some fair-seeming address, and finding himself powerless to overcome a mind so firm, and to deceive the man, has he turned his attack on me, as one endowed with a more susceptible mind? And is this word "Hail" (Grace be with you) spoken as the sign of gracelessness hereafter? Is this benediction and salutation uttered in irony? Is there not some poison concealed in the honey? Is it not the address of one who brings good tidings, while the end of the same is to make me the designer's prey? And how is it that he can thus salute one whom he knows not?"

These things she pondered in perplexity with herself, and expressed in words. Then again the archangel addressed her with the announcement of a joy which all may believe in, and which shall not be taken away, and said to her: "Fear not, Mary, for you have found favor with God. Soon you will have the proof of what has been said. For I will not only let you understand that there is nothing to fear, but I show you the very key to the absence of all cause for fear. For through me all the heavenly powers hail you, the Holy Virgin. Yes rather, He Himself, who is Lord of all the heavenly powers and of all creation, has selected you as the holy one and the wholly fair. And through your holy, chaste, pure, and undefiled womb the enlightening Pearl comes forth for the salvation of all the world, since of all the race of man you are by birth the holy one, and the more honorable, and the purer, and the more pious than any other.

"You have a mind whiter than the snow, and a body made purer than any gold, however fine, and a womb such as the object which Ezekiel saw, and which he described in these terms: 'And the likeness of the living creatures upon the head was as the firmament, and as the appearance of the terrible crystal, and the likeness of the throne above them was as the appearance of a sapphire-stone: and above the throne it was as the likeness of a man, and as the appearance of amber; and within it there was, as it were, the likeness of fire round about' (Ezek. 1:22, 26, 27).

Thus, the prophet clearly beheld in type Him who was born of the Holy Virgin, whom you, O Holy Virgin, would have had no strength to bear if you did not beam forth for that time with all that is glorious and virtuous. Then, with what words of praise can we describe her virgin-dignity? With what indications and proclamations of praise shall we celebrate her stainless figure? With what spiritual song or word shall we honor her who is most glorious among the angels?

She is planted in the house of God like a fruitful olive that the Holy Spirit overshadowed. And by her means are we called sons and heirs of the kingdom of Christ. She is the ever-blooming paradise of incorruptibility, in which is planted the Tree that gives life, and that furnishes to all the fruits of immortality. She is the pride and glory of virgins, and the exultation of mothers. She is the sure support of the believing, and the helper of the pious. She is the garment of light, and the house of virtue. She is the ever-flowing fountain, in which the Water of Life sprang and produced the Lord's incarnate manifestation. She is the monument of righteousness; and all who become lovers of her, and set their affections on virgin-like ingenuousness and purity, shall enjoy the grace of angels.

All who keep themselves from wine and intoxication, and from the wanton enjoyments of strong drink, shall be made glad with the products of the life-bearing plant. All who have preserved the unextinguished lamp of virginity shall be privileged to receive the eternally beautiful crown of immortality. All who have possessed themselves of the stainless robe of temperance shall be received into the mystical bride-chamber of righteousness. All who have come nearer the angelic degree than others shall also enter into the more real enjoyment of their Lord's beatitude. All who have possessed the illuminating oil of understanding, and the pure incense of conscience, shall inherit the promise of spiritual favor and the spiritual adoption.

All who worthily observe the Feast of the Annunciation of the Virgin Mary, the Theotokos, shall receive as their proper reward the fuller significance in the message, "Hail, to you, O highly favored one!"

It is our duty, therefore, to keep this feast, seeing that it has cultivated the whole world with joy and gladness. So let us keep it with psalms, and hymns, and spiritual songs...

She wrapped in swaddling-clothes Him Who is covered with light as with a garment (cf. Psa. 103:2). She wrapped in swaddling-clothes Him Who made every creature. She laid in a manger Him Who sits above the Cherubim, and is praised by myriads of angels. In the manger set apart for ignorant brutes did the Word of God repose, in order that He might impart to men, who are really irrational by free choice, the perceptions of true reason. In the board from which cattle eat was laid the heavenly Bread, in order that He might provide participation in spiritual sustenance for men who live like the beasts of the earth.

Nor was there even room for Him in the inn. He found no place, Who by His word established heaven and earth; "for though He was rich, for our sakes He became poor" (2 Cor. 8:9), and showed extreme humiliation on behalf of the salvation of our nature, in His inherent goodness toward us.

He Who fulfilled the whole administration of unutterable mysteries of the economy in heaven in the bosom of the Father, and in the cave in the arms of the mother, reposed in the manger. Angelic choirs encircled Him, singing of glory in heaven and of peace on earth. In heaven He was seated at the right hand of the Father; and in the manger He rested, as it were, upon the cherubim. Even there was in truth His cherubic throne; there was His royal seat. Holy of the holy, and alone glorious upon the earth, and holier than the holy, was that in which Christ our God rested.

To Him be glory, honor, and power, together with the Father undefiled, and the altogether Holy and Life-Giving Spirit, now and ever, and unto ages of ages. Amen.

"In the Sixth Month"

St. Gregory Thaumaturgus[18]

Again have we the glad tidings of joy, again the announcements of liberty, again the restoration, again the return, again the promise of gladness, again the release from slavery. An angel talks with the Virgin in order that the serpent may no more have converse with the woman.

In the sixth month, it is said, the angel Gabriel was sent from God to a virgin espoused to a man (Lk. 1:26, 27). Gabriel was sent to declare the worldwide salvation; Gabriel was sent to bear to Adam the signature of his restoration; Gabriel was sent to a virgin, to transform the dishonor of the female gender into honor; Gabriel was sent to prepare the worthy chamber for the pure spouse; Gabriel was sent to wed the creature with the Creator;

[18] St. Gregory Thaumaturgus, *Homily 3 on the Annunciation,* ANF v. 6, pp. 152-155.

Gabriel was sent to the living palace of the King of the angels; Gabriel was sent to a virgin espoused to Joseph, but preserved for Jesus the Son of God.

The incorporeal servant was sent to the Virgin undefiled. One free from sin was sent to one that admitted no corruption. The light was sent that should announce the Sun of Righteousness. The dawn was sent that should precede the light of the day. Gabriel was sent to proclaim Him Who is in the bosom of the Father, and Who yet was to be in the arms of the mother. Gabriel was sent to declare Him Who is upon the throne, and yet also in the cavern. The subaltern was sent to utter aloud the mystery of the great King; the mystery, I mean, which is discerned by faith, and which cannot be searched out by officious curiosity; the mystery which is to be adored, not weighed; the mystery which is to be taken as a thing divine, and not measured.

"Now in the sixth month Gabriel was sent...to a virgin" (Lk. 1:26, 27). What is meant by this sixth month? What? It is the sixth month from the time when Elisabeth received the glad tidings, from the time that she conceived John. And how is this made plain? The archangel himself gives us the interpretation, when he says to the virgin: "Now indeed, Elizabeth your relative has also conceived a son in her old age; and this is now the sixth month for her who was called barren" (Lk. 1:36).

"In the sixth month"—that is evidently, therefore, the sixth month of the conception of John. For it was meet that the subaltern should go before; it was meet that the attendant should precede; it was meet that the herald of the Lord's coming should prepare the way for Him. In the sixth month the angel Gabriel was sent to a virgin espoused to a man; espoused, not united; espoused, yet kept intact. And for what purpose was she espoused? In order that the spoiler might not learn the mystery prematurely. For that the King was to come by a virgin, was a fact known to the wicked one. For he too heard these words of Isaiah: "Behold, the Virgin shall conceive, and bear a Son" (Isa. 7:14).

And on every occasion, consequently, he kept watch upon the virgin's words, in order that, whenever this mystery should be fulfilled, he might prepare her dishonor. Therefore the Lord came by an espoused virgin, in order to elude the notice of the wicked one; for one who was espoused was pledged in fine to be her husband's. "In the sixth month the angel Gabriel was sent to a virgin espoused to a man whose name was Joseph."

Hear what the prophet says about this man and the virgin: "This book that is sealed shall be delivered to a man that is learned" (Isa. 29:11). What is meant by this sealed book, but just the virgin undefiled? From whom is this to be given? From the priests evidently. And to whom? To the artisan Joseph. As, then, the priests espoused Mary to Joseph as to a prudent husband, and committed her to his care in expectation of the time of marriage, and as it behoved him then on obtaining her to keep the virgin untouched, this was announced by the prophet long before, when he said: "This book that is sealed shall be delivered to a man that is learned." And that man will say, I cannot read it. But why canst thou not read it, O Joseph? I cannot read it, he says, because the book is sealed. For whom, then, is it preserved? It is preserved as a place of sojourn for the Maker of the universe. But let us return to our immediate subject.

In the sixth month Gabriel was sent to a virgin—he who received, indeed, such injunctions as these: "Come here now, archangel, and become the minister of a dread mystery which has been kept hidden, and be the agent in the miracle. I am moved with compassion to descend to earth to recover the lost Adam. Sin has decayed him who was made in My Image, has corrupted the work of My hands, has obscured the beauty which I formed. The wolf devours My child. The home of Paradise is desolate, the Tree of Life is guarded by the flaming sword, the location of enjoyments is closed. My pity is evoked for the object of this enmity, and I desire to seize the enemy. Yet I wish to keep this mystery, which I confide to you alone, still hidden from all the powers of heaven. Go, therefore, to the Virgin Mary. Pass on to that living city of which the prophet said, 'Glorious things are spoken of you, O city of God' (Psa. 86:3).

"Proceed, then, to My rational paradise; proceed to the gate of the east; proceed to the place of sojourn that is worthy of My word; proceed to that second heaven on earth; proceed to the light cloud, and announce to it the shower of My coming. Proceed to the sanctuary prepared for Me; proceed to the hall of the Incarnation; proceed to the pure chamber of My generation after the flesh. Speak in the ears of My rational ark, so as to prepare for Me the accesses of hearing. But neither disturb nor vex the soul of the Virgin. Manifest yourself in a manner befitting that sanctuary, and hail her first with the voice of gladness. And address Mary with the salutation, 'Hail to you, O Full of Grace!' That I may show compassion for Eve in her depravation."

The archangel heard these things, and considered them within himself, as was reasonable, and said: "Strange is this matter; passing comprehension is this thing that is spoken. He Who is the object of dread to the Cherubim, He Who cannot be looked upon by the Seraphim, He Who is incomprehensible to all the heavenly powers, does He give the assurance of His connection with a maiden? Does He announce His own personal coming? Yes more, does He hold out an access by hearing? And is He Who condemned Eve, urgent to put such honor upon her daughter? For He says, 'So as to prepare for Me the accesses of hearing.' But can the womb contain Him who cannot be contained in space? Truly this is a dread mystery."

While the angel is indulging such reflections, the Lord said to Him: "Why are you troubled and perplexed, O Gabriel? Have you not already been sent by Me to Zacharias the priest? Have you not conveyed to him the glad tidings of the nativity of John? Did you not inflict upon the doubtful priest the penalty of speechlessness? Did you not punish the aged man with speechlessness? Did you not make your declaration, and I confirmed it? And has not the actual fact followed your announcement of good? Did not the barren woman conceive? Did not the womb obey the word? Did not the sickness of sterility depart? Did not the lifeless disposition of nature escape? Is not [Elizabeth] now one who shows fruitfulness, who before was never pregnant? Can anything be impossible with Me, the Creator of all? Why, then, are you tossed with doubt?"

What is the angel's answer to this? "O Lord," he says, "to remedy the defects of nature, to do away with the blast of evils, to recall the dead members to the power of life, to enjoin on nature the potency of generation, to remove barrenness in the case of members that have passed the common limit, to change the old and withered stalk into the appearance of fertile energy, to set forth the fruitless soil suddenly as the producer of corn sheaves —to do all this is a work which, as always the case, demands Your power. And Sarah is a witness to this, as well as Rebecca and Anna, who all, though bound by the dread ill of barrenness, were afterwards gifted by You with deliverance from that sickness. But that a virgin should bring forth, without knowledge of a man, is something that goes beyond all the laws of nature; and do You yet announce Your coming to the maiden? The bounds of heaven and earth do not contain You, and how shall the womb of a virgin contain You?"

And the Lord says: "How did the tent of Abraham contain Me (cf. Gen. 18)?"

And the angel says: "As there were there the depths of hospitality, O Lord, You showed Yourself there to Abraham at the door of the tent, and passed quickly by it, as He who fills all things. But how can Mary sustain the fire of the divinity? Your throne blazes with the illumination of its splendor, and can the Virgin receive You without being consumed?"

Then the Lord says: "Yes, if the fi re in the wilderness injured the bush, then My coming would also injure Mary. But if that fire which served as the type of the advent of the fire of divinity from heaven fertilized the bush and did not burn it, what will you say of the Truth that does not descend in a flame of fire, but in the form of rain (cf. Psa. 71:6)?"

Thereupon the angel set himself to carry out the commission given to him, and appeared to the Virgin and addressed her with a loud voice, saying: "Hail, to you, O highly favored one! The Lord is with you. No longer shall the Devil be against you; for where of old that adversary inflicted the wound, there now first of all does the Physician apply the ointment of deliverance. Where death came from, there has life now prepared its entrance. By a woman came the flood of our ills, and by a woman also our blessings have their spring.

"Hail, to You O highly favored one! Do not be ashamed, as if you were the cause of our condemnation. For you will be the mother of Him Who is Judge and Redeemer. Hail to you, O pure mother of the Bridegroom of an empty world! Hail to the one who has defeated Eve's death in your womb! Hail to you, O living temple of God! Hail, O home of heaven and earth! Hail, O most worthy vessel of the Infinite One!"

But as these things are so, through her the Physician has come for the sick; for those who are sitting in darkness, the Sun of Righteousness; for all those who are tossed and tempest-beaten, the Anchor and the Port undisturbed by storm. For the servants in irreconcilable enmity have been born the Lord; and One has sojourned with us to be the bond of peace and the Redeemer of those led captive, and to be the peace for those involved in hostility. For He is our peace (Eph. 2:14); and of that peace may it be granted that we all may receive the enjoyment, by the grace and kindness of our Lord Jesus Christ to Whom be the glory, honor, and power, now and ever, and unto all the ages of the ages. Amen.

Third Sunday

THE HOLY VISITATION

Meditations on the Third Sunday of the Blessed Month of Kiahk

Gospel Reading of the Third Sunday

Luke 1:39-56

Now Mary arose in those days and went into the hill country with haste, to a city of Judah, and entered the house of Zacharias and greeted Elizabeth. And it happened, when Elizabeth heard the greeting of Mary, that the babe leaped in her womb; and Elizabeth was filled with the Holy Spirit. Then she spoke out with a loud voice and said, "Blessed are you among women, and blessed is the fruit of your womb! But why is this granted to me, that the mother of my Lord should come to me? For indeed, as soon as the voice of your greeting sounded in my ears, the babe leaped in my womb for joy. Blessed is she who believed, for there will be a fulfillment of those things which were told her from the Lord."

And Mary said: "My soul magnifies the Lord, And my spirit has rejoiced in God my Savior. For He has regarded the lowly state of His maidservant; for behold, henceforth all generations will call me blessed. For He who is mighty has done great things for me, And holy is His name. And His mercy is on those who fear Him From generation to generation. He has shown strength with His arm; He has scattered the proud in the imagination of their hearts. He has put down the mighty from their thrones, and exalted the lowly. He has filled the hungry with good things, and the rich He has sent away empty. He has helped His servant Israel, in remembrance of His mercy, As He spoke to our fathers, To Abraham and to his seed forever."

And Mary remained with her about three months, and returned to her house.

"Conformed to His Glory"

The Scholar Origen[19]

As soon as she conceived, the mother of Jesus had formerly stayed with the mother of John, also at that time with child. The Former then communicated to the formed with some exactness His own Image, and caused him to be conformed to His glory.

So after the testimonies of John to Him, Jesus is Himself seen by the Baptist coming to him. Previously, when the voice of Mary's salutation came to the ears of Elizabeth, the babe John leaped in the womb of his mother, who then received the Holy Spirit, as it were, from the ground. For it came to pass, we read, "when Elizabeth heard the greeting of Mary, the babe leaped in her womb; and Elizabeth was filled with the Holy Spirit. Then she spoke out with a loud voice, "Blessed are you among women, and blessed is the fruit of your womb!"

On this occasion, similarly, John sees Jesus coming to him and says, "Behold the Lamb of God Who takes away the sin of the world." For with regard to matters of great moment one is first instructed by hearing and afterwards one sees them with one's own eyes. Anyone who has grasped our proof that John is a voice but that Jesus is the Word will understand that the Lord helped shape the form of John when he was still in the process of formation and Christ was in His mother's womb. For when Elizabeth was filled with the Holy Spirit at the greeting of Mary, there was a great voice in her, as the words themselves bear; for they say, "And she spoke out with a loud voice."

Elizabeth, it is plain, did this, "and she spoke." For the voice of Mary's greeting coming to the ears of Elizabeth filled John with itself. Therefore, John leaps, and his mother becomes, as it were, the mouth of her son and a prophetess, crying out with a loud voice and saying, "Blessed are you among women, and blessed is the fruit of your womb."

Now we see clearly how it was that through Mary's hasty journey to the hill country, her entrance into the house of Zacharias, and her greeting to Elizabeth that she communicated some of the power she derived from Him that she had conceived to John, yet in his mother's womb. Also, John

---

[19] Origen, *Commentary on St. John,* ANF, v. 10, pp. 654-656.

communicated to his mother some of the prophetic grace which had come to him. These transactions took place most appropriately in the hill country, since no great thing can be entertained by those who are low and, therefore, called valleys...

Also note that Mary, being the greater, comes to Elizabeth, who is the less, and the Son of God comes to the Baptist. This should encourage us to render help without delay to those who are in a lower position and to cultivate for ourselves a moderate station.

"Proof of His Divinity"

St. Ephrem the Syrian[20]

This is He Who was begotten from the Godhead according to His nature, and from manhood not after His nature, and from baptism not after His custom; that we might be begotten from manhood according to our nature, and from Godhead not after our nature, and by the Spirit not after our custom. He then was begotten from the Godhead, He that came to a second birth; to bring us to the birth that is discoursed of, even His generation from the Father—not that it should be searched out, but that it should be believed —and His birth froth the woman, not that it should be despised, but that it should be exalted. Now His death on the Cross witnesses to His birth from the woman. For He that died was also born.

The Annunciation of Gabriel declares His generation by the Father that, "the power of the Most High will overshadow you." If then it was the power of the Most High, it is plain that it was not the seed of mortal man. So then His conception in the womb is bound up with His death on the Cross; and His first generation is bound up with the declaration of the Angel. So that whoever denies His birth may be baffled by His crucifixion; that whoever thinks that His beginning was from Mary, may be admonished that His Godhead is before all; and that whoever concludes His beginning is physical, may be proved wrong that His issuing forth from the Father is reported.

The Father begat Him, and through Him created the creatures. Flesh bare Him and through Him slew lusts. Baptism brought Him forth, that

[20] St. Ephrem the Syrian, "Homily on our Lord," NPNF, S. 2, v. 13, p. 108.

through Him it might wash away stains. Hades brought Him forth, that through Him its treasures might be emptied out. He came to us from beside His Father by the way of them that are born; and by the way of them that die, He went forth to go to His Father, so that by His coming through birth, His advent might be seen; and by His returning through resurrection, His departure might be confirmed.

"The Barren Woman and the Virgin"

St. John Chrysostom[21]

Well, this consideration indeed is able to school us in moral character, but it is necessary also to state the cause for which those women were barren. What then was the reason? Why then were those women barren? So that when you hear about the Virgin bringing forth our common Master, you might not disbelieve. Therefore exercise your mind in the womb of the barren so that when you have seen the womb, disabled and bound as it is, being opened to the bearing of children from the grace of God, you may not marvel at hearing that a virgin has brought forth.

Or rather even marvel and be astounded, but do not disbelieve the marvel. When the Jew says to you, "How did the virgin bear?" ask him, "How did she bear who was barren and enfeebled by old age?" In this case then, there were two hindrances, both the unreasonableness of her age and the unserviceableness of nature, but in the case of the Virgin, there was one hindrance only, the not having shared in marriage.

The barren ones therefore prepare the way for the Virgin. And that you may learn that it was on this account that the barren ones had anticipated it, in order that the Virgin's childbirth might be believed, hear the words of Gabriel which were addressed to her—For when he said to her, "You will conceive in your womb and bear a son, and you will call his name Jesus," the Virgin was astonished and marveled, and said, "How can this be to me, since I do not know a man." What then did the Angel say? "The Holy Sprit shall come upon you." Seek not the sequence of nature, he

---

[21] St. John Chrysostom, "Upon Not Publishing the Errors of the Brethren," NPNF, s. 1, v. 9, pp. 390-391

says, when that which takes place is above nature. Look not round for marriage and the pains of childbirth, when the manner of the birth is too grand for marriage.

"And how will this be," she says, "since I do not know a man?" And truly on this account shall this be, since you know no husband. For if you knew a husband, you would not have been deemed worthy to serve this ministry. So that, for the same reason why you disbelieve, for this believe. You would not have been deemed worthy to serve this ministry—not because marriage is an evil, but because virginity is superior.

Thus, the entry of the Master should be more glorious than ours; for it was royal, and the King enters through one more glorious. It was necessary that He should both share as to birth, and be diverse from ours. Therefore both these things are accomplished. For the being born from the womb is common in respect to us, but the being born without marriage is a thing greater than on a level with us. And the gestation and conception in the belly belongs to human nature; but that the pregnancy should take place without intimate relations is too impressive for human nature. And for this purpose both these things took place in order that you may learn both the preeminence and the fellowship with you of Him Who was born...

Consider the wisdom of all that was done. Neither did the preeminence injure the likeness and kinship to us, nor did the kinship to us dim the preeminence, but both were displayed by all the circumstances. (The being born from a womb) had our condition in its entirety, while the (being born of a virgin) was diverse compared with us. But just as I was saying, on this account the barren ones went before, in order that the Virgin's childbirth might be believed, and that she might be led by the hand to faith in that promise and undertaking which she heard from the angel, saying, "The Holy Spirit shall come upon you, and the power of the Most High shall overshadow you"— thus, he says, you are able to bear.

Do not look to the earth; it is from the heavens that the operation will come. That which takes place is a grace of the Spirit; do not inquire about nature and laws of marriage. But since those words were too high for her, he offers another demonstration. Observe how the barren one leads her on the way to the belief in this. For since that demonstration was too high for the Virgin's intelligence, hear how he brought down what he said to lower things also, leading her by the hand by sensible facts. "Now indeed," he says, "Elizabeth your relative has also conceived a son in her old age; and this is now the sixth month for her who was called barren." See that the barren one was for the sake of the Virgin? For what reason did (Gabriel) mention to her the childbearing of her relative? Why did he say, "in her old age?" Why did he add, "who was called barren?" It was to induce her by all these things, manifestly, to believe the glad annunciation. For this reason he spoke of both the age and the disabling effect of nature; for this cause he awaited for the time also which had elapsed from the conception; for he did not tell to her the glad tidings immediately from the beginning, but waited for a six month period to have passed for the barren one, in order that the puerperal swelling might, for the rest, be a pledge of the pregnancy, and an indisputable demonstration might arise of the conception.

Again, examine the intelligence of Gabriel. For he neither reminded her of Sarah, nor of Rebecca, nor of Rachel. And though they were also old and barren, miracles took place. However, the stories were ancient. Now things new and recent and occurring in our generation are accustomed to induce us into the belief of marvels more than those which are old. On this account having let those women alone, that she should understand from her own relative, Elizabeth herself, what was coming upon her, he brought it forward; so as from (Elizabeth) to lead (St. Mary) to her own— that most awesome and noble childbirth. For the childbirth of the barren one lays between ours and that of the Master, and less indeed than that of the Virgin, but greater than ours. On this account it was by Elizabeth lying between, just as by some bridge, that he lifted up the mind of the Virgin from the travail which is according to nature, to that which is above nature.

"My Soul Magnifies the Lord"

St. Irenaeus of Lyons[22]

God became the Son of Man so that man would become the son of God. Mary, rejoicing because of this, cried out, and prophesied on behalf of the Church, "My soul magnifies the Lord, and my spirit has rejoiced in God my Savior. He has helped His servant Israel, in

[22] St. Irenaeus of Lyons, *Against the Heresies,* ANF v. 1, p. 877.

remembrance of His mercy, as He spoke to our fathers, to Abraham and to his seed forever." By these and similar passages the gospel points out that it was God who spoke to the fathers. It was He who, by Moses, instituted the legal dispensation, by which giving of the law we know that He spoke to the fathers. This same God, after His great goodness, poured His compassion upon us, through which compassion "the Dayspring from on high has visited us; to give light to those who sit in darkness and the shadow of death, and to guide our feet into the way of peace."

"The Mighty Lord"

St. Gregory Thaumaturgus[23]

"He has scattered the proud in the imagination of their hearts."

Yes, He has scattered the Devil himself and all the demons that serve under him. For he was arrogantly proud in his heart, seeing that he dared to say, "I will set my throne above the clouds, and I will be like the Most High" (Isa. 14:14). And now, how He scattered him the prophet has indicated in what follows, where he says, "Yet now you shall be brought down to hell" (Isa. 14:15), and all your hosts with you. For He has overthrown everywhere his altars and the worship of vain gods, and He has prepared for Himself a peculiar people out of the heathen nations.

"He has put down the mighty from their thrones, and exalted the lowly."

In these terms is made know in brief the extrusion of the Jews and the admission of the Gentiles. For the elders of the Jews and the scribes in the law, and those who were richly privileged with other prerogatives, because they used their riches ill and their power lawlessly, were cast down by Him from every seat, whether of prophecy or of priesthood, whether of legislature or of doctrine, and were stripped of all their ancestral wealth, and of their sacrifices and multitudinous festivals, and of all the honorable privileges of the Kingdom. Spoiled of all these boons, as naked fugitives they were cast out into captivity. And in their stead the humble were exalted, namely, the gentile peoples who hungered after righteousness. For, discovering their own lowliness, and the hunger that pressed upon them for the knowledge of God, they pleaded for the Divine Word, though it

[23] St. Gregory Thaumaturgus, *Second Homily on the Annunciation*, ANF v. 6, p. 149-150.

were but for crumbs of the same, like the woman of Canaan; and for this reason they were filled with the riches of the divine mysteries. For the Christ who was born of the Virgin, and who is our God, has given over the whole inheritance of divine blessings to the Gentiles.

Fourth Sunday

NATIVITY OF ST. JOHN THE BAPTIST

Meditations on the Fourth Sunday of the Blessed Month of Kiahk

GOSPEL READING OF THE FOURTH SUNDAY

LUKE 1:57-80

Now Elizabeth's full time came for her to be delivered, and she brought forth a son. When her neighbors and relatives heard how the Lord had shown great mercy to her, they rejoiced with her. So it was, on the eighth day, that they came to circumcise the child; and they would have called him by the name of his father, Zacharias. His mother answered and said, "No; he shall be called John."

But they said to her, "There is no one among your relatives who is called by this name." So they made signs to his father—what he would have him called. And he asked for a writing tablet, and wrote, saying, "His name is John." So they all marveled. Immediately his mouth was opened and his tongue loosed, and he spoke, praising God. Then fear came on all who dwelt around them; and all these sayings were discussed throughout all the hill country of Judea. And all those who heard them kept them in their hearts, saying, "What kind of child will this be?"

And the hand of the Lord was with him. Now his father Zacharias was Filled with the Holy Spirit, and prophesied, saying: "Blessed is the Lord God of Israel, for He has visited and redeemed His people, and has raised up a horn of salvation for us in the house of His servant David as He spoke by the mouth of His holy prophets, who have been since the world began, that we should be saved from our enemies and from the hand of all who hate us, to perform the mercy promised to our fathers and to remember His holy covenant, the oath which He swore to our father Abraham: to grant us that we, being delivered from the hand of our enemies, might serve Him without fear, in holiness and righteousness before Him all the days of our life. "And you, child, will be called the prophet of the Highest; for you will go before the face of the Lord to prepare His ways, to give knowledge of salvation to His people by the remission of their sins, through the tender mercy of our God, with which the Dayspring from on high has visited us; to give light to those who sit in darkness and the shadow of death, to guide our feet into the way of peace." So the child grew and became strong in spirit, and was in the deserts till the day of his manifestation to Israel."

"In Praise of the Baptist"

St. Ephrem the Syrian[24]

The daughter of Aaron the priest (Elizabeth) gave birth to the voice in the wilderness (cf. Isa. 40:3; Mt. 3:3), and the daughter of King David (St. Mary), to the Word of the heavenly King.

St. Cyril of Jerusalem[25]

John alone while carried in the womb leaped for joy (cf. Lk. 1:44), and although he could not see with the eyes of the flesh, he knew his Master by the Spirit. For since the grace of Baptism was great, it required greatness in its founder also.

St. Cyril of Alexandria[26]

The blessed Isaiah knew the work of the Forerunner in proclaiming Christ, and styled John His minister and servant, and said that he was a lamp advancing before the true Light (cf. Isa. 9:2), the morning star heralding the Sun (cf. Mal. 4:2). He foreshadowed the coming of the day that was about to shed its rays upon us; and that he was a voice, not a word, forerunning Jesus, as the voice does the word.

St. John Chrysostom[27]

Conceive, for example, how great a thing it was to see a man after thirty years coming down from the wilderness, being the son of a

---

[24] St. Ephrem the Syrian, *Commentary on Tatian's Diatessaron*

[25] St. Cyril of Jerusalem, *Catechetical Lecture 3*, NPNF, s. 2, v. 7, p. 16.

[26] St. Cyril of Alexandria, Homily 6 on St. Luke, p. 69

[27] St. John Chrysostom, Homily 16 on St. John, NPNF, s.2, v. 10, pp. 56, 57

chief priest (cf. Lk. 1:3), who had never known the common wants of men, and was on every account venerable, and had Isaiah with him...For so great was the earnestness of the Prophets touching these things, that not their own Lord only, but him also who was to minister to Him, they proclaimed a long time beforehand. And they not only mentioned him, but the place too in which he was to abide, and the manner of the doctrine which he had to teach when he came, and the good effect that was produced by him.

St. Cyril of Alexandria[28]

The blessed Baptist was entirely devoted to piety unto Christ; nor was there in him the slightest regard either for fleshly lusts or for the things of this world. Having altogether abandoned, therefore, the vain and unprofitable distractions of this world, he labored at that one and very urgent task of blamelessly fulfilling the ministry entrusted to him.

St. John Chrysostom[29]

See, at least, how both the Prophet and the Baptist arrive at the same ideas, although not upon the same words. Thus the Prophet says that he shall come saying, "Prepare the way of the Lord, make straight the paths of our God" (Isa. 40:3). And (St. John) himself when he was come said, "Bear fruits worthy of repentance" (Mt. 3:8), which corresponds with, "Prepare the way of the Lord" (Mt. 3:3). See that both by the words of the Prophet, and by his own preaching, this one thing is manifested alone: that he came making a way and preparing beforehand, not bestowing the gift, which was the remission, but ordering in good time the souls of such as should receive the God of all.

St. John Chrysostom[30]

The character and heavenly wisdom of the witness showed that his testimony proceeded, not from flattery, but from truth; which is

---

[28] St. Cyril of Alexandria, Homily 39 on St. Luke, p. 166.

[29] St. John Chrysostom, Homily 10 on St. Matthew, NPNF, s. 1, v. 10, p. 63.

[30] St. John Chrysostom, Homily 16 on St. John, pp. 56-57.

plain also from this, that no man prefers his neighbor to himself, nor, when he may lawfully give honor to himself, will yield it up to another, especially when it is so great as that of which we speak.

St. Ambrose of Milan[31]

Moses was not the Bridegroom (cf. Ex. 3:5)...nor Joshua of Nun (cf. Josh. 5:16)....None other is the Bridegroom but Christ alone, of Whom John the Baptist spoke (cf. Jn. 3:29). Therefore, they loosen their sandals, but His sandal cannot be loosed, even as St. John said, "Whose sandal strap I am not worthy to loose" (Jn. 1:27).

"A Life of Simplicity"

St. Jerome[32]

A widow who is "released from the law of her husband" (cf. Rom. 7:2) has, for her one duty, to continue to be a widow. But, you will say, a somber dress vexes the world. In that case, John the Baptist would vex it, too; and yet, among those who are born of women, there has not been a greater than he. He was called an angel; he baptized the Lord Himself, and yet he was clothed in raiment of camel's hair, and girded with a leathern girdle. Is the world displeased because a widow's food is coarse? Nothing can be coarser than locusts, and yet this was the food of John. The women who should scandalize Christians are those who paint their eyes and lips with lipstick and cosmetics, whose chalked faces, unnaturally white, are like those of idols; upon whose cheeks every chance tear leaves a furrow; who fail to realize that years make them old; who heap their heads with hair not their own; who smooth their faces, and rub out the wrinkles of age; and who, in the presence of their grandsons, behave like trembling school-girls. A Christian woman should blush to do violence to nature, or to stimulate desire by bestowing care upon the flesh. "Those who are in the flesh," the apostle Paul tells us, "cannot please God" (Rom. 8:8).

---

31 St. Ambrose of Milan, "Of the Christian Faith," NPNF s. 1, v. 3, p. 253.

32 St. Jerome, *Letter 38* (to Marcella and Blaesilla), NPNF, s. 2, v. 6, pp. 160-161.

"Samson in the Old is Saint John in the New"

St. Irenaeus of Lyons[33]

The little boy, therefore, who guided Samson by the hand, pre-typified John the Baptist, who showed to the people the faith in Christ. And the house in which they were assembled signifies the world, in which dwell the various heathen and unbelieving nations, offering sacrifice to their idols. Moreover, the two pillars are the two covenants. The fact, then, of Samson leaning himself upon the pillars, indicates this, that the people, when instructed, recognized the mystery of Christ.

"Life in the Desert"

St. Jerome[34]

John the Baptist had a religious mother and his father was a priest. Yet neither his mother's affection nor his father's wealth could induce him to live in his parents' house at the risk of his chastity. He lived in the desert, and seeking Christ with his eyes refused to look at anything else. His rough garb, his girdle made of skins, his diet of locusts and wild honey were all alike designed to encourage virtue and continence. The sons of the prophets, who were the monks of the Old Testament, built for themselves huts by the waters of Jordan and forsaking the crowded cities lived in these on pottage and wild herbs.

As long as you are at home make your cell your paradise, gather there the varied fruits of scripture, let this be your favorite companion, and take its precepts to your heart. If your eye, foot, or hand offends you, cast it from you. Save your soul; save nothing else.

The Lord says: "whoever looks to a woman to lust for her has already committed adultery with her in his heart" (Mt. 5:28). "Who can say," writes the wise man, "I have made my heart clean?" (Prov. 20:9). The stars

---

[33] St. Irenaeus of Lyons, *Fragment 27*, ANF v. 1, p. 1186

[34] St. Jerome, *Letter 75* (to Rustics), NPNF, s. 2, v. 6, pp. 556-557. Rustics, a young monk of Tailless who is advised by Jerome not to become an anchorite but to continue in a community. Rules are suggested for the monastic life and a vivid picture is drawn of the difference between a good monk and a bad. The date of the letter is 411 A.D.

are not pure in the Lord's sight; how much less men whose whole life is one long temptation. Woe to us who commit fornication every time that we cherish lust. "My sword," God says, "has drunk its fill in heaven" (Isa.34:5); much more then upon the earth with its crop of thorns and thistles. The chosen vessel who had Christ's name ever on his lips kept under his body and brought it into subjection. Yet even he was hindered by carnal desire and had to do what he would not. As one suffering violence he cries: "O wretched man that I am! Who will deliver me from this body of death?" (Rom. 7:24).

Is it likely then that you can pass without fall or wound, unless you keep your heart with all diligence, and say with the Savior: "My mother and My brothers are those who hear the word of God and do it" (Lk. 8:21). This may seem cruel, but it is really affection. What greater proof can there be of affection than for a holy mother to guard her holy son? She, too, desired your eternal welfare and is willing to forego seeing you for a time that she may see you forever with Christ. She is like Hannah who brought forth Samuel not for her own solace but for the service of the tabernacle.

"The Baptism of Saint John"

St. Jerome[35]

"Behold, I send my messenger (angel) before your face, who shall prepare your way before you." He must have been an angel who after lodging in his mother's womb at once began to frequent the desert wilds, and while still an infant played with serpents; who, when his eyes had once gazed on Christ thought nothing else worth looking at; who exercised his voice, worthy of a messenger of God, in the words of the Lord, which are sweeter than honey and the honey-comb...

The baptism of John did not so much consist in the forgiveness of sins as in being a baptism of repentance for the remission of sins, that is, for a future remission, which was to follow through the sanctification of Christ.

[35] St. Jerome, *Dialogue Against the Luciferians,* NPNF s. 2, v. 6, pp. 706-707. This Dialogue was written about 379, seven years after the death of Lucifer, the bishop of Cagliari in Sardinia. Lucifer came into prominent notice about 354. After returning from his hermit life in the desert of Chalcis, St. Jerome writes this dialogue

For it is written, "John came baptizing in the wilderness and preaching a baptism of repentance for the remission of sins" (Mk. 1:4). And soon after, "And all the land of Judea, and those from Jerusalem, went out to him and were all baptized by him in the Jordan River, confessing their sins" (Mk. 1:5). For as he himself preceded Christ as His forerunner, so also his baptism was the prelude to the Lord's baptism. "He who is of the earth," he said, "is earthly and speaks of the earth. He Who comes from heaven is above all" (Jn. 3:31). And again, "I indeed baptize you with water, but he will baptize you with the Holy Spirit" (Mk. 1:5). But if John, as he himself confessed, did not baptize with the Spirit, it follows that he did not forgive sins either, for no man has his sins remitted without the Holy Spirit. Or if you contentiously argue that, because the baptism of John was from heaven, therefore sins were forgiven by it, tell me why would there be an additional need for us to get in Christ's baptism. Because it forgives sins, it releases from Gehenna. Because it releases from Gehenna, it is perfect. But no baptism can be called perfect except that which depends on the Cross and resurrection of Christ.

Thus, although John himself said, "He must increase, but I must decrease" (Jn. 3:30), in your perverse scrupulosity you give more than is due to the baptism of the servant, and destroy that of the Master to which you leave no more than to the other. What is the drift of your assertion? Just this—it does not strike you as strange that those who had been baptized by John, should afterwards by the laying on of hands receive the Holy Spirit, although it is evident that they did not obtain even remission of sins apart from the faith which was to follow. But you who receive a person baptized by the Arians and allow him to have perfect baptism, after that admission do you invoke the Holy Spirit as if this were still some slight defect, whereas there is no baptism of Christ without the Holy Spirit? But I have wandered too far, and when I might have met my opponent face to face and repelled his attack, I have only thrown a few light darts from a distance. The baptism of John was so far imperfect that it is plain that they who had been baptized by him were afterwards baptized with the baptism of Christ. For thus history relates: "And it happened, while Apollos was at Corinth, that Paul, having passed through the upper regions, came to Ephesus. And finding some disciples he said to them, 'Did you receive the Holy Spirit when you believed?' And they said to him, 'We have not so much as heard whether there is a Holy Spirit.' And he said, 'Into what then were you baptized?' And they said, 'Into John's baptism.' Then Paul said, 'John indeed baptized with a baptism of repentance, saying to the people that they should believe on Him who would come after him, that is, on Jesus.' And when they heard this, they were baptized in the name of the Lord Jesus. And when Paul had laid hands on them, the Holy Spirit came upon them" (Acts 19:1-6).

If, then, they were baptized with the true and lawful baptism of the Church, and thus received the Holy Spirit, you also follow the apostles and baptize those who have not had Christian baptism, and you will be able to invoke the Holy Spirit.

"Who Are You?"

St. John Chrysostom[36]

In the case of Christ all was the contrary of this. His family was lowly, (as they often objected to Him, saying, "Is this not the carpenter's son? Is not his mother called Mary? And His brothers James and Joses?") (Mt. 13:55); and that which was supposed to be His country was held in such evil repute, that even Nathanael said, "Can anything good come out of Nazareth?" (Jn. 1:46). His mode of living was ordinary, and His garments not better than those of the many. For He was not girt with a leathern girdle, nor was His raiment of hair, nor did He eat honey and locusts. But He fared like all others, and was present at the feasts of wicked men and publicans, that He might draw them to Him. Which thing the Jews not understanding reproached Him with, as He also says Himself, "The Son of Man came eating and drinking, and they say, 'Look a gluttonous man and a winebibber, a friend of tax collectors and sinners" (Mt. 11:19).

When then John continually sent (his disciples) from himself to Jesus, who seemed to them a more lowly person, being ashamed and vexed at this, and wishing rather to have him for their teacher, they did not dare to say so plainly, but send to him, thinking by their flattery to induce him to confess that he was the Christ. They did not therefore send to him lowly men, as in the case of Christ, for when they wished to lay hold on Him, they sent servants, and then Herodians, and the like, but in this instance, "priests and Levites" (Jn. 1:19), and not merely "priests," but those "from

[36] St. John Chrysostom, *Commentary on St. John*, NPNF, s. 1, v. 14, pp. 137-138

Jerusalem," that is, the more honorable; for the Evangelist did not notice this without a cause.

And they were sent to ask, "Who are You?" (Jn. 1:19). Yet the manner of his birth was well known to all, so that all said, "What manner of child shall this be?" (Lk. 1:66); and the report had gone forth into all the hill country.

Afterwards when (St. John) came to Jordan, all the cities were set on the wing, and came to him from Jerusalem, and from all Judaea, to be baptized. Why then do they now ask? Not because they did not know him, (how could that be, when he had been made manifest in so many ways?) but because they wished to bring him to do that which I have mentioned. Hear then how this blessed person (St. John) answered to the intention with which they asked the question, not to the question itself. When they said, "Who are You?" he did not at once give them what would have been the direct answer, "I am the voice of one crying in the wilderness." But what did he say? He removed the suspicion they had formed; for, the Evangelist said, being asked, "Who are you?" "He confessed, and denied not; but confessed, I am not the Christ" (Jn. 1:20).

"The Baptist and Elijah"

The Scholar Origen[37]

The words, "Elijah has already come" (Mt. 17:11), and that following which was spoken by the Savior refers to John the Baptist...I do not think that this refers to Elijah's soul, or else I would fall into the dogma of transmigration, which is foreign to the church of God, and not handed down by the Apostles, nor anywhere set forth in the Scriptures. For it is also in opposition to the saying that "things seed are temporal," and that "this age shall have a consummation," and also to the fulfillment of the saying, "Heaven and earth shall pass away," and "the fashion of this world passes away," and "the heavens shall perish," and what follows.

I have thought it necessary to dwell some time on the examination of the doctrine of transmigration, because of the suspicion of some who suppose that the soul under consideration was the same in Elijah and in John, being called in the former case Elijah, and in the second case John.

[37] Origen, *Commentary on St. Matthew*, Book 13, ANF v. 10, pp. 846-851.

And that, not apart from God, had he been called John, as is plain from the saying of the angel who appeared to Zacharias, "Do not be afraid, Zacharias, for your prayer is heard, and your wife Elizabeth will bear you a son, and you shall call his name John" (Lk. 1:13). From the fact that Zacharias regained his speech after he had written in the tablet, that he who had been born should be called John (cf. Lk. 1:63). But if it were the soul of Elijah, then, when he was begotten a second time, he should have been called Elijah; or for the change of name some reason should have been assigned, as in the case of Abram and Abraham, Sarah and Sarai, Jacob and Israel, Simon and Peter. And yet not even thus would their argument in the case be tenable, for in the case of the aforesaid, the change of names took place in one and the same life.

But some one might ask, if the soul of Elijah was not first in the Tishbite and secondly in John, what might that be in both which the Savior called Elijah? And I say that Gabriel in his words to Zacharias suggested what the substance was in Elijah and John that was the same; for he says, "And he will turn many of the children of Israel to the Lord their God. He will also go before Him in the spirit and power of Elijah" (Lk. 1:16, 17). For, observe, he did not say in the "soul" of Elijah, in which case the doctrine of transmigration might have some ground, but "in the spirit and power of Elijah." For the Scripture well knows the distinction between spirit and soul, as, "Now may the God of peace Himself sanctify you completely; and may your whole spirit, soul, and body be preserved blameless at the coming of our Lord Jesus Christ" (1 Thess. 5:23).

This differs from the passage, "Bless the Lord, you spirits and souls of the righteous" (Dan. 3:86) as it stands in the book of Daniel, according to the Septuagint, represents the difference between spirit and soul. Elijah, therefore, was not called John because of the soul, but because of the spirit and the power, which in no way conflicts with the teaching of the Church, though they were formerly in Elijah, and afterwards in John; and "the spirits of the prophets are subject to the prophets" (1 Cor. 14:32), but the souls of the prophets are not subject to the prophets, and "the spirit of Elijah rested on Elisha" (2 Kgs. 2:15).

But we should inquire whether the spirit of Elijah is the same as the spirit of God in Elijah, or whether they are different from each other, and whether the spirit of Elijah which was in him was something supernatural, different from the spirit of each man which is in him, for the Apostle Paul clearly indicates that the Spirit of God, though it is in us, is different from the spirit of each man which is in Him, when he says, "The Spirit Himself bears witness with our spirit that we are the children of God" (Rom. 8:16); and elsewhere, "For what man knows the things of a man except the spirit of the man which is in him? Even so no one knows the things of God except the Spirit of God" (1 Cor. 2:11). But do not marvel in regard to what is said about Elijah, if, just as something strange happened to him different from all the saints who are recorded, in respect of his having been caught up by a whirlwind into heaven (cf. 2 Kgs. 2:11), so his spirit had something of choice excellence, so that not only did it rest on Elisha, but also descended along with John at his birth; and that John, separately, "was filled with the Holy Spirit even from his mother's womb," and separately, "came before Christ in the spirit and power of Elijah" (Lk. 1:15, 17).

For it is possible for several spirits not only worse, but also better, to be in the same man. David accordingly asks to be established by a free spirit, and that a right spirit be renewed in his inward parts (cf. Psa. 51:10, 12). But if, in order that the Savior may impart to us of "the spirit of wisdom and understanding, the spirit of counsel and might, the spirit of knowledge and reverence" (Isa. 11:2), he was filled also with the spirit of the fear of the Lord.

It is also possible that these several good spirits may be conceived as being in the same person. And this also we have brought forward, because of John having come before Christ "in the spirit and power of Elijah," in order that the saying, "Elijah has already come" (Mt. 17:12), may be referred to the spirit of Elijah that was in John; as also the three disciples who had gone up with Him understood that He spoke to them about John the Baptist (cf. Matt. 17:13).

Upon Elisha, then, only the spirit of Elijah rested, but John came before (cf. Lk. 1:17), not only in the spirit, but also in the power of Elijah. Therefore, also, Elisha could not have been called Elijah, but John was Elijah himself. But if it is necessary to adduce the Scripture from which the scribes said that Elijah must come first, listen to Malachi who says, "And behold I will send to you Elijah the Tishbite," etc., down to the words, "Lest I come and smite the earth utterly" (Mal. 4:5,6). And it seems to be indicated by these words that Elijah was to prepare for the glorious coming of Christ by certain holy words and dispositions in their souls, those who had been made fittest for this, which those upon earth could not have endured, because of the excellence of the glory, unless they had been prepared before hand by Elijah. And likewise, by Elijah, in this place, I do not understand the soul of that prophet but his spirit and his power; for these it is by which all things shall be restored, so that when they have been restored (cf. Matt. 17:11), and, as a result of that restoration, become capable of receiving the glory of Christ, the Son of God who shall appear in glory may sojourn with them.

But if also Elijah be in some sort a word inferior to "the Logos who was in the beginning with God, God the Logos" (Jn. 1:1), this word also might come as a preparatory discipline to the people prepared by it, that they might be trained to the reception of the perfect Logos.

The Blessed Month of Tubah

INTRODUCTION TO THE SUNDAY READINGS OF TUBAH

> This is My Beloved Son, in Whom I am well pleased. This is He Who is named the son of Joseph, and Who is according to the divine essence My Only-Begotten. This is My Beloved Son—He Who is hungry, and yet maintains myriads; Who is weary, and yet gives rest to the weary; Who has no where to lay His head, and yet bears up all things in His hand; Who suffers, and yet heals sufferings; Who is smitten, and yet confers liberty on the world; Who is pierced in the side, and yet repairs the side of Adam.
>
> — *St. Hippolytus of Rome*

The fifth month of the Coptic Calendar is Tubah (**ⲦⲰⲂⲒ** in Bohairic; **ⲦⲰⲂⲈ** in Sahidic). The days of this month range from January 9/10 until February 7/8. This month was originally called Botti, because during this month, the ancient Egyptians celebrated a great festival known as the Swelling of the Barley.

The Sunday gospels of Tubah all deal with Baptism as a means of salvation, for in this month we celebrate the blessed Feast of Epiphany or Theophany, after which our Lord commenced His ministry among the people of Israel. Thus, these four weeks present to us the theme of salvation.

The First Sunday deals with the declaration of salvation to the Gentiles in Egypt with the visit of the Holy Family. As the great Exodus from Egypt to Israel was a symbol of Baptism in the Old Testament, the journey of the Holy Family from Israel to Egypt symbolizes a return to the sinful nation to save it from sin and idolatry. The 144,000 slain children of

Bethlehem, which we remember in the Vespers gospel, is a symbol of Baptism "by blood."

The Second Sunday deals with the Holy Epiphany or Theophany in which our Lord Jesus Christ was baptized in the Jordan to fulfill all righteousness. Those who follow in deed and word will receive the salvation through Baptism (cf. Lk. 11:28).

During the Third Sunday of Tubah, we focus on the ministry of the St. John the Baptist and his testimony that Jesus was the Christ, Messiah, and Lamb of God.

Finally, on the Fourth Sunday of Tubah we read of another symbol of Baptism through the miracle of our Lord healing the man born blind (Jn. 9). Through repentance and Baptism, we come to know the Lord personally.

SUNDAY	PASSAGE	TOPIC
First Sunday	Matt. 2:13-23	Entry Into Egypt
Second Sunday	John 1:18-34	Holy Theophany
Third Sunday	John 3:22-36	St. John the Baptist Exalts Christ
Fourth Sunday	John 9:1-38	Light of the World

First Sunday

FROM EGYPT TO NAZARETH

Meditations on the First Sunday of the Blessed Month of Tubah

Gospel Reading of the First Sunday

Matthew 2:13-23

Now when they had departed, behold, an angel of the Lord appeared to Joseph in a dream, saying, "Arise, take the young Child and His mother, flee to Egypt, and stay there until I bring you word; for Herod will seek the young Child to destroy Him." When he arose, he took the young Child and His mother by night and departed for Egypt, and was there until the death of Herod, that it might be fulfilled which was spoken by the Lord through the prophet, saying, "Out of Egypt I called My Son."

Then Herod, when he saw that he was deceived by the wise men, was exceedingly angry; and he sent forth and put to death all the male children who were in Bethlehem and in all its districts, from two years old and under, according to the time which he had determined from the wise men. Then was fulfilled what was spoken by Jeremiah the prophet, saying: "A voice was heard in Ramah, lamentation, weeping, and great mourning; Rachel weeping for her children, refusing to be comforted, because they are no more."

But when Herod was dead, behold, an angel of the Lord appeared in a dream to Joseph in Egypt, saying, "Arise, take the young Child and His mother, and go to the land of Israel, for those who sought the young Child's life are dead." Then he arose, took the young Child and His mother, and came into the land of Israel. But when he heard that Archelaus was reigning over Judea instead of his father Herod, he was afraid to go there. And being warned by God in a dream, he turned aside into the region of Galilee. And he came and dwelt in a city called Nazareth, that it might be fulfilled which was spoken by the prophets, "He shall be called a Nazarene."

"Why Egypt?"

St. John Chrysostom[38]

Why are you angry, O Herod when you were tricked by the wise men? Did you not know that the birth was divine? Did you not summon the chief princes? Did you not gather the Scribes? Did they not, being called, bring the prophet also with them into your court of judgment, proclaiming these things beforehand from of old? Did you not see how the old things agreed with the new? Did you not hear that a star also ministered to these men? Did you not reverence the zeal of the barbarians? Did you not marvel at their boldness? Were you not horrorstruck at the truth of the prophet? Did you not from the former things perceive the very last also? Why did you not reason with yourself from all these things, that this event was not of the craft of the wise men, but of a Divine Power, fittingly dispensing all things? And even if you were deceived by the wise men, what is that to the young children, who have done no wrong?...

But why is the young Child sent into Egypt? First, the evangelist himself says, "That it might be fulfilled through the prophet, saying, 'Out of Egypt have I called my Son'" (Matt. 2:15). And at the same time, beginnings of fair hopes were thus proclaimed to the world. When Babylon, Egypt, and most of the world were burning with the flame of ungodliness, by going to Egypt He signifies from the beginning that He will correct and amend both, and inducing men by this to expect His bounties concerning the whole world likewise, He sent to the one the wise men, and the other He Himself visited with His mother.

By this we learn to expect temptations and plots from the beginning. See, for instance, how this was the case even at once from His swaddling clothes. Thus, you see at His birth, first a tyrant raging, then flight ensuing, and departure beyond the border. And for no crime His mother is exiled into the land of the barbarians so that you, hearing these things (supposing you thought yourself worthy to minister to any spiritual matter, and then to see yourself suffering incurable ills and enduring countless dangers), should not be greatly troubled, nor say, "How can this be? Yet surely I should instead be crowned and celebrated, and be glorious and

---

[38] St. John Chrysostom, *Commentary on Matthew*, NPNF s. 1, v. 10, pp. 139-142

illustrious for fulfilling the Lord's commandment." But having this example, you might bear all things nobly, knowing that this especially is the order of all things spiritual, to have temptations everywhere as the Holy Family did. See at least how this is the case not only concerning the mother of the young Child, but also of those Gentile wise men, since they retire secretly in the condition of fugitives. The mother of the young Child again, who had never passed over the threshold of her house, is commanded to undergo so long a journey of affliction because of this wonderful birth and her spiritual travail.

And behold another wonder: Palestine plots, and Egypt receives and preserves Him Who is the object of the plots. For, as it appears, not only in the instance of the sons of the patriarch did types take place, but also in our Lord's own case. In many instances, we are sure, His doings were prophetic declarations of what was to happen afterwards, as, for example, in the matter of the donkey and the colt (cf. Zech. 9:9).

Now the angel having thus appeared, does not talk with Mary, but with Joseph, and what does he say? "Arise, and take the young Child and His mother." Here, the angel no longer says, "your wife," but "His mother." For after the birth had taken place, and the suspicion was done away, and the husband appeased, the angel talks openly, calling neither Child nor wife his, but "take the young Child and His mother, and flee into Egypt." And the angel mentions the cause of the flight: "For Herod," he says, "will seek the young Child's life." So He escapes and withdraws Himself as any mortal would, for the working of miracles was not yet appropriate. For if from His earliest infancy He had shown forth wonders, He would not have been accounted a Man.

Because of this, let me add, a temple is not framed at once. Rather, a regular conception takes place, and a time of nine months, and pangs, and a delivery, and giving suck, and silence for so long a space, and He awaits the age proper to manhood; that by all means acceptance might be won for the mystery of His Economy...

"But what kind of sin had these children," it may be asked, "that they should do it away? For regarding those who are of full age, and have been guilty of much negligence, one might easily with the demonstration of reason answer such a question. But they who underwent such a premature death, what sort of sins did they put away by their sufferings?" Did you not hear me say, that although there were no sins, there is a recompense of rewards hereafter for those who suffer ill here?

How then were the young children hurt in being slain for such a cause, and taken away speedily into that waveless harbor? "Because," you say, "they would in many instances have achieved, had they lived, many and great deeds of goodness." Why, for this cause He lays up for them beforehand no small reward, the ending of their lives for such a cause. Besides, if the children were to have been any great persons, He would not have allowed them to be snatched away beforehand. For if they that eventually will live in continual wickedness are endured by Him with so great long-sufferings, much more would He not have allowed these to be so taken off had He foreknown they would accomplish any great things.

And these are the reasons we have to give; and yet these are not all. But there are also others more mysterious than these, which He knows perfectly, who Himself orders these things. Let us then give up unto Him the more perfect understanding of this matter, and apply ourselves to what follows, and in the calamities of others let us learn to bear all things nobly. Yes, for it was no little scene of woe, which then befell Bethlehem, for the children were snatched from their mother's breast and dragged to this unjust slaughter.

And if you are still faint-hearted and not equal to controlling yourself in these things, learn the end of him who dared all this, and recover yourself a little. For very quickly Herod was overtaken by punishment for these things. And he paid the due penalty of such an abominable act, ending his life by a grievous death, and more pitiable than that which he now dared inflict, suffering also countless additional ills, which you may know of by reading carefully Josephus' account of these events. But, lest we should make our discourse long, and interrupt its continuity, we have not thought it necessary to insert that account in what we are saying.

"The Blessings of Egypt"

St. Gregory of Nazianzen[39]

I will address myself as is right to those who have come from Egypt; for they have come here eagerly, having overcome ill-will by zeal,

[39] St. Gregory of Nazianzen, *Oration 34*, NPNF, s. 2, v. 7, p. 650.

from that Egypt which is enriched by the River, raining out of the earth, and like the sea in its season—if I too may follow in my small measure those who have so eloquently spoken of these matters; and which is also enriched by Christ my Lord, Who once was a fugitive into Egypt, and now is supplied by Egypt. The first, when He fled from Herod's massacre of the children; and now by the love of the fathers for their children, by Christ the new Food of those who hunger after good; the greatest alms of corn of which history speaks and men believe; the Bread which came down from heaven and gives life to the world, that Life which is indestructible and indissoluble, concerning Whom I now seem to hear the Father saying, "Out of Egypt have I called My Son."

"The 144,000"

St. Gregory of Nazianzen[40]

One thing connected with the Birth of Christ I would have you hate...the murder of the infants by Herod. Or, rather, you must venerate this, too: the sacrifice of the same age as Christ, slain before the Offering of the New Victim. If He flees into Egypt, joyfully become a companion of His exile. It is a grand thing to share the exile of the persecuted Christ. If He tarries long in Egypt, call Him out of Egypt by a reverent worship of Him there. Travel without fault through every stage and faculty of the Life of Christ. Be purified, be circumcised, strip off the veil which has covered you from your birth. After this teach in the Temple, and drive out the sacrilegious traders. Submit to be stoned if need be, for I wish you to be hidden from those who cast the stones. You shall escape even through the midst of them, like God. If you are brought before Herod, answer him not for the most part. He will respect your silence more than most people's long speeches. If you are scourged, ask for what they leave out. Taste gall for the taste's sake; drink vinegar; seek for spitting; accept blows, be crowned with thorns, that is, with the hardness of the godly life. Put on the purple robe, take the reed in hand, and receive mocks from those who mock at the truth. Lastly, be crucified with Him, and share in His death and burial gladly, that you may rise with Him, be glorified with Him and reign with Him. Look at, and be looked at, by the

[40] St. Gregory of Nazianzen, *Oration 38* (On the Theophany), NPNF, s. 2, v. 7, pp. 682-683.

Great God, Who in Trinity is worshipped and glorified, and Whom we declare to be now set forth as clearly before you as the chains of our flesh allow, in Jesus Christ our Lord, to Whom be the glory forever. Amen.

"History of the Flight"

The Scholar Origen[41]

But, moreover, taking the history, contained in the Gospel according to Matthew, of our Lord's descent into Egypt, Celsus refuses to believe the miraculous circumstances attending it, that is, neither that the angel gave the divine intimation or that our Lord's quitting Judea and residing in Egypt was an event of any significance. But instead he invents something altogether different, admitting somehow the miraculous works done by Jesus, by means of which He induced the multitude to follow Him as the Christ. And yet he desires to throw discredit on them, as being done by help of magic and not by divine power, for he asserts "that (Jesus), having been brought up as an illegitimate child, and having served for hire in Egypt, and then coming to the knowledge of certain miraculous powers, returned from there to his own country, and by means of those powers proclaimed himself a god."

Now I do not understand how a magician should exert himself to teach a doctrine which persuades us always to act as if God were to judge every man for his deeds, and should have trained his disciples, whom he was to employ as the ministers of his doctrine, in the same belief. For did the latter make an impression upon their hearers, after they had been so taught to work miracles, or was it without the aid of these? The assertion, therefore, that they did no miracles at all, but that, after yielding their belief to arguments which were not at all convincing, like the wisdom of Grecian dialectics, they gave themselves up to the task of teaching the new doctrine to those persons among whom they happened to take up their abode, is altogether absurd. For in what did they place their confidence when they taught the doctrine and disseminated the new opinions? But if they indeed worked miracles, then how can it be believed that magicians

[41] The Scholar Origen, *Against Celsus,* 1.38, ANF, v. 4.

exposed themselves to such hazards to introduce a doctrine which forbade the practice of magic?

Second Sunday

THE HOLY THEOPHANY

Meditations on the Second Sunday of Blessed Month of Tubah

GOSPEL READING OF THE SECOND SUNDAY

JOHN 1:18-34

No one has seen God at any time. The Only-Begotten Son, Who is in the bosom of the Father, He has declared Him.

Now this is the testimony of John, when the Jews sent priests and Levites from Jerusalem to ask him, "Who are you?" He confessed, and did not deny, but confessed, "I am not the Christ." And they asked him, "What then? Are you Elijah?" He said, "lam not." "Are you the Prophet?" And he answered, "No." Then they said to him, "Who are you, that we may give an answer to those who sent us? What do you say about yourself?" He said: "I am 'The voice of one crying in the wilderness: "Make straight the way of the Lord," as the prophet Isaiah said."

Now those who were sent were from the Pharisees. And they asked him, saying, "Why then do you baptize if you are not the Christ, nor Elijah, nor the Prophet?" John answered them, saying, "I baptize with water, but there stands One among you Whom you do not know. It is He Who, coming after me, is preferred before me, Whose sandal strap I am not worthy to loose." These things were done in Bethabara beyond the Jordan, where John was baptizing.

The next day John saw Jesus coming toward him, and said, "Behold! The Lamb of God Who takes away the sin of the world! This is He of Whom I said, After me comes a Man Who is preferred before me, for He was before me.' I did not know Him; but that He should be revealed to Israel, therefore I came baptizing with water." And John bore witness, saying, "I saw the Spirit descending from heaven like a dove, and He remained upon Him. I did not know Him, but He Who sent me to baptize with water said to me, 'Upon Whom you see the Spirit descending, and remaining on Him, this is He Who baptizes with the Holy Spirit.' And I have seen and testified that this is the Son of God."

"WHO BAPTIZED?"

St. Augustine[42]

It may perhaps surprise you why it is said, that "Jesus made and baptized more than John" (Jn. 4:1), and after this was said, "though Jesus Himself did not baptize, but His disciples" (Jn. 4:2). What then? Was the statement made false, and then corrected by this addition? Or, are both true, that is, that Jesus both did and also did not baptize? He did in fact baptize, because it was He that cleansed; and He did not baptize, because it was not He that touched. The disciples supplied the ministry of the body; He afforded the aid of His majesty. Now, when could He cease from baptizing, so long as He ceased not from cleansing? Of Him it is said by the same John, in the person of the Baptist, who said, "This is He Who baptizes" (Jn. 1:33). Jesus, therefore, is still baptizing; and so long as we continue to be baptized, Jesus baptizes. Let a man come without fear to the minister below, for he has a Master above.

But it may be that one says, "Christ does indeed baptize, but in spirit, not in body." As if, indeed, it were by the gift of another than He that any is imbued even with the sacrament of corporal and visible Baptism. Would you know that it is He Who baptizes not only with the Spirit, but also with water? Hear the Apostle Paul: "Just as Christ," he said, "loved the Church and gave Himself for her, that He might sanctify and cleanse her with the washing of water by the Word, that He might present her to Himself a glorious Church, not having spot or wrinkle or any such thing" (Eph. 5:25-27). Purifying it. How? "With the washing of water by the Word" (Eph. 5:26) What is the Baptism of Christ? The washing of water by the Word. Take away the water, it is not Baptism; take away the Word, it is not Baptism.

---

[42] St. Augustine, *Commentary on the Gospel of John,* NPNF, s. 1, v. 7, p. 198.

"Untying the Sandal Straps"

The Scholar Origen[43]

Now let us consider what is stated by Mark. Mark's account of John's preaching agrees with the other. The words are, "There comes one after me He Who is mightier than I" (Mk. 1:7), which amounts to the same thing as "He Who comes after me is preferred before me" (Jn. 1:15). There is a difference, however, in what follows, "Whose sandal strap I am not worthy to stoop down and loose" (Mk. 1:7). For it is one thing to loose a person's sandals—they must, it is evident, have been untied already from the feet of the wearer—and it is another thing to stoop down and untie the strap of his shoes.

And it follows, since believers cannot think that either of the evangelists made any mistake or misrepresentation, that the Baptist must have made these two utterances at different times and have meant them to express different things. It is not the case, as some suppose, that the reports refer to the same incident, and turned out differently because of a looseness of memory as to some of the facts or words. Now it is a great thing to loose the sandals of Jesus, a great thing to stoop down to the bodily features of His mission, to that which took place in some lower region, so as to contemplate His image in the lower sphere, and to untie each difficulty connected with the mystery of His incarnation, as it were His sandal straps. For the fetter of obscurity is one, as the key of knowledge also is one. Not even he who is greatest among those born of women is sufficient of himself to loose such things or to open them, for He Who tied and locked at first, is He Who also grants to whom He wishes to loose His sandal straps and to unlock what He has shut.

If the passage about the sandals has a mystical meaning we should not scorn to consider it. Now I consider that the Incarnation when the Son of God assumes flesh and bones is one of His sandals, and that the other (sandal) is the descent to Hades, whatever that Hades be, and the journey with the Spirit to the prison. As to the descent into Hades, we read in the sixteenth Psalm, "You will not abandon my soul to Hades" (Ps. 16:10), and as for the journey in prison with the Spirit we read in Peter in his Catholic Epistle, "Being put to death," he says, "in the flesh but made alive by the

---

[43] The Scholar Origen, *Commentary on Gospel of St. John,* ANF, v. 10, pp. 639-640.

Spirit, by Whom also He went and preached to the spirits in prison, who formerly were disobedient, when once the long-suffering of God waited in the days of Noah, while the ark was being prepared" (1 Pet. 3:18-20).

He, then, who is worthily able to set forth the meaning of these two journeys is able to untie the straps of the sandals of Jesus. He, bending down in his mind and going with Jesus as He goes down into Hades, and descending from heaven and the mysteries of Christ's deity to the advent He of necessity made with us when He took on man (as His sandals). Now He Who put on man also put on the dead, for "to this end Christ died and rose and lived again, that He might be Lord both of the dead and the living" (Rom. 14:9). This is why He put on both the living and the dead, that is, the inhabitants of the earth and those of Hades, that He might be the Lord of both the dead and the living. Who, then, is able to stoop down and untie the straps of such sandals, and having untied them not to let them drop, but by the second faculty he has received to take them up and bear them, by bearing the meaning of them in his memory?

"The Baptism of John and Christ"

St. Augustine[44]

It seems to you an odious thing to say that baptism as given to some after John had baptized them, and yet that baptism is not to be given to men after heretics have baptized them. But it may be said with equal justice to be an odious thing that baptism was given to some after John had baptized them, and yet that baptism is not to be given to men after intemperate persons have baptized them. I name this sin of intemperance rather than others, because those in whom it reigns are not able to hide it: and yet what man, even though he be blind, does not know how many addicted to this vice are to be found everywhere?

And yet among the works of the flesh, of which it is said that those who do them shall not inherit the Kingdom of God, the Apostle places this in an enumeration in which heresies also are specified: "Now the works of the flesh," he says, "are evident, which are: adultery, fornication, uncleanness, lewdness, idolatry, sorcery, hatred, contentions, jealousies, outbursts of wrath, selfish ambitions, dissensions, heresies, envy, murders,

[44] St. Augustine, *Letter* 93.11, NPNF, s. 1, v. 1, p. 792.

drunkenness, revelries, and the like; of which I tell you beforehand, just as I also told you in time past, that those who practice such things will not inherit the kingdom of God" (Gal. 5:19-21).

Baptism, therefore, although it was administered after John, is not administered after a heretic, on the very same principle according to which, though administered after John, it is not administered after an intemperate man: for both heresies and drunkenness are among the works which exclude those who do them from inheriting the Kingdom of God.

Does it not seem to you as if it were a thing intolerably improper, that although baptism was repeated after it had been administered by him who, not even moderately drinking wine, but wholly refraining from its use, prepared the way for the Kingdom of God, and yet that it should not be repeated after being administered by an intemperate man, who shall not inherit the Kingdom of God?

What can be said in answer to this, but that the one was the Baptism of John, after which the Apostle administered the Baptism of Christ, and that the other, administered by an intemperate man, was the Baptism of Christ? There is a great difference between John the Baptist and an intemperate man, they are almost opposites. But between the Baptism of Christ and the Baptism of John there is no inconsistence, but a great difference. Between the Apostle and an intemperate man there is a great difference; but there is none between the Baptism of Christ administered by an Apostle, and the Baptism of Christ administered by an intemperate man. Likewise, between John and a heretic there is a great difference, as of opposites; and between the Baptism of John and the Baptism of Christ which a heretic administers there is no contrariety, but there is a great difference. But between the Baptism of Christ which an apostle administers, and the Baptism of Christ which a heretic administers, there is no difference. For the form of the sacrament is acknowledged to be the same even when there is a great difference in point of worth between the men by whom it is administered.

"On the Holy Theophany"

St. Gregory Thaumaturgus[45]

O you who are the friends of Christ, and the friends of the stranger, and the friends of the brethren, receive in kindness my speech today, and open your ears like the doors of hearing, and admit within them my discourse, and accept from me this saving proclamation of the Baptism of Christ, which took place in the river Jordan, in order that your loving desires may be made alive after the Lord, who has done so much for us in the way of condescension. For even though the festival of the Epiphany of the Savior is past, the grace of the same still abides with us through all. Let us therefore enjoy it with insatiable minds; for insatiate desire is a good thing in the case of what pertains to salvation—yes, it is a good thing.

Come therefore, all of us, from Galilee to Judea, and let us go forth with Christ; for blessed is he who journeys in such company on the way of life. Come, and with the feet of thought let us make for the Jordan, and see John the Baptist as he baptizes One who needs no Baptism, and yet submits to the rite in order that He may bestow freely upon us the grace of Baptism. Come, let us view the image of our regeneration, as it is emblematically presented in these waters.

"Then Jesus came from Galilee to John at the Jordan to be baptized by him" (Matt. 3:13). O how vast is the humility of the Lord! O how vast His condescension! The King of the heavens hastened to John, His own forerunner, without setting in motion the camps of His angels, without dispatching beforehand the incorporeal powers as His precursors. But presenting Himself in utmost simplicity, in soldier-like form, He comes to His own subordinate.

He approached him as one of the multitude. He humbled Himself among the captives though He was the Redeemer. He extended Himself with those under judgment though He was the Judge. He joined Himself with the lost sheep though He was the Good Shepherd—who on account of the straying sheep—came down from heaven without forsaking His heavens. He was mingled with the tares though He was that heavenly grain that springs unsown.

---

[45] St. Gregory the Wonder-Worker, *Homily 4,* ANF v. 6, pp. 157-162

And when the Baptist John then saw Him, recognizing Him Whom before in his mother's womb he had recognized and worshipped, and discerning clearly that this was He on Whose account, in a manner surpassing the natural time, he had leaped in the womb of his mother. In violation of the limits of nature, the Baptist drew his right hand within his double cloak, and bowing his head like a servant full of love to his Master, addressed Him in these words: "I need to be baptized by You, and are You coming to me? (Matt. 3:14). What are you doing, my Lord? Why do You reverse the order of things? Why do You seek along with the servants, at the hand of Your servant, the things that are proper to servants? Why do You desire to receive what You do not require? Why do You burden me, Your servant, with Your mighty condescension? I need to be baptized by You, but You have no need to be baptized by me.

"The less is blessed by the Greater; the Greater is not blessed and sanctified by the less. The light is kindled by the Sun; the Sun is not made to shine by the rush-lamp.[46] The clay is wrought by the Potter; the Potter is not molded by the clay. The creature is renewed by the Creator; the Creator is not restored by the creature. The sick is healed by the Physician; the Physician is not cured by the sick. The poor man receives contributions from the Rich; the Rich do not borrow from the poor. I need to be baptized by You, and are You coming to me?

"Can I be ignorant of who You are, and from what source You have Your light, and where You come from? Or, because You have been born even as I have been, am I, then, to deny the greatness of Your divinity? Or, because You have condescended so far to me as to have approached my body, and bear me wholly in Yourself to effect the salvation of the whole of mankind, am I, on account of that body of Yours which is seen, to overlook that divinity of Yours which is only apprehended?

"Or, because on behalf of my salvation You have taken to Yourself the offering of my first-fruits, should I ignore the fact that You "cover Yourself with light as with a garment?" (Ps. 103:2). Or, because You wear the flesh that is related to me, and appear to men as they are able to see You, should I forget the brightness of Your glorious divinity? Or, because I see my own form in You, am I to reason against Your divine substance, which is invisible and incomprehensible?

---

[46] This lamp held a fat-soaked rush stem, and was a less expensive light source than a candle

"I know You, O Lord; I know You clearly. I know You, since I have been taught by You. For no one can recognize You, unless He enjoys Your illumination. I know You, O Lord, clearly, for I saw You spiritually before I beheld this light. When You were altogether in the incorporeal bosom of the heavenly Father, You were also altogether in the womb of Your handmaid and mother. And although I was held in the womb of Elizabeth by nature, as in a prison, and bound with the unbreakable bonds of unborn children—I leapt and celebrated Your birth with anticipating celebration. Shall I, then, who indicated Your sojourn on earth before Your birth, fail to apprehend Your coming after Your birth? Shall I, who in the womb was a teacher of Your coming, be now a child in understanding in view of perfect knowledge?

"I cannot but worship You, Who are adored by the whole creation. I cannot but proclaim You, of Whom heaven gave the indication by the star, and for whom earth offered a kind reception by the wise men, while the choirs of angels also praised You in joy over Your condescension to us, and the shepherds who kept watch by night hymned You as the Chief Shepherd of the rational sheep. I cannot keep silent while You are present, for I am a voice —yes, 'I am the voice,' as it is said, 'of one crying in the wilderness, "Prepare the way of the Lord' (Mark 1:3)." I need to be baptized by You, and are You coming to me?

"I was born, and by this removed the barrenness of the mother that bore me. While I was still a child I became the healer of my father's speechlessness, having received of You from my childhood the gift of the miraculous. But You, being born of the Virgin Mary, as You did will, and as You alone do know, did not do away with her virginity. But You preserved it, and simply gifted her with the name of 'mother'. Her virginity neither precluded Your birth, nor did Your birth injure her virginity. But these two things, so utterly opposite—bearing and virginity—harmonized with one intent; for such a thing abides, possible with You, the Framer of nature. I am, but a man and a partaker of the divine grace. But You are God, and at the same time, man— for You are by nature man's friend. I need to be baptized of You, and are You coming to me?

"You Who were in the beginning, and were with God, and was God; You Who are the brightness of the Father's glory (cf. Heb. 1:3); You Who are the perfect image of the perfect Father; You who are the true Light that gives light to every man coming into the world (Jn. 1:9); You Who was in the world, and did come where You were; You Who took flesh, and yet was not changed into the flesh; You Who tabernacled in us, and did manifest Yourself to Your servants in the form of a servant; You Who bridged earth and heaven together by Your Holy Name—You come to me?

"One so great comes to someone like me? The King to the Forerunner? The Lord to the servant? But though You were not ashamed to be born in the lowly measures of humanity, yet I have no ability to pass the measures of nature. I know how great is the measure of difference between earth and the Creator. I know how great is the distinction between the clay and the Potter. I know how vast is the superiority possessed by You, Who are the Sun of Righteousness, over me who am but the torch of Your grace. Even though You surrounded with the pure cloud of the body, I can still recognize Your lordship. I acknowledge my own servitude; I proclaim Your glorious greatness; I recognize Your perfect lordship; I recognize my own perfect insignificance. I am not worthy to unloose the straps of Your sandals.

"And how shall I dare to touch Your stainless head? How can I stretch out the right hand upon You, who did stretch out the heavens like a curtain, and did set the earth above the waters? How shall I spread those menial hands of mine upon Your head? How shall I wash You, who are undefiled and sinless? How shall I enlighten the Light? What manner of prayer shall I offer up over You, You who receive the prayers even of those who are ignorant of You?

"When I baptize others, I baptize into Your name, in order that they may believe in You, Who come with glory. But when I baptize You, of whom shall I make mention and into whose name shall I baptize You? Into that of the Father? But You have the Father altogether in Yourself, and You are altogether in the Father. Or into that of the Son? But beside You there is no other Son of God by nature. Or into that of the Holy Spirit? But He is ever-together with You, as being of one essence, of one will, of one judgment, of one power, and of one honor with You. He receives, along with You, the same adoration from all.

"Therefore, O Lord, You baptize me, if You please. Baptize me, the Baptist. Restore one whom You created. Extend Your awesome right hand, which You have prepared for Yourself, and crown my head by Your touch, in order that I may run the course before Your kingdom, crowned like a forerunner, and diligently announce the good tidings to the sinners, addressing them with this earnest call: 'Behold the Lamb of God Who takes away the sin of the world!' (Jn. 1:29).

"O river Jordan, accompany me in the joyous choir, and leap with me, and stir your waters rhythmically, as in the movements of the dance—for your Maker stands by you in the body. Long ago, when you saw Israel pass through you, you divided your floods and waited in expectation of the passage of the people. Now divide yourself more decidedly, flow more easily, and embrace the unblemished limbs of Him who at that ancient time did convey the Jews through you. You mountains and hills, you valleys and torrents, you seas and rivers, bless the Lord, Who has come upon the Jordan River. For through these streams He transmits sanctification to all streams."

And Jesus answered and said to him:

"Permit it to be so now, for thus it is fitting for us to fulfill all righteousness' (Matt. 3:15). Permit it to be so now; grant the favor of silence, O Baptist, to the season of My Economy. Learn to will whatever is My will. Learn to minister to Me in those things on which I am concerned of, and do not pry curiously into all that I wish to do.

"Permit it to be so now; do not yet proclaim My divinity. Do not yet herald My Kingdom with your lips, in order that the tyrant may not learn the fact and give up the counsel he has formed with respect to Me.

"Permit the Devil to come upon Me, and enter the conflict with Me as though I were but a common man, and receive thus his mortal wound. Permit Me to fulfill the object for which I have come to earth. It is a mystery that is being gone through this day in the Jordan. My mysteries are for Myself and My own. There is a mystery here, not for the fulfilling of My own need, but for the designing of a remedy for those who have been wounded. There is a mystery, which gives in these waters the representation of the heavenly streams of the regeneration of men.

"Permit it to be so now. When you see Me doing what seems to Me good among the works of My hands, in a manner befitting divinity, then attune your praises to the acts accomplished. When you see Me cleansing the lepers, then proclaim Me as the framer of nature. When you see Me make the lame ready runners, then with quickened pace do you also prepare your tongue to praise Me. When you see Me cast out demons, then hail My Kingdom with adoration. When you see Me raise the dead from their graves by My word, then, in concert with those thus raised, glorify Me as the Prince of Life. When you see Me on the Father's right hand, then acknowledge Me to be divine, as the equal of the Father and the Holy Spirit, on the throne, in eternity, and in honor.

"Permit it to be so now, for thus it is fitting for us to fulfill all righteousness. I am the Lawgiver, and the Son of the Lawgiver. I desire to first to pass through all that is established, and then to set forth everywhere the intimations of My free gift. I desire to fulfill the law, and then to bestow Grace. I desire to adduce the shadow, and then the reality.

"I desire to finish the Old Covenant, then to dictate the New, to write it on the hearts of men, to subscribe it with My Blood, and to seal it with My Spirit. I desire to ascend the Cross, and to be pierced with its nails, and to suffer after the manner of that nature which is capable of suffering, and to heal sufferings by My suffering, and by the tree to cure the wound that was inflicted upon men by the medium of a tree. I desire to descend even into the very depths of the grave on behalf of the dead who are detained there. I desire to, by My three days' dissolution in the flesh, to destroy the power of the ancient enemy, death. I desire to kindle the torch of My body for those who sit in darkness and in the shadow of death. I desire to ascend in the flesh to that place where I am in My divinity. I desire to introduce to the Father, the Adam reigning in Me. I desire to accomplish these things, for on account of these things I have taken My position with the works of My hands. I desire to be baptized with this Baptism for the present, and afterwards to bestow the Baptism of the consubstantial Trinity upon all men.

"Lend Me, therefore, O Baptist, your right hand for the present Economy, even as Mary lent her womb for My birth. Immerse Me in the streams of the Jordan, even as she who bore Me wrapped Me in children's swaddling-clothes. Grant Me your Baptism even as the Virgin granted Me her milk. Lay hold of this head of Mine, which the Seraphim revere. With your right hand lay hold of this head, that is related to yourself in kinship. Lay hold of this head, which nature has made to be touched. Lay hold of this head, which for this very purpose has been formed by Myself and My Father. Lay hold of this head of Mine, which, if one does lay hold of it in piety, will save him from ever-suffering shipwreck.

"Baptize Me, Who am destined to baptize those who believe on Me with water, and with the Spirit, and with fire: with water, capable of washing away the defilement of sins; with the Spirit, capable of making the earthly spiritual; with fire, naturally fitted to consume the thorns of transgressions."

On hearing these words, the Baptist directed his mind to the object of the salvation, and comprehended the mystery which he had received, and discharged the divine command. For he was at once pious and ready to obey. And stretching forth slowly his right hand, which seemed both to tremble and to rejoice, he baptized the Lord.

"The Meaning of the Jordan"

The Scholar Origen[47]

Let us look at the words of the gospel now before us. "Jordan" means "their going down." The name "Jared" is etymologically akin to it, if I may say so. It also yields the meaning "going down," for Jared was born to Maleleel, as it is written in the Book of Enoch, if any one cares to accept that book as sacred...

Should this be so, what river will "their going down" be, to which one must come to be purified, a river going down, not with its own descent, but "theirs," that, namely, of men, what but our Savior Who separates those who received their lots from Moses from those who obtained their own portions through Jesus (Joshua)? His current, flowing in the descending streams, makes glad, as we find in the Psalms, the City of God, not the visible Jerusalem—for it has no river beside it—but the blameless Church of God, built on the foundation of the apostles and prophets, Christ Jesus our Lord being the chief Cornerstone (Ps.117:22).

Under the Jordan, accordingly, we have to understand the Word of God Who became flesh and tabernacled in us: Jesus, Who gives us as our inheritance the humanity which He assumed, for that is the Chief Cornerstone, which being taken up into the deity of the Son of God, is washed by being so assumed, and then receives into itself the pure and guileless dove of the Spirit, bound to it and no longer able to fly away from

[47] The Scholar Origen, *Commentary on Gospel of St. John,* ANF, v. 10, pp. 647-8.

it. For "Upon whom," we read, "you see the Spirit descending, and remaining on Him, this is He Who baptizes with the Holy Spirit" (Mk. 1:33). Hence, he who receives the Spirit abiding on Jesus Himself is able to baptize those who come to him in that abiding Spirit. But John baptizes beyond Jordan, in the regions verging on the outside of Judea, in Bethabara, being the forerunner of Him Who came to call not the righteous but sinners (cf. Matt. 9:13), and Who taught that the healthy have no need of a physician, but those who are sick (cf. Mk. 2:17). For it is for forgiveness of sins that this washing is given.

"On the Holy Theophany"

St. Hippolytus of Rome[48]

Good, yes, very good, are all the works of our God and Savior—all of those which eye sees and mind perceives, all that reason interprets and hand handles, all that intellect comprehends and human nature understands.

For what richer beauty can there be than that of the circle of heaven? For what form of blooming fairness is more than that of earth's surface? Is there anything that travels quicker than the chariot of the sun? Or is there anything more graceful than the moon's sphere? Or any work more wonderful than the compact mosaic of the stars? Or anything more productive than the seasonable winds? Or anything more spotless mirror than the light of day? Or any work more excellent creature than man? So, then all the works of our God and Savior are very good.

And what more requisite gift, again, is there than the element of water? For with water all things are washed and nourished, and cleansed and bedewed. Water bears the earth, water produces the dew, water exhilarates the vine, water matures the corn in the ear, water ripens the grape cluster, water softens the olive, water sweetens the palm-date, water reddens the rose and decks the violet, water makes the lily bloom with its brilliant cups. And why should I speak at length? Without the element of water, none of the present order of things can subsist. So necessary is the element of water; for the other elements took their places beneath the

[48] St. Hippolytus, *Discourse on the Holy Theophany,* ANF v. 5, pp. 491-496.

highest vault of the heavens, but the nature of water obtained a seat also above the heavens. And to this the prophet himself is a witness, when he exclaims, "Praise the Lord, you heavens of heavens, and the water above the heavens" (Ps.148:4).

Nor is this the only thing that proves the dignity of the water. But there is also that which is more honorable than all—the fact that Christ, the Maker of all, came down as the rain, and was known as a spring, and diffused Himself as a river, and was baptized in the Jordan. For you have just heard how Jesus came to John, and was baptized by him in the Jordan. O things strange beyond comparison! How should the boundless rivers that make glad the city of God have been dipped in a little water?! The illimitable Spring that bears life to all men, and has no end, was covered by poor and temporary waters! He Who is present everywhere and absent nowhere, Who is incomprehensible to angels and invisible to men, comes to the Baptism according to His own good pleasure.

When you hear these things, beloved, take them not as if spoken literally, but accept them as presented in a figure. Whence also the Lord was not unnoticed by the watery element in what He did in secret, in the kindness of His condescension to man. "For the waters saw You, and they were afraid" (Ps. 76:17). The waters well near broke from their place, and burst away from their boundary. Hence the prophet, having this in his view many generations ago, puts the question, "What troubles you, O sea, that you become red; and you, Jordan, that you were driven back? (cf. Ps. 114:3)" And they in reply said, "We have seen the Creator of all things in the form of a servant, and being ignorant of the Mystery of the Economy, we were lashed with fear."

But we, who know the Economy, adore His mercy, because He has come to save and not to judge the world (cf. Jn. 12:47). Therefore John, the Forerunner of the Lord, who did not know this mystery previously, upon learning that He is the Lord in truth, cried out, and spoke to those who came to be baptized of him: "O Brood of vipers" (cf. Matt. 3:7), why look you so earnestly at me? I am not the Christ; I am the servant, and not the Lord; I am the subject, and not the King; I am the sheep, and not the Shepherd; I am a man, and not God. By my birth I loosed the barrenness of my mother; I did not make virginity barren. I was brought up from beneath; I did not come down from above. I bound the tongue of my father; I did not unfold divine grace. I was known by my mother, and I was not announced by a star. I am worthless, and the least; but 'after me there comes One Who is before me' (Jn. 1:26)—after me, indeed, in time, but before me by reason of the inaccessible and unutterable light of divinity. 'There comes One after me Who is mightier than I, whose sandal straps I am not worthy to stoop down and loose: He shall baptize you with the Holy spirit and fire' (Matt. 3:11; Mk. 3:7). I am subject to authority, but He has authority in Himself. I am bound by sins, but He is the Remover of sins. I apply the law, but He brings Grace to light. I teach as a slave, but He judges as the Master. I have the earth as my couch, but He possesses heaven. I baptize with the Baptism of repentance, but He confers the Grace of adoption: "He shall baptize you with the Holy Spirit and fire." Why do you give your attention to me? I am not the Christ."

As John says these things to the multitude, and as the people watch in eager expectation of seeing some strange spectacle with their bodily eyes, and the Devil is struck with amazement at such a testimony from John, behold, the Lord appears plain, solitary, uncovered, without escort, having on Him the body of man like a garment, and hiding the dignity of the Divinity, that He may elude the snares of the Dragon. And not only did He approach John as Lord without royal escort; but even like a mere man, and one involved in sin, He bent His head to be baptized by John. Therefore John, on seeing so great a humbling of Himself, was struck with astonishment at the affair, and began to prevent Him, saying, as you have just heard: "'I need to be baptized by You, and are You coming to me?' (Matt. 3:13). Why, O Lord? You teach things not according to rule. I have preached one thing (regarding You), and You perform another; the Devil has heard one thing, and perceives another. Baptize me with the fire of Divinity; why do You wait for water? Enlighten me with the Spirit; why do You attend to a creature? Baptize me, the Baptist, so that Your superiority may be known. I, O Lord, baptize with the Baptism of repentance, and I cannot baptize those who come to me unless they first confess fully their sins. If it is then that I baptize You, what have You to confess? You are the Remover of sins, and you will be baptized with the Baptism of repentance? Though I should venture to baptize You, the Jordan dares not to come near You. 'I need to be baptized by You, and You are coming to me?'"

And what does the Lord say to him? "'Permit it to be so now, for thus it is fitting for us to fulfill all righteousness' (Matt 3:15). Permit it to be so now, John, for you are not wiser than I. You see as man; I foreknow as God. It is fitting for Me to do this first, and thus to teach. I engage in nothing unfitting, for I am invested with honor. Do you marvel, O John, that I have not come in My dignity? The purple robe of kings suits not one in private station, but military splendor suits a king. Have I come to a prince, and not to a friend? Permit it to be so now for thus it is fitting for us to fulfill all righteousness.

"I am the Fulfiller of the law; I seek to leave nothing wanting to its whole fulfillment, that so after me Paul may exclaim, 'For Christ is the fulfilling of the law for righteousness to everyone who believes' (Rom. 10:4). Permit it to be so now, for thus it is fitting for us to fulfill all righteousness.

"Baptize me, John, in order that no one may despise Baptism. I am baptized by you, the servant, that no one among kings or dignitaries may scorn to be baptized by the hand of a poor priest. Allow Me to go down into the Jordan in order that they may hear My Father's testimony and recognize the power of the Son. Permit it to be so now, for thus it is fitting for us to fulfill all righteousness."

Then at length John allowed Him. "When He had been baptized, Jesus came up immediately out of the water; and behold, the heavens were opened to Him, and He saw the Spirit of God descending like a dove and resting upon Him. And suddenly a voice came from heaven, saying, 'This is My Beloved Son, in Whom I am well pleased'" (Matt. 3:16, 17).

Do you see, beloved, how many and how great blessings we would have lost, if the Lord had yielded to the exhortation of John, and declined Baptism? For the heavens were shut before this; the region above was inaccessible. We would in that case descend to the lower parts, but we would not ascend to the upper parts. But was it only that the Lord was baptized? He also renewed the old man, and committed to him again the scepter of adoption. For immediately "the heavens were opened to Him."

A reconciliation took place of the visible with the invisible; the celestial orders were filled with joy; the diseases of earth were healed; secret things were made known; those at enmity were restored to amity. For you have heard the words of the Evangelist, saying, "The heavens were opened to Him" (Matt. 3:16) on account of three wonders. For when Christ the Bridegroom was baptized, it was meet that the bridal-chamber of heaven should open its brilliant gates. And in like manner also, when the Holy Spirit descended in the form of a dove, and the Father's voice spread everywhere, it was meet that "the gates of heaven should be lifted up." "And, behold, the heavens were opened to Him; and a voice was heard, saying, 'This is My Beloved Son, in Whom I am well pleased.'"

If love generates love, is light immaterial and light inaccessible? "This is My Beloved Son," He Who, being manifested on earth and yet not separated from the Father's Bosom, was manifested, and yet did not appear. For the appearing is a different thing, since in appearance the baptizer here is superior to the baptized. For this reason the Father sent down the Holy Spirit from heaven upon Him Who was baptized. For as in the Ark of Noah the love of God toward man is signified by the dove, so also now the Spirit, descending in the form of a dove, bearing as it were the fruit of the olive, rested on Him to Whom the witness was born.

For what reason? That the faithfulness of the Father's voice might be made known, and that the prophetic utterance of a long time past might be ratified. And what utterance is this? "The voice of the Lord is on the waters, the God of glory thundered; the Lord is upon the many waters" (Ps. 28:3). And what voice?

"This is My Beloved Son, in Whom I am well pleased. This is He Who is named the son of Joseph, and Who is according to the divine essence My Only-Begotten. This is My Beloved Son—He Who is hungry, and yet maintains myriads; Who is weary, and yet gives rest to the weary; Who has no where to lay His head, and yet bears up all things in His hand; Who suffers, and yet heals sufferings; Who is smitten, and yet confers liberty on the world; Who is pierced in the side, and yet repairs the side of Adam."

But give me now your best attention, I ask you, for I wish to go back to the Fountain of Life, and to view the Fountain that gushes with healing. The Father of immortality sent the immortal Son and Word into the world, Who came to man to wash him with water and the Spirit. And He, begetting us again to incorruption of soul and body, breathed into us the breath (spirit) of life, and endued us with an incorruptible splendor.

If, therefore, man has become immortal, he will also be God. And if he is made God by water and the Holy Spirit after the regeneration of the laver he is found to be also joint-heir with Christ (Rom. 8:17), after the

Resurrection from the dead. Therefore I preach to this effect: Come, all you kindreds of the nations, to the immortality of the Baptism. I bring good tidings of life to you who tarry in the darkness of ignorance. Come into liberty from slavery, into a kingdom from tyranny, into incorruption from corruption.

"And how," one says, "shall we come?" How? By water and the Holy Spirit. This is the water in conjunction with the Spirit, by which Paradise is watered, by which the earth is enriched, by which plants grow, by which animals multiply, and (to sum up the whole in a single word) by which man is begotten again and endued with life, in which also Christ was baptized, and in which the Spirit descended in the form of a dove.

This is the Spirit that at the beginning "hovering over the face of the waters" (Gen. 1:2); by Whom the world moves; by Whom creation consists, and all things have life; Who also worked mightily in the prophets, and descended in flight upon Christ. This is the Spirit that was given to the apostles in the form of fiery tongues. This is the Spirit that David sought when he said, "Create in me a clean heart, O God, and renew a right spirit within me" (Ps.50:12). Of this Spirit Gabriel also spoke to the Virgin, "The Holy Spirit will come upon you, and the power of the Highest will overshadow you" (Lk. 1:35). By this Spirit Peter spoke that blessed word, "You are the Christ, the Son of the Living God" (Matt. 16:16). By this Spirit the rock of the Church was established. This is the Spirit, the Comforter, that is sent because of you, that He may show you to be the Son of God.

Come then, be begotten again, O man, into the adoption of God. "And how?" says one: if you practice adultery no more, and do not commit murder, and do not serve idols. If you are not overmastered by pleasure; if you do not suffer the feeling of pride to rule you; if you clean off the filth of impurity, and put off the burden of sin; if you cast off the armor of the Devil, and put on the breastplate of faith, even as Isaiah says, "'Wash yourselves, and make yourselves clean. Put away the evils from your souls before My eyes. Cease your evils. Learn to do good. Seek judgment and redeem the wronged. Defend the orphans and justify the widow. Come now and let us reason together,' says the Lord, 'although your sins are like crimson, I shall make them white like snow; and although they are like scarlet, I shall make them white like wool. If you are willing and obedient, you shall eat the good things of the land" (Isa. 1:16-19).

Do you see, beloved, how the prophet spoke beforetime of the purifying power of Baptism? For whoever descends in faith to the laver of regeneration, renounces the Devil, and joins himself to Christ; who denies the enemy, and makes the confession that Christ is God; who puts off the bondage, and puts on the adoption—he comes up from the Baptism brilliant as the sun, flashing forth the beams of righteousness, and, which is indeed the chief thing, he returns a son of God and joint-heir with Christ. To Him be the glory and the power, together with His most holy, good, and Life-Giving Spirit, now and ever, and to all the ages of the ages. Amen.

"Hymn on the Epiphany"

St. Ephrem the Syrian[49]

To You be praise from Your flock in the day of Your Epiphany!

1. The heavens He has renewed, for that fools all the luminaries. He has renewed the earth, for that in Adam it was wasted. That which He fashioned has become new by His spittle, and the All-Sufficing has restored bodies with souls.

2. Gather yourselves again, sheep and without labor receive cleansing! For one does not need, as Elisha, to bathe seven times in the river, nor again to be wearied as the priests are wearied with sprinklings.

3. Seven times Elisha purified himself in a mystery of the seven spirits, and the hyssop and blood are a mighty symbol. There is no room for division; He is not divided from the Lord of all Who is Son of the Lord of all.

4. Moses sweetened in Marah the waters that were bitter, because the people complained and murmured. Thus he gave a sign of Baptism, in which the Lord of life makes sweet those that were bitter.

5. The cloud overshadowed and kept off the burning heat from the camp— it showed a symbol of the Holy Spirit, which overshadows you in Baptism— tempering the flaming fire that it harm not your bodies.

[49] St. Ephrem the Syrian, *Hymns for the Feast of Epiphany*, Hymn 1, NPNF, s. 2, v. 13.

6. Through the sea the people then passed, and showed a symbol of the Baptism in which you were washed. The people passed through that and believed not — the Gentiles were baptized in this and believed and received the Holy Spirit.

7. The Word sent the voice to proclaim His Coming, to prepare for Him the way by which He came, and to betroth the Bride until He should come, that she might be ready when He should come and take her from the water.

8. The voice of prophesy stirred the son of the barren woman, and he went forth wandering in the desert and crying," Behold! The Son of the Kingdom comes! Prepare the way that He may enter and abide in your dwellings!"

9. John cried, "He who comes after me, He is before me"— I am the voice but not the Word; I am the torch but not the Light; the star that rises before the Sun of Righteousness."

10. In the wilderness this John had cried and said, "Repent you sinners of your evils, and bear fruits worthy of repentance; for behold He comes winnowing the wheat from the tares."

11. The Light-giver has prevailed and marked a mystery, by the degrees He ascended. Behold, there are twelve days since He ascended, and today this is the thirteenth—a perfect Mystery of Him, the Son, and His twelve!

12. Darkness was overcome to make manifest that Satan was overcome, and the Light prevailed that he should proclaim that the Firstborn triumphs. Darkness was overcome with the Dark Spirit, and our Light prevailed with the Light-giver.

13. In height and depth the Son had two heralds: the star of light proclaimed Him from above, while John likewise preached Him from beneath— two heralds, the earthly and the heavenly.

14. The star of light, contrary to nature, shone forth all of a sudden — less than the sun yet greater than the sun. Less was it than he in manifest light; and greater than he in secret might because of its mystery.

15. The star of light shed its rays among them that were in darkness, and guided them as though they were blind; so that they came and met the great Light. They gave offerings and received Life, adored and departed.

16. The herald from above showed His Nature to be from the Most High; likewise he (John) who was from beneath showed His Body to be from humankind, mighty marvel — that His divinity and His humanity were proclaimed by both of them!

17. Thus whoever considers Him as of earth, the star of light will convince him that He is of heaven; and whoever considers Him as of Spirit, this John will convince him that He is also bodily.

18. John drew near with his parents and worshipped the Sun, and brightness rested on His Face. He was not moved as when in the womb. Mighty marvel! that here he worships and there he leaped!

19. The whole creation became for Him as one mouth and cried out concerning Him. The Magi cry out in their gifts; the barren cry out with their children; the star of light, lo! it cries out in the air, "Behold the Son of the King!"

20. The heavens are opened, the waters break forth, the dove is in glory! The voice of the Father is stronger than thunder, as it utters the word, "This is My Beloved." The Watchers brought the tidings, the children acclaimed Him in their Hosannas.

"A Hymn Concerning Our Lord and John"

St. Ephrem the Syrian[50]

Glory to You, my Lord, for You — with joy Heaven and earth worship!

1. My thought bore me to Jordan, and I saw a marvel when there was revealed the glorious Bridegroom who to the Bride shall bring freedom and holiness.

---

[50] St. Ephrem the Syrian, *Hymns for the Feast of Epiphany*, Hymn 14, NPNF, s. 2, v. 13.

2. I saw John filled with wonder, and the multitudes standing about him, and the glorious Bridegroom bowed down to the Son of the barren that he might baptize Him.

3. At the Word and the Voice my thought marveled. For, behold John was the Voice—our Lord was manifested as the Word, that what was hidden should become revealed.

4. The Bride was espoused but knew not who was the Bridegroom on whom she gazed; the guests were assembled, the desert was filled, and our Lord was hidden among them.

5. Then the Bridegroom revealed Himself; and He drew near to John at the voice: and the Forerunner was moved and said of Him: "This is the Bridegroom Whom I proclaimed."

6. He came to Baptism Who baptizes all, and He showed Himself at Jordan. John saw Him and drew back, deprecating, and thus he spoke.

7. "How, my Lord, do You will to be baptized, You Who in Your Baptism atones all? Baptism looks to You—do You shed on it holiness and perfection?"

8. Our Lord said, "I will it so; draw near, baptize Me that My Will may be done. You cannot resist My Will: I shall be baptized by you, for thus I will it."

9. "I entreat, my Lord, that I be not compelled, for this is hard that You have said to me, 'I need you to baptize Me,' for it is You that with Your hyssop purifies all."

10. "I have asked it, and it pleases Me that thus it should be; and you, John, why do you deny? Allow righteousness to be fulfilled, and come, baptize Me; why are you standing there?"

11. "How can one openly grasp in his hands the fire that burns? O You that are fire have mercy on me, and bid me not come near You, for it is hard for me!"

12. "I have revealed to You My Will, what do you question? Draw near, baptize Me, and you shall not be burned. The bridal chamber is ready; keep Me not back from the wedding-feast that has been made ready."

13. "The Watchers fear and dare not gaze on You lest they be blinded; and I, how, O my Lord, shall I baptize You? I am too weak to draw near; blame me not!"

14. "You fear; therefore deny not against My Will in what I desire—and Baptism has respect to Me. Accomplish the work to which you have been called!"

15. "Lo! I proclaimed You at Jordan in the ears of the people that believed not and if they shall see You baptized of me, they will doubt that You are the Lord."

16. "Lo! I am to be baptized in their sight, and the Father Who sent Me bears witness of Me that I am His Son and in Me He is well pleased, to reconcile Adam who was under His wrath."

17. "It is fitting for me, O my Lord, to know my nature that I am molded out of the ground, and You the molder Who forms all things—I, then, why should I baptize You in water?"

18. "It is fitting for you to know why I have come, and for what cause I have desired that you should baptize Me. It is the middle of the way in which I have walked; withhold not Baptism."

19. "Small is the river to which You have come, that You should lodge in it and it should cleanse You. The heavens suffice not for Your mightiness— how much less shall Baptism contain You!"

20. "The womb is smaller than Jordan, yet was I willing to lodge in the Virgin. And as I was born from woman, so too am I to be baptized in Jordan."

21. "Lo! the hosts are standing! The ranks of Watchers, lo! they worship! And if I draw near, my Lord, to baptize You, I tremble for myself with quaking."

22. "The hosts and multitudes call you happy, all of them, for that you baptize Me. For this I have chosen you from the womb—fear not, for I have willed it.

23. "I have prepared the way as I was sent; I have betrothed the Bride as I was commanded. May Your Epiphany be spread over the world now that You are come, and let me not baptize You!"

24. "This is My preparation, for so have I willed; I will go down and be baptized in Jordan and make bright the armor for them that are baptized, that they may be white in Me and I not be conquered."

25. "Son of the Father, why should I baptize You? For lo! You are in Your Father and Your Father in You. Holiness to the priests You give— why do You ask for water that is common?"

26. "The children of Adam look to Me, that I should work for them the new birth. A way in the waters I will search out for them, and if I am not baptized this cannot be."

27. "Pontiffs of You are consecrated, priests by Your hyssop are purified; the anointed and the kings You make — baptism, how shall it profit You?"

28. "The Bride you betrothed to Me awaits Me, that I should go down, be baptized, and sanctify her. Friend of the Bridegroom withhold Me not from the washing that awaits Me."

29. "I am not able, for I am weak, Your blaze in my hands to grasp. Lo! Your legions are as flame; bid one of the Watchers baptize You!"

30. "Not from the Watchers was My Body assumed, that I should summon a Watcher to baptize Me. The body of Adam, lo! I have put on, and you, son of Adam, are to baptize Me."

31. "The waters saw You, and greatly feared; the waters saw You, and lo, they tremble! The river foams in its terror; and I that am weak, how shall I baptize You?"

32. "The waters in My Baptism are sanctified, and fire and the Spirit from Me shall they receive; and if I am not baptized they are not made perfect — to be fruitful of children that shall not die."

33. "Fire, if to Your fire it draw near, shall be burnt up of it as stubble. The mountains of Sinai endured You not, and I that am weak, how shall I baptize You?"

34. "I am the flaming fire, yet for man's sake I became a babe in the virgin womb of the maiden. And now I am to be baptized in Jordan."

35. "It is very meet that You should baptize me, for You have holiness to purify all. In You it is that the defiled are made holy; but You Who are holy, why are You to be baptized?"

36. "It is very right that you should baptize Me, as I bid, and should not deny. Behold, I baptized you within the womb; baptize me in Jordan!"

37. "I am a bondman and I am weak. You Who frees all have mercy on me! Your sandal straps to unloose I am not able; Your exalted head, who will make me worthy to touch?"

38. "Bondmen in My Baptism are set free; handwritings in My washing are blotted out; slaves are sealed in the water; and if I am not baptized all these come to nothing."

39. "A mantle of fire the air wears, and waits for You, above Jordan; and if You consent to it and will to be baptized, You shall baptize Yourself and fulfill all."

40. "This is meet, that you should baptize Me, that none may err and say concerning Me, 'Had He not been alien from the Father's house, why feared the Levite to baptize Him?'"

41. "The prayer, then, when You are baptized, how shall I complete over Jordan? When the Father and the Spirit are seen over You, Whom shall I call on, as priest?"

42. "The prayer in silence is to be complete—come, your hand alone lay on Me—and the Father shall utter in the priest's stead that which is meet concerning His Son."

43. "They that are bidden, lo! all of them stand; the Bridegroom's guests, lo! they bear witness that day by day I said among them, 'I am the Voice and not the Word.'"

44. "Voice of him that cries in the wilderness, fulfill the work for which you came, that the desert to which you went out may resound with the mighty peace you preached in it."

45. "The shout of the Watchers has come to my ears. Lo! I hear from the Father's house the hosts that sound forth the cry, 'In Your Epiphany, O Bridegroom, the worlds have life.'"

46. "The time hastes on, and the marriage guests—look to Me to see what is doing. Come, baptize Me, that they may give praise to the Voice of the Father when it is heard!"

47. "I hearken, my Lord, according to Your Word, come to Baptism as Your love constrains You! The dust worships that to which he has attained, that on Him Who fashioned him he should lay his hand."

48. The heavenly ranks were silent as they stood, and the Bridegroom went down into Jordan; the Holy One was baptized and straightway went up, and His Light shone forth on the world.

49. The doors of the highest were opened above, and the voice of the Father was heard, "This is my Beloved in Whom I am well pleased." All you peoples, come and worship Him.

50. They that saw were amazed as they stood, at the Spirit Who came down and bore witness to Him. Praise to Your Epiphany that gladdens all, You in Whose revelation the worlds are lightened!

"Victory and Blessings"

St. Ephrem the Syrian[51]

Blessed is He Who blots out in water misdeeds that are without measure!

1. Descend my sealed brethren, put on our Lord and be rejoined to His lineage, for He is Son of a great lineage, as He has said in His Word.

2. From on high is His nature, and from beneath His Vesture. Each that puts off his vesture, commingled that vesture with His Vesture forever.

3. You, too, in the water, receive from him the vesture that wastes not or is lost, for it is the vesture that vests them that are vested in it forever.

4. But the blessed Priest, is arbiter between two: the covenant shall be made before Him, He is the arbiter of his Lord, and surety on our part.

5. The Godhead in the water, behold has mingled His leaven for the creatures of dust, that leaven raises up, and the Godhead joins them.

[51] St. Ephrem the Syrian, *Hymns for the Feast of Epiphany*, Hymn 4, NPNF, s. 2, v. 13.

6. For it is the leaven of the Lord, that can glide into the bondman, and raise him to freedom; it has joined the bondman to the lineage of Him Who is the Lord of all.

7. For the bondman who has put on Him, Who makes all free in the waters, although he is a bondman on earth, he is son of the free on high, for he has put on freedom.

8. The freeman who has put on that Angel in the waters is as the fellow of servants, that he may be made like the Lord, Who became bondman to bondmen.

9. He Who enriches all came down and put on poverty, that He might divide to the poor the stores that were hidden out of the treasure-house of the water.

10. The lowly one again that has put on the Giver of all greatness in the water, even though he is base in the sight of fools, yet is great in the sight of the Watchers, for that he is clad in greatness.

11. For like as He Who is great, Who became lowly in His love, by the unbelievers was persecuted, and by the Watchers was worshipped, was made lowly and makes the lowly great.

12. Thus let then be lowly as He Who is great, that in him the lowly may be great. Let us be like Him Who is greater than all, Who became less than all. He was made lowly, and makes all men great.

13. The meek man who has put on Him Who is great, in the water, though his countenance is humble, very great is his discernment, for He Who is exalted above all dwells in him.

14. For who could be found to despise the thorn bush, the despised and humble, in which the Majesty in fire, made its dwelling within?

15. Who again could be found to despise Moses, the meek and slow of speech, when that excelling glory dwelt upon his meekness?

16. Those who despised him despised his Lord; the wicked who despised him the earth swallowed up in anger; the Levites who scorned Him, the fire devoured in fury.

17. Of Him Christ commanded, "You shall not call him Raca," who is baptized and has put Him on, for whoever despises the despised, despises with him the Mighty.

18. In Eden and in the world are parables of our Lord, and what tongue can gather the similitudes of His mysteries? For He is figured all of Him in all things.

19. In the Scriptures He is written of; on Nature He is impressed; His crown is figured in kings, in prophets His truth, His atonement in priests.

20. In the rod was He of Moses, and in the hyssops of Aaron, and in the crown of David: to the prophets pertains His similitude to the apostles His Gospel.

21. Revelations beheld You, proverbs looked for You, mysteries expected You, similitudes saluted You, parables showed types of You.

22. The Covenant of Moses looked forward to the Gospel—all things of old time, flew on and alighted thereon, in the New Covenant.

23. Behold, the prophets have poured out on Him their glorious mysteries! The priests and kings have poured out upon Him their wonderful types; they all have poured them out on all of Him.

24. Christ overcame and surpassed, by His teachings the mysteries, by His interpretations the parables; as the sea into its midst receives all streams.

25. For Christ is the sea, and He can receive the fountains and brooks, the rivers and streams, that flow from the midst of the Scriptures.

Third Sunday

ST. JOHN THE BAPTIST EXALTS OUR LORD

Meditations on the Third Sunday of the Blessed Month of Tubah

GOSPEL READING OF THE THIRD SUNDAY

JOHN 3:22-36

Now John also was baptizing in Aenon near Salim, because there was much water there. And they came and were baptized. For John had not yet been thrown into prison. Then there arose a dispute between some of John's disciples and the Jews about purification.

And they came to John and said to him, "Rabbi, He who was with you beyond the Jordan, to whom you have testified—behold, He is baptizing, and all are coming to Him!" John answered and said, "A man can receive nothing unless it has been given to him from heaven. You yourselves bear me witness, that I said, I am not the Christ,' but, I have been sent before Him.' He who has the bride is the Bridegroom; but the friend of the Bridegroom, who stands and hears him, rejoices greatly because of the Bridegroom's voice. Therefore this joy of mine is fulfilled.

"He must increase, but I must decrease. He Who comes from above is above all; he who is of the earth is earthly and speaks of the earth. He Who comes from heaven is above all. And what He has seen and heard, that He testifies; and no one receives His testimony. He who has received His testimony has certified that God is true. For He Whom God has sent speaks the words of God, for God does not give the Spirit by measure. The Father loves the Son, and has given all things into His hand. He who believes in the Son has everlasting life; and he who does not believe the Son shall not see life, but the wrath of God abides on him."

"Why Our Lord Did Not baptize"

St. John Chrysostom[52]

"After these things Jesus and His disciples came into the land of Judea, and there He remained with them and baptized" (Jn. 3:22).

The Evangelist says, "Jesus Himself did not baptize, but His disciples" (Jn. 4:2), when it is clear that this is his meaning here also. Why did Jesus not baptize? The Baptist had said before, "He will baptize you with the Holy Spirit and fire" (Matt. 3:11). Now He had not yet given the Spirit, and it was therefore with good cause that He did not baptize. But His disciples did so, because they desired to bring many to the saving doctrine. And why, when the disciples of Jesus were baptizing, did John not cease to do so? Why did he continue to baptize, and even until he was led to prison? He says:

"Now John also was baptizing in Aenon near Salim...For John had not yet been thrown into prison" (Jn. 3:23, 24).

These he said to declare that until that time John did not cease to baptize. But why did he baptize until then? For he would have made the disciples of Jesus seem more reverend had he desisted when they began. Why then did he baptize?"

It was that he might not excite his disciples to even stronger rivalry, and make them more contentious still. For even if he had proclaimed Christ ten thousand times, yielded to Him the chief place, and made himself so much inferior, he still could not persuade them to run to Him. He also added that he would have made them yet more hostile. On this account it was that Christ began to preach more constantly when John was removed. And moreover, I think that the death of John was allowed, and that it happened very quickly, in order that the whole attention of the multitude might be shifted to Christ and that they might no longer be divided in their opinions concerning the two.

Besides this, even while John was baptizing, he did not cease continually to exhort them, and to show them the high nature of Jesus, full

---

[52] St. John Chrysostom, *Commentary on the Gospel of St. John*, NPNF, s. 1, v. 14, pp. 235-237.

of awe. For he baptized them, and told them no other thing than that they must believe on Him that came after him. Now how would a man who acted thus by desisting have made the disciples of Christ seem worthy of reverence? On the contrary, he would have been thought to do so through envy and passion. But to continue preaching gave a stronger proof; for he desired not glory for himself, but sent on his hearers to Christ, and wrought with Him not less, but rather much more than Christ's own disciples, because his testimony was unsuspected and he was by all men far more highly esteemed than they. And this the Evangelist implies, when he says, "Jerusalem, all Judea and all the region around the Jordan went out to him and were baptized" (Matt. 3:5, 6). Even when the disciples were baptizing, yet many did not cease to run to him.

If any one should inquire, "And in what was the Baptism of the disciples better than that of John?" we will reply, "In nothing." Both were alike without the Gift of the Spirit, both parties alike had one reason for baptizing, and that was, to lead the baptized to Christ. For in order that they might not be always running about to bring together those that should believe, as in Simon's case his brother did, and Philip to Nathaniel, they instituted Baptism, in order to bring by it all men to them easily, and to prepare a way for the faith which was to be.

"All Things Are in His Hand"

St. Athanasius the Apostolic[53]

For, "The Father loves the Son, and has given all things into His hand" (Jn. 3:35) and, "All things have been delivered to Me by My Father" (Matt. 11:27); and, "I can of Myself do nothing, but as I hear, I judge" (Jn. 5:30). Such passages do not indicate that the Son never lacked these prerogatives. For He eternally has what the Father has—who is the Only Word and Wisdom of the Father in essence, who also says, "All things that the Father has are Mine" (Jn. 16:15), and what are Mine, are the Father's. For if the things of the Father are the Son's and the Father has them forever, it is plain that what the Son has, being the Father's, were always in the Son.

[53] St. Athanasius, *Against the Arians*, NPNF s. 2, v. 4 pp. 1024-1026.

Thus He did not say this because He lacked them, but because, although the Son has these eternally, yet He has them from the Father.

For unless a man, perceiving that the Son has all that the Father has from the exact likeness and identity of that He has, should wander into the irreligion of Sabellius, considering Him to be the Father, therefore He has said, "Was delivered to Me," and "I received," and "were delivered to Me," only to show that He is not the Father, but the Father's Word, and the Eternal Son, who because of His likeness to the Father, has eternally what He has from Him, and because He is the Son, has from the Father what He has eternally. Moreover that "was delivered" and "were delivered," and the like, do not impair the Godhead of the Son, but rather show Him to be truly Son, we may learn from the passages themselves. For if all things are delivered to Him, first, He is other than that all which He has received; next, being Heir of all things, He alone is the Son and proper according to the Essence of the Father. For if He were one of all, then He were not "heir of all," but every one had received according as the Father willed and gave.

But now, as receiving all things, He is other than them all, and alone proper to the Father. Moreover that "was delivered" and "were delivered" do not show that once He had them not, we may conclude from a similar passage, and in like manner concerning them all; for the Savior Himself says, "For as the Father has life in Himself, so He has granted the Son to have life in Himself" (Jn. 5:26). Now from the words "Has granted," He signifies that He is not the Father; but in saying "so," He shows the Son's natural likeness and propriety towards the Father.

If then once the Father had not, plainly the Son once had not; for as the Father, "so" also the Son has. But if this is irreligious to say, and religious on the contrary to say that the Father had ever, is it not unseemly in them when the Son says that, "as" the Father has, "so" also the Son has, to say that He has not "so," but otherwise? Rather then is the Word faithful, and all things which He says that He has received, He has always, yet has from the Father; and the Father indeed not from any, but the Son from the Father. For as in the instance of the radiance, if the radiance itself should say, "All places the light has given me to enlighten, and I do not enlighten from myself, but as the light wills," yet, in saying this, it does not imply that it once had not, but it means, "I am proper to the light, and all things of the light are mine;" so, and much more, must we understand in the instance of the Son. For the Father, having given all things to the Son, in the Son still has all things; and the Son having, still the Father has them; for the Son's Godhead is the Father's Godhead, and thus the Father in the Son exercises His Providence over all things.

"The Food of Angels"

St. Augustine[54]

"After these things Jesus and His disciples came into the land of Judea, and there He remained with them and baptized" (Jn. 3:22).

Being baptized, He baptized. Not with that Baptism with which He was baptized did He baptize. The Lord, being baptized by a servant gives Baptism, showing the path of humility and leading to the Baptism of the Lord, that is, His own Baptism, by giving an example of humility, in not Himself refusing Baptism from a servant. And in the Baptism by a servant, a way was prepared for the Lord. The Lord also being baptized, made Himself a way for them that come to Him. Let us hear Himself: "I am the way, the truth, and the life" (Jn. 14:6).

If you seek truth, keep the way, for the way and the truth are the same. The way that you are going is the same as the place you are going; you are not going by a way as one thing, and to an object as another thing. Not coming to Christ by something else as a way, you come to Christ by Christ. How by Christ to Christ? By Christ the man, to Christ God; by the Word made flesh, to the Word which in the beginning was God with God; from that which man ate, to that which angels daily eat.

For so it is written, "He gave them the bread of heaven; man ate the bread of angels" (Ps. 77:24, 25). What is the bread of angels? "In the beginning was the Logos, and the Logos was with God, and the Logos was God" (Jn. 1:1). How has man eaten the bread of angels? "And the Logos became flesh and tabernacled in us" (Jn. 1:14).

But though we have said that angels eat, do not fancy, brethren, that this is done with teeth. For if you think so, God, of whom the angels eat, is as it were torn in pieces. Who tears righteousness in pieces? But still, some one asks me, "And who is it that can eat righteousness?" Well, how is

[54] St. Augustine, *Commentary on John*, NPNF, s. 1, v. 7, pp. 173-175.

it said, "Blessed are those who hunger and thirst after righteousness, for they shall be filled" (Matt. 5:6)? The food which you eat carnally perishes, to refresh you; to repair your waste it is consumed. Eat righteousness, and while you are refreshed, it continues entire. Just as by seeing this corporeal light, these eyes of ours are refreshed, and yet it is a corporeal thing that is seen by corporeal eyes. Many there have been, when too long in darkness, whose eyesight is weakened by fasting, as it were, from light. The eyes, deprived of their food (for they feed on light), become wearied by fasting, and weakened, so that they cannot bear to see the light by which they are refreshed; and if the light is too long absent, they are quenched, and the very sense of sight dies as it were in them. What then?

Does the light become less, because so many eyes are daily fed by it? Your eyes are refreshed, and the light remains entire. As God was able to show this in the case of corporeal light to corporeal eyes, does He not show that other light to clean hearts as unwearied, continuing entire, and in no respect failing? What light? "In the beginning was the Word, and the Word was with God" (Jn. 1:1). Let us see if this is light. "For with You is the fountain of light, and in Your light shall we see light" (Ps. 35:10). On earth, a fountain is one thing, light another. When thirsting, you seek a fountain, and to get to the fountain you seek light; and if it is not day, you light a lamp to get to the fountain. That fountain is the very light: to the thirsting a fountain, to the blind a light. Let the eyes be opened to see the light, let the lips of the heart be opened to drink of the fountain; that which you drink, you see, you hear. God becomes all to you; for He is to you all of these things which you love.

If you regard things visible, God is neither bread nor water; neither light nor garment, nor house. For all these are visible things, and single separate things. What bread is, water is not; and what a garment is, a house is not; and what these things are, God is not, for they are visible things. God is all this to you: if you hunger, He is bread to you; if you thirst, He is water to you; if you are in darkness, He is light to you, for He remains incorruptible. If you are naked, He is a garment of immortality to you, when this corruptible shall put on incorruption, and this mortal shall put on immortality (cf. 1 Cor. 15:54).

All things can be said of God, and nothing is worthily said of God. Nothing is wider than this poverty of expression. If you seek a fitting name for Him, you cannot find it. If you want to speak of Him in any way whatever, you find that He is all. What is the similarity between the lamb and the lion? Both is said of Christ. "Behold the Lamb of God!" (Jn. 1:29). How a lion? "The Lion of the tribe of Judah has prevailed" (Rev. 5:5).

"WHY DID SAINT JOHN BAPTIZE?"

St. Augustine[55]

Let us hear John: "Jesus baptized" (Jn. 4:1). We said that Jesus baptized. How Jesus? How the Lord? How the Son of God? How the Word? Well, but the Word was made flesh. "Now John also was baptizing in Aenon near to Salim" (Jn. 3:23). A certain lake, "Aenon." How do we know it was a lake? "Because there was much water there, and they came and were baptized. For John was not yet cast into prison" (Jn. 3:23, 24). If you remember (see, I say it again), I told you why John baptized: because the Lord must be baptized.

And why must the Lord be baptized? Because many there would be to despise Baptism, that they might appear to be endowed with greater grace than they saw other believers endowed with. For example, a catechumen, now living continently, might despise a married person, and say of himself that he was better than the other believer. That catechumen might possibly say in his heart, "What do I need to receive Baptism, to have just what that other man has, than whom I am already better?" Therefore, lest that neck of pride should hurl to destruction certain men much elated with the merits of their own righteousness, the Lord was willing to be baptized by a servant, as if addressing His chief sons: "Why do you extol yourselves? Why lift yourselves up because you have, one prudence, another learning, another chastity, another the courage of patience? Can you possibly have as much as I who gave you these? And yet I was baptized by a servant, and do you disdain to be baptized by the Lord?" This is the meaning of the phrase" to fulfill all righteousness" (Matt. 3:15).

But some one will say, "It were enough, then, that John baptized only the Lord; what need was there for others to be baptized by John?" Now we have said this too, that if John had baptized only the Lord, men would not be without this thought, that John had a better Baptism than the Lord had. They would say, in fact, "So great was the Baptism of John that

[55] St. Augustine, *Commentary on John*, NPNF, s. 1, v. 7, pp. 175-176.

Christ alone was worthy to be baptized with it." Therefore, to show that the Baptism which the Lord was to give was better than that of John, that the one might be understood as that of a servant, the other as that of the Lord, the Lord was baptized to give an example of humility.

But He was not the only one baptized by John, lest John's Baptism should appear to be better than the Baptism of the Lord. To this end, however, our Lord Jesus Christ showed the way, as you have heard, brethren, lest any man, claiming to himself that he has abundance of some particular grace, should disdain to be baptized with the Baptism of the Lord. For whatever the catechumen's proficiency, he still carries the load of his iniquity; it is not forgiven him until he shall have come to Baptism. Just as the people of Israel were not rid of the Egyptians until they had come to the Red Sea, so no man is rid of the pressure of sins until he has come to the font of Baptism.

"From Above and Above All"

St. John Chrysostom[56]

A dreadful thing is the love of glory, dreadful and full of many evils; it is a thorn hard to be extracted, a wild beast untamable and many headed, arming itself against those that feed it. For as the worm eats through the wood from which it is born, as rust wastes the iron from which it comes from, and moths the fleeces, so vainglory destroys the soul which nourishes it; and therefore we need great diligence to remove this passion. Observe here how long a charm John uses over the disciples affected by it, and can scarcely pacify them. For he softens them with other words besides those already mentioned. And what are these other words? "He Who comes from above," he says, "is above all; he who is of the earth is earthly and speaks of the earth" (Jn. 3:31). Since you make much trouble with my testimony, and in this way say that I am more worthy of credit than He, you must know this, that it is impossible for One who comes from heaven to have His credit strengthened by one that inhabits earth.

And what does "above all" mean, what is the expression intended to show to us? That Christ has need of nothing, but is Himself sufficient for Himself, and incomparably greater than all. About himself, John speaks as

[56] St. John Chrysostom, *Commentary on John*, NPNF s. 1, v. 14, pp. 243-245.

being "of the earth, and speaking of the earth." Not that he spoke of his own mind, but as Christ said, "If I have told you earthly things and you do not believe" (Jn. 3:12), so calling Baptism, not because it was an "earthly thing," but because He compared it when He spoke with His own Ineffable Generation, so here John said that he spoke "of earth," comparing his own with Christ's teaching. For the "speaking of earth" means nothing else than this, "My things are little and low and poor compared with His, and such as it was probable that an earthly nature would receive. In Him 'are hid all the treasures of wisdom'" (Col. 2:5). That he speaks not of human reasoning's is plain from this. "He that is of the earth," he says, "is earthly." Yet not all in him was earthly, but the higher parts were heavenly, for he had a soul, and was a partaker of a Spirit which was not of earth. How then does he say that he is "earthly"? See not that he means only, "I am small and of no esteem, going on the ground and born in the earth; but Christ came to us from above." Having by all these means quenched their passion, he afterwards speaks more openly of Christ. For before this it was useless to utter words which could never have gained a place in the understanding of his hearers; but when he has pulled up the thorns, he then boldly casts in the seed, saying:

"He Who comes from above is above all. And what He has seen and heard He speaks, that He testifies; and no one receives His testimony" (Jn. 3:31, 32).

Having uttered something great and sublime concerning Him, he again brings down his discourse to a humbler strain. For the expression, "what He has seen and heard," is suited rather to a mere man. What He knew, He knew not from having learned it by sight, or from having heard it, but He included the whole in His Nature, having come forth perfect from the Bosom of His Father, and needing none to teach Him. For, "As the Father," He said, "knows Me, even so I know the Father" (Jn. 10:15). What then means, "What He has seen and heard, that He testifies"? Since by these senses we gain correct knowledge of everything, and are deemed worthy of credit when we teach on matters which our eyes have embraced and our ears have taken in, as not in such cases inventing or speaking falsehoods, John desiring here to establish this point, said, "What He has seen and heard;" that is, "nothing that comes from Him is false, but all is true." Thus, when we are making curious inquiry into anything, often ask, "Did you hear it? Did you see it?"

And if this is proved, the testimony is indubitable, and so when Christ Himself says, "As I hear, I judge" (Jn. 5:30); and, "What I have heard from My Father, that I speak" (Jn. 15:15); and, "We speak what We have seen" (Jn. 3:11); and whatever other sayings He utters of the kind, are uttered not that we might imagine that He says what He does being taught of any, (it were extreme folly to think this,) but in order that nothing of what is said may be suspected by the shameless Jews. For because they had not yet a right opinion concerning Him, He continually betakes Himself to His Father, and hence makes His sayings credible.

And why do you wonder if He likens Himself to the Father, when He often resorts to the Prophets and the Scriptures as when He said, "These are they which testify of Me" (Jn. 5:39)? Shall we then say that He is inferior to the Prophets, because He draws testimonies from them? Away with the thought. It is because of the infirmity of His hearers that He so orders His discourse, and said that He spoke what He spoke having heard it from the Father, not because He needed a teacher, but that they might believe that nothing that He said was false. John's meaning is of this kind: "I desire to hear what He says, for He comes from above, bringing from there those tidings which none but Life knows rightly; for 'what He has seen and heard,' is the expression of one who declares this." "And no man receives His testimony." Yet He had disciples, and many others gave heed to His words. How then says John, "No man"? He says "no man," instead of "few men," for had he meant "no man at all," how could he have added,

"He who has received His testimony has certified that God is true" (Jn. 3:33).

Here, John touches his own disciples, as not being likely for a time to be firm believers. And that they did not even after this believe in Him, is clear from what is said afterwards; for John even when dwelling in prison sent them thence to Christ, that he might the more bind them to Him. Yet even then they scarcely believed, to which Christ alluded when He said, "And blessed is he who is not offended because of Me" (Matt. 11:6). And therefore now he said, "no one receives His testimony" (Jn. 3:32) to make sure his own disciples; all but saying, "Do not, because for a time few shall believe on Him, therefore deem that His words are false; for, He speaks 'all what He has seen.'" Moreover he says this to touch also the insensibility of the Jews. A charge which the Evangelist at commencing brought against them, saying, "He came to His own, and His own did not receive Him" (Jn. 1:11). For this is no reproach against Him, but an accusation of those who received Him not.

"He Must Increase; I Must Decrease"

St. Augustine[57]

"He must increase, but I must decrease" (Jn. 3:30).

What is this? He must be exalted, but I must be humbled. How is Jesus to increase? How is God to increase? The perfect does not increase. God neither increases nor decreases. For if He increases, He is not perfect; if He decreases, he is not God. And how can Jesus increase, being God? If to man's estate, since He deigned to be man and was a child; and, though the Word of God, lay an infant in a manger; and, though His mother's Creator, yet sucked the milk of infancy of her, then Jesus having grown in age of the flesh, that perhaps is the reason why it is said, "He must increase, but I must decrease."

But why in this? As regards the flesh, John and Jesus were of the same age, there being six months between them. They had grown up together; and if our Lord Jesus Christ had willed to be here longer before His death, and that John should be here with Him, then, as they had grown up together, so would they have grown old together.

In what way, then, "He must increase, but I must decrease"? Above all, our Lord Jesus Christ being now thirty years old, does a man who is already thirty years old still grow? From that same age, men begin to go downward, and to decline to graver age, and from there to old age. Again, even had they both been lads, he would not have said, "He must increase, but, we must increase together." But now each is thirty years of age. The interval of six months makes no difference in age; the difference is discovered by reading rather than by the look of the persons.

What means, then, "He must increase, but I must decrease"? This is a great mystery! Before the Lord Jesus came, men were glorying of themselves; He came a man, to lessen man's glory, and to increase the glory of God. Now He came without sin, and found all men in sin. If thus He came to put away sin, God may freely give, man may confess. For

---

57 St. Augustine, *Commentary on John*, NPNF s. 1, v. 7, pp. 188-190.

man's confession is man's lowliness; God's pity is God's loftiness. Therefore, since He came to forgive man his sins, let man acknowledge his own lowliness and let God show His pity.

"He must increase, but I must decrease," that is, He must give, but I must receive; He must be glorified, but I must confess. Let man know his own condition, and confess to God. Hear the apostle Paul as he says to a proud, elated man bent on extolling himself: "What do you have that you did not receive? Now if you did receive it, why do you boast as if you had not receive it?" (1 Cor. 4:7). Then let man understand that he has received; and when he would call that his own which is not his, let him decrease, for it is good for him that God be glorified in him. Let him decrease in himself, that he may be increased in God. Christ and John by their deaths signified these testimonies and this truth. For John was lessened by the Head: Christ was exalted on the cross so that even there it appeared what this is, "He must increase, but I must decrease."

Again, Christ was born when the days were just beginning to lengthen; John was born when they began to shorten. Thus their very creation and deaths testify to the words of John, when he says, "He must increase, but I must decrease." May the glory of God then increase in us, and our own glory decrease, that even ours may increase in God! For this is what the apostle Paul says, this is what Holy Scripture says: "He who glories, let him glory in the Lord" (1 Cor. 1:31; 2 Cor. 10:17). You will glory in yourself? You will grow; but grow worse in your evil. For whoever grows worse is justly decreased. Let God, then, who is ever perfect, grow, and grow in you. For the more you understand God, and apprehend Him, He seems to be growing in you; but in Himself He grows not, being ever perfect. You did understand a little yesterday; you understand more today, will understand much more tomorrow. The very light of God increases in you as if thus God increases, who remains ever perfect. It is as if one's eyes were being cured of former blindness, and he began to see a little glimmer of light, and the next day he saw more, and the third day still more; to him the light would seem to grow, yet the light is perfect, whether he sees it or not. Thus it is also with the inner man—he makes progress indeed in God, and God seems to be increasing in him; yet man himself is decreasing, that he may fall from his own glory, and rise into the glory of God.

"CHRIST AND THE BAPTIST"

St. Cyril of Alexandria[58]

"Now John also was baptizing in Aenon near Salim, because there was much water there. And they came and were baptized. For John had not yet been thrown into prison" (Jn. 3:23, 24).

After the conversation with Nicodemus had reached its conclusion, the Divine Evangelist again prepares something else most profitable. For enlightened by the Divine Spirit to the exposition of things most needful, he knew that it would exceedingly profit his readers to know clearly, how great the excellence, and by how great measures, the Baptism of Christ surpasses that of John.

For it was indeed not far from his expectation, that certain people would arise who of their folly should dare to say, either that there was no difference whatever between them, but that they should be crowned with equal honors; or, having stumbled into folly even wilder than this, say, that the vote of superiority should to be taken away from Christ's Baptism, and the superiority shamelessly lavished on the Baptism by water. For what daring is not attainable by the ill-instructed, or through what blasphemy do they not rush, who rising up against the holy doctrines of the Church, pervert all equity, as it is written?

The most-wise Evangelist then, that he might destroy beforehand the plea for their vain babbling, introduces the holy Baptist laying before his disciples the solution to the question. Christ therefore baptizes through His own disciples, as John also did, and not altogether by the hands of others, nor yet did he baptize in those same fountains. Christ was seen doing this near Salim, as it is written, and in one of the neighboring fountains. And through the very distinction of the fountains of waters does he show the difference of the Baptism, and signify as in a figure that his Baptism is not the same as that of our Savior Christ. But it was similar to it—a kind of preparation and introduction to the more perfect Baptism. As the law of Moses is said to be a shadow of the good things to come, not the very image of the things (for the Mosaic letter is a kind of preparatory exercise and pre-instruction for the worship in the Spirit, travailing with

[58] St. Cyril of Alexandria, *Commentary on John*, 2.1-2.

the truth hidden within), so, too, you will also conceive of the Baptism unto repentance.

"Then there arose a dispute between some of John's disciples and the Jews about purification. And they came to John and said to him" (Jn. 3:25, 26).

The Jews being powerless to commend the purifications of the law, and not able to advocate the cleansing through the ashes of an heifer, plan something against John's disciples, by which they should cause his disciples no slight vexation, although easily defeated in their own matters.

Because those who attended the blessed Baptist appeared to be more excellent and of more understanding than the Pharisees, admiring the Baptism of their own teacher, and opposing the purifications after the law— they are angry at these things who are diligent in reviling only, and most ready to all wickedness. And even overturning their own case, the Pharisees praise Christ's Baptism, not rightly disposed, nor pouring forth true praise on it, but exasperated to the mere distressing of John's disciples, and lending out a statement against their opinion, until their purpose should attain its accomplishment.

Thus, the Pharisees cannot find any reasonable proof, nor do they even support Christ out of the Holy Scriptures (for from where would such understanding come to the uninstructed?). But the Pharisees merely allege in confirmation of their own arguments that very few in number are those who come to John, but that they flock together to Christ. For happily, the Pharisees in their exceeding folly thought that they should carry off the vote of victory, and might speak out on behalf of the legal purifications, as having already conquered, by giving the palm over John's to the Baptism bestowed by Christ on those who come to Him. And they trouble those with whom their dispute was, but they get off with difficulty and leave the disciples of John, much more beaten by their ill-considered dispute. For they crown with compulsory praises, and against their will, the Lord.

"'Rabbi, He who was with you beyond the Jordan, to whom you have testified— behold, He is baptizing, and all are coming to Him!' John answered and said..." (Jn. 3:26, 27).

The disciples bitten by the words of the Pharisees, and looking to the very nature of the thing, were not able to convict them as liars, but were reasonably at a loss, and being ignorant of the great dignity of our Savior, are exceedingly startled at John's shortcoming. And mingling words of love with reverence and admiration, the disciples of John desire to learn why He Who was witnessed to by his voice prevents him in honor, outstrips him in grace, and in baptizing takes in His net, not a portion of the whole Jewish multitude, but even all of them. And they made the inquiry as it seems not without the Will of God, and for this reason the Baptist invites them to an accurate and long explanation respecting the Savior, and introduces the clearest distinction between the Baptisms.

"A man can receive nothing unless it has been given to him from heaven."

He says that there is nothing good in man, but every good thing is the gift of God. Thus, creation hears Him saying, "What do you have that you did not receive?" (1 Cor. 4:7). So, we should be content with the measures allotted to us, and to rejoice in the honors apportioned to us from heaven. But we should by no means stretch out beyond, nor in desire of what is greater -unthankfully, nor to despise the decree from above, and fight against the judgment of the Lord, in shame that one should appear to receive what is less than the more perfect. But whatever God wishes to honor us with, we should value it highly. Therefore, he says do not let my disciple be ashamed if I do not overleap the measure given me, if I do not contemplate the greater, and am contracted to the glory befitting a man.

"You yourselves bear me witness, that I said, 'I am not the Christ,' but, 'I have been sent before Him'" (Jn. 3:28).

He brings his disciples to the recollection of the words which they have already often heard, in part, correctly rebuking them, as being steeped in forgetfulness of things profitable, and slumbering in respect to this so most dread doctrine. And in part also, he is persuading them to remember the Divine Scripture, as having been nourished in zeal for the knowledge of these things; Whom it preaches as the Christ to come, whom again as the Baptist the Forerunner. Thus, if they received the knowledge of these things, they would not be angry, seeing them in the state befitting each. I shall need then, he says, no other witnesses to this, I have my own disciples as ear-witnesses. I confessed my state of servitude, when I fore-announced, I was sent, I am not the Christ. Let Him overcome, prevail, shine forth yet more as Lord and God.

"He who has the bride is the Bridegroom; but the friend of the Bridegroom, who stands and hears him, rejoices greatly because of the Bridegroom's voice. Therefore this joy of mine is fulfilled" (Jn. 3:29).

The discourse again took its rise from likeness to our affairs, but leads us to the knowledge of subtle thoughts. For types of things spiritual are those which endure the touch of the hand, and the grossness of corporeal examples introduces oftentimes a most accurate proof of things spiritual.

Christ then, he says, is the Bridegroom and Ruler of the assembly, I the bidder to the supper and conductor of the bride, having as my chief joy and illustrious dignity to be only enrolled among His friends, and to hear the Voice of Him Who feasts.

Therefore, I have had my dearest wish fulfilled, that which I have I longed for. For not only do I preach that Christ would come, but I have already seen Him here, and I lay up in my ears His very Voice. But you, most wise disciples, seeing the human nature that is betrothed to Christ, going to Him, and beholding the nature which was cut off and a run-away from its love to Him attaining to spiritual union through holy Baptism, do not grieve, he says, that it befits not me, but rather runs very gladly to the spiritual Bridegroom (for this were in truth just and more fitting).

"He Who has the bride is the Bridegroom." That is, do not seek in me the crown of the Bridegroom, for the Psalmist does not rejoice for me when he says "Listen, O daughter, consider, and incline your ear; forget also your own people and your father's house, for the King has desired your beauty" (Ps. 45:10, 11). For the bride does not seek my chamber when she says, "Tell me, O You Whom my soul loves, where You feed, where You make Your flock to rest at noon" (Song 1:7), for she has the Heavenly Bridegroom. But I will rejoice, having surpassed the honor becoming a bondman, in the title and reality of friendship.

I suppose then that the meaning of the passage has been interpreted very well, and having already sufficiently explained the spiritual marriage, I think it tedious to write any more about it.

"He must increase, but I must decrease" (Jn. 3:30).

He convicts his disciples for being troubled about trifles, for being offended unnecessarily at what should not trouble them, and for not yet accurately knowing Who Emmanuel is and where He came from.

So he says, "He will be honored more than me not because His deeds will be greater, nor because more are baptized by Him, but He attains such a great measure of honor, because He is God. For He must increase in glory, and, through daily additions of miracles, ever mount up to the greater, and shine forth with greater splendor to the world. But I must decrease, abiding in that measure in which I appear, not sinking from what was once given me, but in such a degree inferior to Him that advances ever to an increase of glory, as He moves and passes on." In this way, the blessed Baptist interprets to us.

But our discourse will advance profitably through examples, making the force of what has been said clearer. Let then a stake two cubits long be fixed in the ground. Let there lie near a plant too, just peeping above the ground, putting forth green shoots into the air, and ever thrust up to a greater height by the unrelenting vigor from the roots. If the stake could speak about itself and its neighbor the plant, it would say "This must increase, but I decrease." We would not reasonably suppose that it indicated any harm to itself, nor that its existing measure would be clipped, but it would be affirming its decrease in that sort only, in which it is found less than that which is ever advancing towards increase. Again you may take an example akin to this one, and suppose the brightest of the stars to cry out saying of the sun, "It must increase, but I decrease."

For while in the gloom of night the depth of the atmosphere is darkened, one may well admire the morning star flashing forth its golden light, and conspicuous in its full glory, but when the sun now gives notice of its rising, and covers the world with a moderate light, the star is surpassed by the greater and gives place to it, advancing little by little. And it too might well speak the words of John, being in that same state, which he says is enduring.

"He Who comes from above is above all" (Jn. 3:31).

No great thing is it, [St. John] says, nor exceeding wonderful, if Christ surpasses the glory of human nature. For not thus far does He set the bounds of His own glory, but is over all creation, as God, is above all things made, not as numbered among all, but as excepted from all, and Divinely set over all. He adds the reason, shaming the denier, and silencing the opposer.

He Who comes from above, [St. John] says, is He Who is born of the Root from above, preserving in Himself by Nature the Father's Natural goodness, will confessedly possess the being above all. For it would be impossible that the Son should not altogether appear to be such as He Who begat is conceived of, and rightly. The Son Who excels in sameness of Nature, the Brightness and express Image of the Father, how will He be inferior to Him in glory? Or will not the Property of the Father be dishonored in the Son, and we insult the Image of the Begotten if we count Him inferior? But this I suppose will be manifest to all. Therefore it is also written, "All men should honor the Son just as they honor the Father. He who does not honor the Son does not honor the Father who sent Him" (Jn. 5:23). He who glories in equal honor with God the Father, by reason of being of Him by Nature, how will He not be conceived of as surpassing the essence of things originate? For this is the meaning of "is above all."

But I perceive that the mind of the fighters against Christ will never rest, but they will come, as is probable, vainly babbling and say, "When the blessed Baptist says that the Lord sprang from above, what reason will compel us to suppose that He came of the Essence of the Father, by reason of the word from above, and not rather from heaven, or even from His inherent superiority above all, so that for this reason He should be conceived of and said to be also above all?"

Therefore, when they attack us with such words, they shall hear in return, "We will not follow your very corrupt analysis, but rather we will only follow the Divine Scriptures and the Sacred Writings." We must then search in them (and see) how they define to us the meaning of "from above." So, let them hear one clothed in the Spirit crying, "Every good gift and every perfect gift is from above, and comes down from the Father of lights" (Jam. 1:17).

Behold, [St. John] plainly says that the Father is from above. Knowing that nothing else surpasses things originate except the Ineffable Nature of God, he rightly attached to it the term "from above." For all things else fall under the yoke of bondage, God alone rises above being ruled, and reigns, from where He is truly above all. But the Son, being by Nature God and of God, will not be excluded from the glory in respect of this. But if you deem that "from above" should be taken as of heaven, let the word be used of every angel and rational power. For they come to us from heaven who inhabit the city that is above, and ascend and descend, as the Savior somewhere says, upon the Son of Man (cf. Jn. 1:51). What then persuaded the blessed Baptist to attribute that which was in the power of many to the Son Alone specially, and as to One coming down from above to call Him, "He Who comes from above"? For surely he should have made the dignity common to the rest, and say that they who come from above are above all. But he knew that the expression was due to the One Son, as sprung of the Supreme Root.

Therefore "from above" does not mean from heaven, but will be piously and truly understood, in the sense we spoke of before. For how is He "above all" at all, if "from above" does not signify from the Father, but rather from Heaven? If this were so, every one of the angels would also be "above all," as coming from there. But if each one escapes being reckoned among all, of whom at last will all be composed? Or how will the word "all" remain intact, preserving accurately its meaning, while such a multitude of angels overpass and break down the boundary of all? For "all" it is no longer, if they remain outside, who were "In all." But the Logos that shone forth ineffably from God the Father, having His Proper Birth from above, and being of the Essence of the Father as of a fountain, will not by His coming wrong the word "all," seeing He escapes being reckoned among all as if a part, but rather will be above all, as Other than they, both by Nature and God-befitting Power and all other Properties of Him Who begat Him.

But if they are ashamed at the absurd result of the investigation that "from above" means not from heaven, but from His inherent superiority above all, then let us more accurately test the force of what is said and see how their attempt will end.

First then, it is wholly foolish and without understanding, to say that the Son Himself has come from His Own Dignity, and that as from a certain place or out of one, He One and the Same advances from His Own Excellency to be above all. In addition to this, I would also most gladly inquire of them, in respect of the excellence above all, whether they will grant it to the Son Essentially and Irrevocably, or added from without in the nature of accident. If then they say that He has the Excellence by acquisition, and is honored with dignities from without, one must acknowledge that the Only-Begotten could exist deprived of glory, and be stripped of the acquired (as they call it) grace, and be deprived of being above all, and appear bare of the excellence which they now admire, since an accident may be lost, seeing that it does not belong to the essence of its subject. Therefore, there will be change and varying in the Son. The Psalmist will lie hymning Him with vain words, "The heavens will vanish away like smoke, the earth will grow old like a garment, and those who dwell in it will die in like manner; but My salvation will be forever, and My righteousness will not be abolished" (cf. Ps. 101:26, 27; Isa. 51:6).

For how is He the Same, if with us He changes, and that He changes for the worse? Vainly too (it seems) He glories of Himself, saying, "I am the Lord, and there is no other. There is no God besides Me" (Isa. 45:5). And how will not the passions of the offspring reach up to the Father Himself too, since He is His Impress and Exact Likeness? God the Father then will be changeable, and has the Supremacy over all accruing to Him; I omit the rest. For what belongs to the Image will of necessity appertain to the Archetype. But they will not say that He has the supremacy from without (shuddering at such difficulties alike and absurdities of their arguments), but Essential rather and irrevocable. Then again, how you will not agree with us even against your will, that the Son being by nature God, is above all, and therefore comes of the lone essence of God the Father?

For if there is nothing of things originate which is not parted off by the force of the Alpha and Omega, but the Son is above all, that is to say, as Other than all, and having the Essential Supremacy over all, and not the same in nature with all, how will He not be at length conceived of as very God? For He Who is essentially separate from the multitude of created beings, and by nature escapes the being classed among things originate, what else can He be except God?

For we see that He is not lowly regarding His existing essence. For the creation is ruled over, and God is conceived of as over it. If then the Son is by nature God, and has been ineffably begotten of God the Father, "from above" signifies the Nature of the Father. Therefore, the Only-Begotten is above all, inasmuch as He also is seen to be of that Nature.

"He who is of the earth is earthly and speaks of the earth" (Jn. 3:31).

The earthborn (he says) will not effect equally in power of persuasion with Him Who is God over all. For he who is of the earth will speak as man, and will rank merely as an adviser, committing to his disciples the whole reins of desire to believe, but He who comes from above, as God, having used discourse with a certain Divine and ineffable grace, sends it into the ears of those who come to Him. But in proportion as He is by nature superior, so much the more effectually will He surely in-work.

The blessed Baptist says these things with much benefit to his disciples. For since they considered him with greater glory than the Savior, and were not even slightly offended, they came to him and said, "Rabbi, He who was with you beyond the Jordan, to whom you have testified—behold, He is baptizing, and all are coming to Him!" (Jn. 3:26). So those dressed in the Spirit, cutting off the sickness of offense, and implanting in his disciples a healthful perception on most necessary points, he explains the Savior's supremacy over all, and teaches no less the cause why all men were already going to Him, leaving the Baptism by water alone, and going to the more Divine and perfect one, which is that by the Holy Spirit.

"He Who comes from heaven is above all" (Jn. 3:31).

This testifies (he says) that there is a very great and incomparable distinction between those of the earth, and the Logos of God Who came down from above and from Heaven. "If I am not fit to teach, and my word alone does not satisfy you, the Son Himself will confirm it, testifying that in an incomprehensible degree differs the earth-born from the Beginning Who is above all."

For disputing some unholy Jews, the Savior said, "You are from beneath; I am from above. You are of this world; I am not of this world" (Jn. 8:23). For He says that the nature of things originate is from beneath, as subject and of necessity in bond service to God Who calls them into being from above; again He calls the Divine and Ineffable and Lordly Nature, as having all things originate under Its feet, and subjecting them to the yoke of His Authority. For the blessed Baptist did not casually add these things to those above. For that he may not be supposed by disciples to be inventing empty arguments, and from fear of seeming with reason inferior to Christ, to call Him greater and from above, himself from beneath and of the earth, he needs to confirm the force of the things that the Savior Himself said and show the explanation to be not as they thought, an empty excuse, but rather a demonstration of the truth. But since the other part of the verse runs like this:

"And what He has seen and heard that He testifies" (Jn. 3:32)

Come, we will also discuss a few things about this. We are so constituted and habituated as to receive the full proof of everything, by means of two especial senses particularly, I mean sight and hearing. For having been both ear-witnesses and eye-witnesses of anything, we come to speak positively of it. Therefore, to persuade them to hasten to belief in Christ (for He speaks, he says, that He knows accurately), he takes again, as it were from the likeness to us, that we may understand it more Divinely, and says, "what He has seen and heard, that He testifies" (Jn. 3:32) what the Savior Himself said.

"And no one receives His testimony" (Jn. 3:32).

Not as though no one receives the testimony, that Christ is God by nature and, sprung from above and the Father, is above all, does the blessed Baptist say this (for many received, and have believed it, and before all Peter said, "You are the Christ, the Son of the Living God" (Jn. 6:69), but as having himself conceived of the great dignity of the Speaker more rightly than they all, does he all but shaking his head, and smiting with right hand on his thigh, marvel at the folly of them that disbelieve Him.

"He who has received His testimony has certified that God is true" (Jn. 3:33).

The only way He could show the wickedness of those who did not believe, was to demonstrate the glorious achievement of the believers. For by the contrast of good things is the evil easily discerned, and the knowledge of what is better convicts the worse. If any, then (he says), have assented to the words of Him Who comes from above, he has sealed and confirmed by his understanding that truth is ever akin and most dear to the Divine Nature. Whence the converse is manifest to them that see. For he who thrusts away the faith will surely witness against himself that God is not true. But we must again take notice, that he removes the Son from consubstantiality with the creation, and shows by what has been said that He is by nature God.

For if he who believes the things spoken by Him and receives the testimony which He gave of Himself sealed and well confirmed that God is true, how shall not Christ be conceived of as by nature God, Who is testified of as true by the credit of the things just said? Or let our opponent again say how the Divine Nature is honored, as being true, by our Savior's testimony being received. For if He is not wholly by nature God, he who believes will not be reverencing the Divine Nature as true, but rather one (according to them) the fairest of creatures. But since, when Christ is believed, the declaration of being true extends to God, it is I suppose altogether clear that He being God, not falsely so called, Himself takes honor to Himself from those who believe.

But the enemy of the truth will not (it seems) agree to these words of ours, but will start up strong, not admitting the Son to be by nature God, and will say again, "Sir, you quibble and contrive many types of arguments only to reject the simple and right meaning." For since the Logos of God has come down from Heaven, calling out, openly, "I have not spoken on My own authority; but the Father who sent Me gave Me a command, what I should say and what I should speak" (Jn. 12:49), and again, "All things that I heard from My Father I have made known to you" (Jn. 15:15); or also, as the holy Baptist declared in the following words, "Or He Whom God has sent speaks the words of God therefore of Him is he saying, 'He who has received His testimony has certified that God is true" (Jn. 3:33). For surely God the Father is true, but you attempt to bring round to the Son what is due to Another.

What then shall we say to these things? Shall we class the Only-Begotten among the prophets, fulfilling the ministry of Prophets, and doing nothing else? For by whom is it not unhesitatingly received that Prophets used to bring us voices from God? Then what excellence is there, in the Son, if He accomplish this alone? How is He above all, if He is still ranked along with Prophets and is clad in slave-befitting measure?

How, as though surpassing them in glory does He say in the gospels, "If He called them gods, to whom the word of God came (and the Scripture cannot be broken), do you say of Him whom the Father sanctified and sent into the world, 'You are blaspheming,' because I said, 'I am the Son of God'?" (Jn. 10:35-36)? For in these words He clearly separates Himself from the company of Prophets, and says that they were called gods, because the Word-of God came to them, but Himself He confesses Son. For to the holy Prophets was imparted grace by measure through the Spirit, but in our Savior Christ it has pleased "all the fullness of the Godhead" to dwell bodily as Paul says (Col. 2:9). Therefore also "of His fullness have all we received," as John affirmed (Jn. 1:16). How then will the Giver be on par with the recipients, or how will the Fullness of the Godhead be reckoned in the portion of the minister?

Let them then from now consider narrowly into how great blasphemy their argument will hazard them. And how one should understand the words, "I have not spoken on My own authority; but the Father who sent Me gave Me a command, what I should say and what I should speak" (Jn. 12:49) will be explained more at large in its proper time and place. But I think that at present the objections of our opponents should be made a foundation of piety, and from what they put forth, we should contend for the doctrines of the Church. They then affirm that the Son has received commandments from the Father and says nothing of Himself, but whatever He heard, as Himself says, these things He is zealous to say to us too. Well, let him hold to this, for we will agree, since this nothing wrongs the Son, as far at least as concerns the question of from where He is; yes rather it brings in a most beautiful economy in respect of the present subject. Therefore when they hear Him say, "I and the Father are One" (Jn. 10:30), "He who has seen Me has seen the Father" (Jn. 14:9), and "I am in the Father, and the Father in Me" (Jn. 14:10), let them receive His testimony, let them set to their seal, that God the Father is true, persuading the Son to speak what He knows accurately. Let them not disbelieve the words of the Savior interpreting to us the things of His Father.

"For He Whom God has sent speaks the words of God" (Jn. 3:34).

The Father then knows that His own Son is in Him the Same by Nature (for this I suppose the words, "are One," signify, and nothing else), and acknowledges Him as Son not creature; Son I mean of His own Essence, and not honored with the bare name of Sonship. For He knows that He is the Exact Image of His own Proper Self, so that He is perfectly seen in Him, and depicts in Himself Him That by Nature Ineffably beamed forth from Him, and has in Himself the Son, is again in the Son, by reason of sameness of Essence.

These things, O heretic, by considering, you will release yourself from bitter disease, and us from trouble in argument and controversy. For He Whom God has sent speaks the words of God. If these words are considered simply, what will there be of marvel in the Son? For was not every one of the holy Prophets also both sent from God, and did they not declare His words? And indeed it is somewhere said to the hierophant Moses, "And now come, I will send you into Egypt, and you will say unto Pharaoh, 'Thus says the Lord...'" (Exod. 4:21, 22). He also said to the most holy Jeremiah, "Do not say, 'I am a youth,' for you shall go to all to whom I send you, and whatever I command you, you shall speak" (Jer. 1:7). What more then is there in the Son by Nature Who speaks the words of God, because He is sent by Him? He will be declared to us again (it seems) as a Prophet, and nothing else, in respect of ministry.

Therefore you will here understand "has sent" either in respect of the Incarnation coming into this world with Flesh, or again you will take it in a more God-befit and higher sense. For the Father hid not the Son but He beamed forth of His Nature, as brightness from light, after the unspeakable and inexplicable mode of Divine Generation, which the Only-Begotten also made known to us, in saying, "I came forth from the Father and have come into the world" (Jn. 16:28). For the Son has come forth from the Father into His Proper Being, even though He is in Him by Nature. "I came forth" there means, the being sent here signifies. The Word then (he has appeared and flashed forth from the Father, in that He is God of God, will use words befitting God, but the words befitting God are true words, and such as reject all stain of falsehood. He then that receives the testimony of the Savior has sealed that God is true; for He is indeed by nature God.)

"...For God does not give the Spirit by measure..."

Promise now special keen attention, my good friend, that with me you may wonder at the sober wisdom of the Saints. [St. John] said therefore that the Son was both sent of God, and speaks the words of God. But He is observed as far as belongs to the simple force of the words to clothe Him with the prophetic measure, as we have just said. [St. John] removes Him then in these words from equality with [the prophets], and through this one token gives us to understand, how great, yes, rather now how incomparable the difference.

For it is impossible, he says, that they who have received the Spirit by measure, could give (the Spirit) to another. For never has a saint to saint been the bestower of the Holy Spirit, but the Son gives to all, as of His own fullness. He then gives not by measure, nor has He, as they, some little portion of the Spirit, and this by participation, but since He was shown also to be the Giver of [the Holy Spirit], it is manifest I suppose that He has [the Spirit] wholly essentially in Himself. He then that has so great superiority over them, will not speak the things of God as one of them, but being God of God, will pour forth words befitting God.

But it will no how interfere with what has been said that certain deem that by Apostolic bands the Spirit was given to some, for we will believe [the apostles] to be invokers of the Spirit rather than truly givers of [the Holy Spirit], since the blessed Moses also was not instructed himself to take of the Spirit that was on him, but God kept this too in His Power alone, saying that be must put forth the seventy, and promising to take of the Spirit that was on him, and put it upon them. For He knew that it befits God alone to perform things God-befitting.

Fourth Sunday

THE LIGHT OF THE WORLD

Meditations on the Fourth Sunday of the Blessed Month of Tubah

GOSPEL READING OF THE FOURTH SUNDAY[59]

JOHN 9:1-38

Now as Jesus passed by, He saw a man who was blind from birth. And His disciples asked Him, saying, "Rabbi, who sinned, this man or his parents, that he was born blind?" Jesus answered, "Neither this man nor his parents sinned, but that the works of God should be revealed in him. I must work the works of Him who sent Me while it is day; the night is coming when no one can work. As long as I am in the world, I am the light of the world." When He had said these things, He spat on the ground and made clay with the saliva; and He anointed the eyes of the blind man with the clay. And He said to him, "Go, wash in the pool of Siloam" (which is translated, Sent). So he went and washed, and came back seeing. Therefore the neighbors and those who previously had seen that he was blind said, "Is not this he who sat and begged?" Some said, "This is he." Others said, "He is like him."He said, "I am he." Therefore they said to him, "How were your eyes opened?" He answered and said, "A Man called Jesus made clay and anointed my eyes and said to me, 'Go to the pool of Siloam and wash.' So I went and washed, and I received sight." Then they said to him, "Where is He?" He said, "I do not know."

They brought him who formerly was blind to the Pharisees. Now it was a Sabbath when Jesus made the clay and opened his eyes. Then the Pharisees also asked him again how he had received his sight. He said to them, "Heput clay on my eyes, and I washed, and I see." Therefore some of the Pharisees

[59] For additional readings, please see the Sixth Sunday of the Great Lent in Volume II of this series.

said, "This Man is not from God, because He does not keep the Sabbath." Others said, "How can a man who is a sinner do such signs?" And there was a division among them. They said to the blind man again, "What do you say about Him because He opened your eyes?" He said, "He is a prophet." But the Jews did not believe concerning him, that he had been blind and received his sight, until they called the parents of him who had received his sight. And they asked them, saying, "Is this your son, who you say was born blind? How then does he now see?" His parents answered them and said, "We know that this is our son, and that he was born blind; but by what means he now sees we do not know, or who opened his eyes we do not know. He is of age; ask him. He will speak for himself." His parents said these things because they feared the Jews, for the Jews had agreed already that if anyone confessed that He was Christ, he would be put out of the synagogue. Therefore his parents said, "He is of age; ask him." So they again called the man who was blind, and said to him, "Give God the glory! We know that this Man is a sinner." He answered and said, "Whether He is a sinner or not I do not know. One thing I know: that though I was blind, now I see." Then they said to him again, "What did He do to you? How did He open your eyes?" He answered them, "I told you already, and you did not listen. Why do you want to hear it again? Do you also want to become His disciples?" Then they reviled him and said, "You are His disciple, but we are Moses' disciples. We know that God spoke to Moses; as for this fellow, we do not know where He is from." The man answered and said to them, "Why, this is a marvelous thing, that you do not know where He is from; yet He has opened my eyes! Now we know that God does not hear sinners; but if anyone is a worshiper of God and does His will, He hears him. Since the world began it has been unheard of that anyone opened the eyes of one who was born blind. If this Man were not from God, He could do nothing." They answered and said to him, "You were completely born in sins, and are you teaching us?" And they cast him out.

Jesus heard that they had cast him out; and when He had found him, He said to him, "Do you believe in the Son of God?" He answered and said, "Who is He, Lord, that I may believe in Him?" And Jesus said to him, "You have both seen Him and it is He who is talking with you." Then he said, "Lord, I believe!" And he worshiped Him.

"WHO SINNED?"

St. Caesarius of Arles[60]

We just heard that Jesus gave sight to the man who was blind from birth. Why do you wonder? Jesus is the Savior. If Jesus is the Savior, He did something in keeping with His Name, for by His kindness he restored what He had given to a lesser degree in the womb. Now when he made his eyes less powerful, surely He did not make a mistake, but deferred it for the miracle.

You might say to me, "How do you know this?" We have heard it from Him—for when the disciples questioned Jesus Christ saying, "Lord who has sinned, this man or his parents, that he should be born blind?" He replied to them, "Neither has this man sinned, nor his parents, but that the works of God should be revealed in him" (Jn. 9:3). Behold, the reason why Christ delayed when He made the eyes less powerful in the womb. Do not think, brethren, that the parents of that blind man had no sin, and that the blind man himself, when he was born, did not contract ancestral sin. But because of ancestral sin even very little children are baptized.

However, that blindness was not due to the sin of his parents, nor due to the sin of the blind man, but in order that the glory of God might be made manifest in him. For when we are born we all contract original sin, and still we are not born physically blind. That blind man, brethren, was prepared as a slave for the human race; he was bodily restored to light, in order that by considering his miracle we might be enlightened in the heart.

"THE BLIND MAN AND ISRAEL"

St. Cyril of Alexandria[61]

While the Jews were raging against Him and now trying to wound Him with stones, He then leaves the temple from among them,

[60] St. Caesarius of Arles, *Sermon 172* in Sister Mary Magdeleine Mueller, O.S.F., trans. *Sermons Volume 2 (81-186)* (Washington, DC: Catholic University of America Press, 1981), pp. 424-425.

[61] St. Cyril of Alexandria, *Commentary on John*, Book VI. For the entire commentary, please see volume 2 of this series, for St. Cyril's commentary on the Sixth Sunday of the Great Lent.

and escapes the unholiness of His pursuers. When passing by, He immediately saw one blind from birth, and set him as a token most clear that He will remove from the abominable behavior of the Jews, and will leave the multitude of the God-opposers, and will rather visit the Gentiles, and to them transfer the abundance of His compassion.

[Christ] likens them to the man blind from birth because their having been made in error and that they are from their first age as it were bereft of the true knowledge of God, and that they have not the light from God, i.e., the illumination through the Spirit. It is meet to observe again what Christ's visiting the blind man as He was passing by signifies.

And I think that Christ strictly speaking did not come for the Gentiles but for Israel's sake alone—as Himself too somewhere says, "I was not sent except to the lost sheep of the house of Israel" (Matt. 15:24)—yet was the recovery of sight given to the Gentiles, Christ transferring His Mercy to them as by the way, because of the disobedience of Israel. This is what Moses sung before, "I will provoke them to jealousy by those who are not a nation; I will move them to anger by a foolish nation" (Deu. 32:21).

For a foolish nation is one that serves the creature more than Creator and like irrational beasts feeds on just all unlearning, and gives heed only to things of the earth. But since Israel which was wise by reason of the law and prudent from having Prophets angered (God), it in its turn was angered by God, they who previously were not cautious being taken into the place belonging to these, for to them through faith was Christ made wisdom and sanctification and redemption (cf. 1 Cor. 1:30), as it is written, that is, both light and recovery of sight.

The Blessed Month of Amshir

INTRODUCTION TO THE SUNDAY READINGS OF AMSHIR

> So then, he who desires to track the footsteps of Christ, he should, as far as possible, be molded after His Pattern. He should not be eager to live in much boasting, nor when he practices virtue be led away in pursuit of praise, nor should he desire to glory immoderately thereat if he enters an extraordinary and exceeding disciplined life, but should desire to be seen alone by the Eyes of the Deity Who reveals hidden things, and that which is performed in secret brings He into clearest apprehension.
>
> — *St. Cyril of Alexandria*

The sixth month in the Coptic Calendar is Mechir (ⲙⲉⲭⲓⲣ in Bohairic; ⲙϣⲓⲣ in Sahidic; *Amshir* in Arabic). The days of its month range from February 8 or 9 until March 9. The ancient Egyptians referred to this month as the "large fire" because it was the coldest time of the year.

As mentioned in the introduction, the blessed month of Amshir is devoted to presenting our Lord Jesus Christ as the Bread of Life. It is preceded by the blessed month of Kiahk which emphasizes the Nativity of our Lord, and the blessed month of Tubah, in which we commemorate the Baptism of our Lord. After speaking of Incarnation and Baptism, the Church focuses the Sunday readings of the sixth Coptic month on Holy Communion and the Lord's table. After the Israelites crossed the Red Sea, a type of holy Baptism, God showered them with the heavenly Manna.

Likewise, after commemorating Holy Baptism during the month of Tubah, we continue during this month to examine Christ, Bread of Life.

The four main Sunday gospels of Amshir are read from the sixth chapter of the gospel of John. The First Sunday focuses on the eternal food that does not perish, the second on the Five Loaves and two fish, and the third on the Bread of Life. After the story in John 6 is read, the Church proceeds with the message from Luke 6 and the story of Zacchaeus. If this month includes a fifth Sunday, then, it is the first Sunday of the Great Lent, in which the appropriate gospel is read. Once Great Lent begins, however, its Sunday readings replace the annual Amshir readings. These readings are summarized as follows:

SUNDAY	TITLE	PASSAGE
First Sunday	Eternal Food	Jn. 6:22-27
Second Sunday	Five Loaves	Jn. 6:5-14
Third Sunday	Bread of Life	Jn. 6:27-46
Fourth Sunday	Zacchaeus	Lk. 19:1-10
Fifth Sunday (if needed)	Sunday of Blessing	Lk. 6:27-38

First Sunday

ETERNAL FOOD

Meditations on the First Sunday of the Blessed Month of Amshir

Gospel Reading of the First Sunday

John 6:22-27

"On the following day, when the people who were standing on the other side of the sea saw that there was no other boat there, except that one which His disciples had entered, and that Jesus had not entered the boat with His disciples, but His disciples had gone away alone—however, other boats came from Tiberias, near the place where they ate bread after the Lord had given thanks—when the people therefore saw that Jesus was not there, nor His disciples, they also got into boats and came to Capernaum, seeking Jesus. And when they found Him on the other side of the sea, they said to Him, "Rabbi, when did You come here?" Jesus answered them and said, "Most assuredly, I say to you, you seek Me, not because you saw the signs, but because you ate of the loaves and were filled. "Do not labor for the food which perishes, but for the food which endures to everlasting life, which the Son of Man will give you, because God the Father has set His seal on Him."

"Do Not Labor for the Food Which Perishes"

St. Cyril of Alexandria[62]

"On the following day, when the people who were standing on the other side of the sea saw that there was no other boat there, except that one which His disciples had entered, and that Jesus had not entered the boat with His disciples, but His disciples had gone away alone—however, other boats came from Tiberias, near the place where they ate bread after the Lord had given thanks" (Jn. 6:22, 23).

The miracle does not escape notice, I mean Jesus walking on the very sea, although it took place by night and in the dark, and was ordered in secret. But the crowd of those wanting to follow Him perceives, assured (as is probable) by much watching, that He had neither sailed with His disciples, nor had crossed in any other ship. For there was there the Apostles' ship alone, which they took and went away before Him. Nothing that is good is hidden even though it is performed in secret, proving that "Nothing is secret that will not be revealed, nor anything hidden that will not be known and come to light" (Lk. 8:17).

So then, he who desires to track the footsteps of christ, he should, as far as possible, be molded after His Pattern. He should not be eager to live in much boasting, nor when he practices virtue be led away in pursuit of praise, nor should he desire to glory immoderately thereat if he enters an extraordinary and exceeding disciplined life, but should desire to be seen alone by the Eyes of the Deity Who reveals hidden things, and that which is performed in secret brings He into clearest apprehension.

"When the people therefore saw that Jesus was not there, nor His disciples, they also got into boats and came to Capernaum, seeking Jesus" (Jn. 6:24).

These men follow Him, marveling perhaps at His miracles, yet not receiving any profit from them unto the duty of faith, but as though they were making some return to the Wonder-worker by merely bestowing on Him a desired praise. For this is a dreary disease of a mind and soul, which is never accustomed to be led to the choice of what is profitable for her.

---

[62] St. Cyril of Alexandria, *Commentary on the Gospel of John*, §24, Book 3, Ch. 4.

They did so because they delighted solely in the pleasures of the flesh, and jumped eagerly at the meanest temporal food, rather than hasten after spiritual goods, and endeavor to gain what would support them to eternal life. This you will also learn clearly by what follows.

"...And when they found Him on the other side of the sea, they said to Him, 'Rabbi, when did You come here?'..."

Their speech is like those who love Him and feigns sweetness, but is convicted of being exceedingly senseless and childish. For after meeting with such a great Teacher, they should not have talked without purpose and taken no pains to learn anything. For what was the need of being eager to ask Him, when He came there? What good would they be likely to get from knowing? We must then seek wisdom from the wise, and prefer prudent silence to undisciplined words. For the disciple of Christ bids that our speech be "seasoned with salt" (Col. 4:6); and another wise one exhorts us, saying, "My son, if you have a word of understanding, answer, if not, lay your hand upon your mouth" (Prov. 30:32). And how evil it is to be condemned for an undisciplined tongue, we shall know from another: for he says, "If anyone among you thinks he is religious, and does not bridle his tongue but deceives his own heart, this one's religion is useless" (Jam. 1:26).

"Jesus answered them and said, 'Most assuredly, I say to you, you seek Me, not because you saw the signs, but because you ate of the loaves and were filled.'" (Jn. 6:26)

We will say something common, yet worn by little use. Great teachers are usually a bit angry when they are questioned about vain and useless matters. And they are so, not out of haughtiness, but rather from annoyance at the folly of the questioners. Therefore, for us and those like us, I think this is rightly said: but the Savior inflicts a warm rebuke upon those who made those inquiries, for speaking without instruction and unwisely inquiring not because it was their duty to seek out the things whereby they might become honest and good, but because they followed Him for carnal reward and that a most mean one.

For what is less than daily food, and that not sumptuous? We must then practice holiness towards Christ and Love of Him, not that we may obtain carnal goods but that we may gain the salvation that is through

Him. Let us not say good words to Him, as these say "Rabbi," nor devise fair-speaking as a foundation of gain and boundless ingathering of riches. Truly he that attempts such things, will not be ignorant that he shall encounter Christ Who keenly convicts him, and reveals his hidden wickedness.

It is also meet to admire also the economy herein. For when He saw that they were enveloped with the aforementioned disease, as a Physician skilful and master of his art, He devised a twofold medicine for them: entwining the helpful reproof with a most glorious miracle.

The miracle then we shall find in His knowing their thoughts; and in the Wonder-worker not telling them what they sought not out of piety to know; you will behold the rebuke. And the advantage is twofold: knowing their plans perfectly, and having accurate perception of them, He shows that they are without understanding, in that they think to escape the Divine Eye, while they heap up wickedness in their heart, and practice sweet words with their tongue.

But this is the part of One Who persuades them to leave their disease and cease from no slight sin. For he who has this conception of God is shameful and lawless. In usefully convicting them of sinning, He restrains in some sort the future course of evil. For that which has no hindrance, creeps on and extends itself; but when caught in the fact, it is well-nigh ashamed, and like a rope contracts into itself. Therefore, the Lord helps them by reproving also, and by those things whereby one thinks that He smites, by these very things He is seen to be their Benefactor. We must then hold that even though some flatter or with mild words wheedle the rulers of the Churches, yet are not sound concerning the faith, it is not meet that they should be carried away by their flattering nor by way of payment for their applause lend in turn to them who need correcting, silence in regard to their faults. Rather, we should boldly rebuke them and persuade them to change for the better, or at least hereby if so be to profit others, according to that spoken by Paul, "Those who are sinning rebuke in the presence of all, that the rest also may fear." (1 Tim. 5:20)

We admit then that our Savior's coming down from the mountain typified His second and future Coming to us from Heaven, and we added as in summary, that He appeared to His disciples while they were watching and toiling, released them from their fear, and brought the ship at once to land. And what is then portrayed to us, as in a type, we have there declared. But now observe, that after Jesus had come down from the mountain, certain miss following Him, and come to Him at last.

For they come on the day following, the Evangelist having not without added this also. Then on meeting with Him, they endeavor to persuade Him with good words, but Christ rebukes them, bringing upon them hot and keen reproof, that we might consider this again, that after the Coming of our Lord to us from Heaven, most vain and profitless unto men is the search after good things, nor will the desire to follow Him find any fitting season. Yes, even though some approach Him, thinking to appease Him with smoothest words, they shall meet the Judge no longer mild and gentle, but rebuking and avenging. For you will see the flattery of those who are reproved, allow the reproof itself in the words of the Savior, when He says, "Many will say to Me in that day, 'Lord, Lord, have we not prophesied in Your name, cast out demons in Your name, and done many wonders in Your name?'" (Matt 7:22). But He says, "And then I will declare to them, 'I never knew you; depart from Me, you who practice lawlessness!'" (Matt 7:23). "For you did not seek Me purely," He says, "nor loved to excel in holiness. For because of this I would have known you. But since you practiced piety in appearance only and in mere imaginaries for the purpose of gain, I justly confess that I have not known you."

What then in that passage is Lord, Lord, here is Rabbi. To whomsoever therefore punishment is a bitter thing, let him not fall into lifelessness nor be variously sick in transgression, looking to the goodness of God, but let him prepare his works for his glory, as it is written, and make it fit for himself in the field, i.e., while he is in the world. For the Savior interpreted that "the field is the world." (Matt. 13:38) Let him prepare to show holiness and righteousness before the Divine Judgment Seat. For he will behold no unseasonably gentle Judge, nor yielding to appeals for mercy, in Him Whom he should have obeyed without delay when He was calling him to salvation, while the time of mercy was granting to him both to beg for forgiveness for his already past transgressions, and to seek for loving-kindness from God Who saves.

"Do not labor for the food which perishes, but for the food which endures to everlasting life." (Jn. 6:27)

Paul teaches us something like this, expanding the discourse universally and more generally, saying, "For he who sows to his flesh will of the flesh reap corruption, but he who sows to the Spirit will of the Spirit reap everlasting life." (cf. Gal 6:8) For he says that they sow to the flesh who giving, as it were, full rein to the pleasures of the flesh, advance at full speed to whatever they will, by no means distinguishing what is profitable for them from what is hurtful and injurious, nor in any way accustomed to approve what seems good unto the Law-giver, but heedlessly hurried off to that alone which is pleasant and agreeable, and preferring nothing to things seen.

Again, he affirms that they sow to the Spirit, who expend the whole aim of their mind on those things wherein the Holy Spirit wills us to excel, employing a mind so intense toward the cultivation of good things, that, did not voice of nature not to be disregarded constrain them to minister needful food to the flesh, they would not endure to descend even to this. I think then that we should take no forethought whatever for the flesh for the lusts thereof, but rather to apply ourselves to what is most needful, and to be zealous in practicing those things, which bring us to the everlasting and Divine Life. For admiration for the delights of the body, and the esteeming nothing better than the superfluities of the belly, is truly brutish and akin to the most extreme folly. But to apply ourselves to good things, and earnestly to strive to excel in virtues, and to be subject to the laws of the Spirit, and with all readiness to seek after the things of God, which are able to support us unto salvation: I will grant that this truly beseems him who knows his own nature, and is not ignorant that he has been made a reasonable creature according to the Image of Him who created him. Therefore as the Savior somewhere says, "Do not ask, what shall we eat? Or, what will we drink? Or, what will we be clothed with? But considering that the soul is more than food, and the body than raiment, let us take thought how the more precious part of us may do well." (Cf. Matt. 6:31, Luke 12:23)

Although the body may be well and fat with succession of delights, it will not profit the miserable soul. But, on the contrary, it will work it much harm. For it will depart into the everlasting fire, since they who have wrought no good, must undergo punishment for it. But if the body has been bridled with due reason, and brought under the law of the Spirit, both must surely be saved together. It is then most absurd, that for the flesh we should so take thought, which is but for a time and even now shall perish, as to think that it ought not to lack any one thing which it loves: and to take care for the soul, by way of appendix, or as though it were nothing of worth. Albeit, I think we should apply ourselves so much the rather to cares for the soul, as it is of more value than the body. For so of a truth preferring what surpasses in the comparison to what is inferior, and giving a just vote in this matter, we shall become holy and wise jurors, and not bestow upon any other the palm of right reasoning, but rather shall put it upon our own heads. Let us then, as the Savior says, not labor for the food which perishes, which when it has passed into the belly, and for a very little while deluded the mind with pettiest pleasure, goes out into the draught, and is conveyed forth again from the belly (cf. Matt. 15:17). But the spiritual food which strengthens the heart, keeps the man unto life everlasting, which also Christ promises to give us, saying, "Which the Son of Man shall give unto you;" at once knitting the human with that which is Divine, and connecting the whole mystery of the economy with Flesh in its order. But He hints, I suppose, at the Mystic and more Spiritual Food, whereby we live in Him, sanctified in body and soul. But we shall see Him speaking more openly of this hereafter. The discourse then must be kept for its fit time and place.

".. .which the Son of Man will give you, because God the Father has set His seal on Him" (Jn. 6:27).

He was not ignorant, as God, of the charges that would result from Jewish folly, nor of the reasons why they were often foolishly enraged. He knew that they would reason in themselves, looking to the flesh alone, and not conceiving of God the Word therein, Who is Th is That seizes upon God-befitting words? For who can give unto men food that keeps them unto everlasting life? For wholly foreign to man's nature is such a thing, and it beseems Him Alone Who is God over all. The Savior therefore defends Himself beforehand, and by seasonable arguments, shames their looked-for shameless talk. For He says that the Son of Man will give them the food which nourishes them unto everlasting life, and immediately affirmed that He is sealed by the Father. Sealed again is either put for anointed (for he who is anointed is sealed), or as skewing that He has been by Nature formed unto the Father. Just as if He had said, I am not unable to give you food, which endures and brings up unto everlasting life and delight. For though I seem as one of you, that is Man with flesh, yet was I anointed and sealed by God the Father to an exact Likeness with Him. For you shall see (He says) that He is in Me, and I again in Him Naturally, even though for your sakes I was born Man of a woman, according to the Ineffable order of the economy. For I can do all things in God-befitting Authority and do not in any way come short of the Might inherent in My Father. And though God the Father gives you the Spiritual Food, which preserves unto everlasting life, it is clear that the Son too will give it, even though made in Flesh, since He is His Exact Image; the Likeness in everything being conceived, not after the lineaments of flesh, nor yet ought conceived of in bodily form, but in God-befitting glory and Equal Power and royal Authority. But we must observe again, that when He says that Son of Man will give the things God-befitting and that He has been sealed unto the Image of God the Father, He does not endure the division of him that separates the Temple of the Virgin from the true Sonship, but defines Himself and wills to be conceived of again as One. For One in truth over us is Christ, bearing as it were the royal purple His Own, I mean His Human Body, or His Temple, to wit of Soul and Body; since One also of Both is Christ.

But, most excellent sir, will the Christ-opposer again say, give the truth the power of overcoming: deal not subtly with the saying, dishonorably turning it about, however you wish. Behold, clearly hereby is the Son proved to be not of the Essence of the Father, but rather a copy of His Essence. Suppose some such thing (say they) as we say: A seal or signet impressed on wax, for example, or any other matter fit to receive it, and engraving a likeness only of itself, is taken away again by him who pressed it on, having lost no part of itself: so the Father, having imposed and imprinted Himself Wholly upon the Son in some way by a most accurate Likeness, from Himself hath He surely no part of His Essence, nor is conceived of as there from but a mere image and accurate likeness.

Let him that is zealous for knowledge see that now too is our opponent darting on us, like a serpent, and rears aloft his head surcharged with venom; but He Who shatters the head of the Dragon, will shatter it too, and will give us power to escape his manifold stubbornness. Let him then tell us, who has just been dinning us with dreadful words, Does not the seal or signet, which is made (it may be) of wood or of iron or of gold, full surely seal with some impress those things whereon it comes, and will it not be and be conceived of as a seal apart from the impress? But I suppose that any one of our opponents too, even against his will constrained by fitness unto the very truth would confess that it will by all means seal with an impress; and without an impress, according to fair reasoning, not at all. Since then, as the Divine Scripture testifies to us, the Son is the Impress of the Person of God the Father, in that He is in It and of It by Nature, where-upon is Himself impressed, or through whom else will the Father seal His Own Impress? For no one will say that the Father is not altogether in God-befitting Form, which is the Son, the Form of Him That begat Him; Whom if any behold spiritually, it is manifest that he will see the Father. Wherefore He says that He too is in Him Naturally, even though He be conceived to be of Him by reason of His Own Existence: as the brightness for instance, is in the brightening and of the brightening, and something different, according to the mode of conception, and again not different, as viewed in relation to it, because it is said to be of it, and again in it. And not I suppose in the way of division and complete essential partition are these things considered of: for they are inherent in respect of identity of essence in those things whence they are, and of which they are believed to be, tending according to expression in idea to something else, of their own, yet not separate. The Word of the Essence of the Father, not bare Word, nor without Flesh, is sealed then by the Father, yes rather through Him are sealed those things which are brought to likeness with God, as far as can be, as we understand in that which certain say, The light of Your Countenance was marked upon us, O Lord. For he says that the Countenance of God the Father, is the Son, Which is again the Impress, but the light thereof is the grace which through the Spirit passes through unto the creation, whereby we are remolds unto God through faith, receiving through Him as with a seal, the conformation unto His Son, Who is the Image of the Father, that our being made after the Image and Likeness of the Creator, might be well preserved in us. But since the Son is confessedly the Countenance of God the Father, He will surely be the Impress too with which God seals.

Yes (says, our opponent), we believe that God through the Spirit seals the Saints, but the things that you are bringing forward have no place in the present question. Wherefore we will recapitulate said say, the seal supposed to be of iron, or may be gold, impresses its own likeness on the matter whereon it comes, losing nothing of its own, but by the operation only of its being pressed on does it mark the things that receive it. Thus do we hold that the Son has been sealed by the Father, not having ought of His Essence but possessing merely an accurate likeness thereof, and being Other than He, as the image to the archetype.

O boundless folly, and perilous conceit! How easily have you forgotten those things just now gone through. For we said that the Son was the Impress of the Father, and that with Him was sealed other than He, and not Himself, lest He be thought to be His Own Impress. But you, having not rightly spurned our argument hereon, do not blush to put about Him a likeness of operation only. In image only then will the Son be God according to you, and by Nature not at all, but merely in that He was fashioned and well formed after the Likeness of Him Who begat. Haply no longer of Him Who begat: for it is time that you should on these accounts take away the begetting also, yes rather there is every need even if you will it not.

On the duty of believing that the Son is begotten of the Father, we have already expended much argument, or shall do so in its place. But it were more fitting that we should proceed to the matter in hand, putting forward to those who are accustomed unrestrainedly to shameless talk the question, Will they not surely say that that which is given may also be taken away, and confess that that which is added can altogether be also lost? For does it not at some time happen that every thing is rejected, which is not firmly rooted in any by nature? It is evident, even should any of them not assent thereto. Some time then or other, according to the argument of possibility, the Son will be bereft of His Likeness. For He was sealed (as you say) by the mere Operation of His Father upon Him, not having the stability that is of natural Endowments, but conceived of and existing wholly other than His Father, and completely severed from His Essence.

Doing then very excellently and foreseeing matters by most cunning reasoning did you secure the Father, by saying that He gives nothing of Himself to the Son, except that He promises Him Likeness only, lest out of passion should be conceived of as about Him. For this is your foolish mystery. For belike you were ignorant that God the Father, Who does all things without passion will also beget without passion, and Is superior to fire (for the argument brings us down to this necessity) which without passion or corporeal division, begets the burning which is of it.

Let those then hear who are zealous in fancies only, and account unrestrained blasphemy to be not an unholy thing, but rather a virtue, that if they say that the Son is classed with the Father, in the propriety of likeness alone, He will abide in no secure possession of good things, but will wholly risk His being by Nature God, and will in possibility at least, admit of change for the worse. For there was also said to that king of Tyre, words which reason necessitates us to attribute to the person of the Devil, "You were the seal of the perfection" (Ezek. 28:12) but he to whom that speech is addresses, is found to have fallen from the likeness.

You see then, and clearly too, by such instances, that the mere being in the likeness of God is no security for an unmoved stability in things spiritual, nor yet does it suffice to perfect endurance in the good things in which they are, to have been duly sealed unto the Nature of the Maker. For they too fall, and stand headfirst, often changing into a worse mind, than they had at the beginning. It is then possible, according to this argument, that the Son, attaining to Likeness with the Father by sameness of work only, and not firm fixed by the support of Nature, but having His stability in the mere motions of His Own Will, should undergo change, or, though He do not suffer it, should find the not so suffering the result of admirable purpose, and not rather the steadfastness of Nature stability, as God.

What then, most noble sirs, is the Son no longer God in truth? And if according to you, He is so found, why do we worship Him? Why is He co-glorified with God the Father? Why is He born, as God, upon the highest Powers? Then, are the Holy Seraphim also so ignorant like us that they greatly err from what is fit, in glorifying Him Who is not by Nature God? They err, it seems, in calling Him Who is honored with equal honor Lord of Sabbaoth.

Or shall we not say, that the highest Powers, Principalities, Thrones, Dominions and Lordships, essay, after their power, to appear conformed to God? For if the very little animal of the earth, in respect of that creation, I mean man, is honored with such beauty, what reason has one not for fully thinking, that to them who are far better than we, far better things are allotted? How then do they both call Him Lord of Sabbaoth, and stand around as guard, as ministering to the King of the universe? Why does He sit with the Father, and that on His Right Hand, the bond with the Lord, the creature with the Creator? For is it not better to bring that which by means of heed and suspicion is free from passion and perfect, to the level of things originate rather than of God by Essence Who by Nature has the inability to suffer? But it is manifest though they do not confess it. Who then will endure these babblers, or how will they not with reason hear, Woe to them that are drunken without wine?

But maybe they will be ashamed of the absurdities of such arguments, and will betake themselves to this, and say, that the Son was sealed by the Father unto a most accurate Likeness, and is Unchangeable in Nature, even though He be not from the Father.

How then, tell me, will that which is not of God by Nature, bear His Attribute, and that be found not without share-essentially of the Excellencies of the Divine Essence, which proceeded not there from, after the true mode of generation? For it is, I suppose, clear and confessed by all, that the Properties of the Godhead are wholly unattainable by the created nature, and that the qualities belonging to It by Nature will not exist in ought else that is, in equal and exact manner: as for example, Immutability is in God Naturally; in us by no means so, but a kind of stability likens us thereto, through heed and vigilance not suffering us readily to go after those things which we ought not. But if it were possible, that according to them, ought of Divine Attributes should be in any who is not of the Divine Nature Essentially, and that they should be so in him as they are in It.

What (tell me) is to prevent all things God-befitting from at length coming down even upon those who are not by nature gods? For if one of them unhindered finds place (I mean Immutability) there will be room for the rest also, and what follows? Utter confusion. For will not the superior pass below, and the inferior mount up into the highest place? And what is there yet to hinder even the Most High God from being brought down to our level, and us again from being gods even as the Father, when there is no longer or is seen any difference intervening, if the qualities which belong to God Only pass to us, and are in us naturally?

Since God the Father contains in Himself Alone, as it seems, those Properties whereby we should be as He, we have remained men, and the angels likewise with us what they are, not mounting up to That which is above all. For if God should reveal Himself not Jealous, by putting His Own Attribute into the power of all, many surely would be those who were by nature gods, able to create earth and heaven and all the rest of the creation. For the Excellencies of Him Who is by Nature the Creator having once passed on, how will not they be as He is? Or what prevents that which is radiant with equal good from appearing in equal glory? But the God-opposer surely sees completely, how great the multitude of strange devices which is hence heaped up upon us and exclaims against the mislearning that is in him. The Godhead then will remain in Its Own Nature, and the creature will partake of It through spiritual relationship, but will never mount up unto the Dignity that unchangeably belongs to It. But our argument being thus arranged, we shall find that Immutability exists Essentially in the Son: He is then God by Nature, and of necessity of the Father, lest ought that is not of Him by Nature should reach to an equal dignity of Godhead.

But since they hold out to us as an incontestable argument their saying that the Son is other than the Father, as Image to archetype, and through this subtlety think to sever Him from the Essence of Him Who begat Him, they shall be caught in no slight folly, and to have studied their assertion to no purpose, of any force in truth to accomplish fairly what they have at heart. For what further are they vainly contending for, or whence do they from only the distinctness of His own Being, sever the Son from the Father? For the fact that He exists Personally does not (I suppose) prove that He is diverse from the Essence of Him who begat Him. For He is confessedly of the Father, as being of His Essence; He is again in the Father, by reason of His being in Him by Nature; and you will hear Him say, at one time, "I came forth from the Father, and have come," (Jn. 16:28) again at another time, "I am in the Father and the Father in Me." (Jn. 14:11) For He will not withdraw into a Personality wholly and completely separated, seeing that the Holy Trinity is conceived of as being in One Godhead; but being in the Father, in mode or position undivided as to consubstantiality, He will be conceived of as likewise of Him, according to the Procession which ineffably manifests Him in respect of beaming forth. For He is Light of Light. Therefore in the Father and of the Father, alike Undivided and separate, in Him as Impress, but as Image to Archetype will He be conceived of in His Own Person.

But we will not simply discourse concerning this, but will confirm it by example from the Law, on all sides fortifying the force of truth against those who think otherwise.

The Law then appointed to the children of Israel to give to every man a ransom for his poll, half a shekel. But one stater contains a shekel. Yes and herein again was shadowed out to us Christ Himself, Who offered Himself for all, as by all, a Ransom to God the Father (1 Tim. 2:6), and is understood in the one drachma, but not separately from the other, because that in the one coin, as we said before, two drachmae are contained.

Thus may both the Son be conceived of in respect of the Father, and again the Father in respect of the Son, Both in One Nature, but Each Separate in part, as existing in His own Person, yet not wholly severed, nor One apart from the Other. And as in the one coin were two drachmae, having equal bulk with one another, and in no ways one less than the other; so you will conceive of the in nothing differing Essence of the Son in respect of God the Father, and again of the Father in respect of the Son, and you will at length receive wholesome doctrine upon all points spoken of concerning Him.

"Master, When Did You Come Here?"

St. John Chrysostom[63]

"And the people that were there saw that there was none other boat there save the one into which the disciples had entered, and that Jesus went not into the boat, but His disciples." (Jn. 6:22)

And why is John so exact? Why said he not that the multitudes having passed over on the next day departed? He desires to teach us something else, namely, that Jesus allowed the multitudes if not openly, at least in a secret manner, to suspect what had taken place. For, "They saw,"

[63] St. John Chrysostom, *Commentary on the Gospel of John*, Homily 63, NPNF, s. 1, v. 14, pp. 357-358.

he says, "that there was none other boat there but one, and that Jesus went not into it with His disciples." And embarking in boats from Tiberias.

"They came to Capernaum seeking Jesus." (Jn. 6:24)

What else then could they suspect, save that He had arrived there crossing the sea on foot? for it was not possible to say that He had passed over in another ship. For "there was one," says the Evangelist, "into which His disciples entered." Still when they came to Him after so great a wonder, they asked Him not how He crossed over, how He arrived there, nor should understand so great a sign. But what say they?

"Master, when did You come here?" (Jn. 6:25)

Unless any one affirm that the "when" is here used by them in the sense of "how." But it is worthwhile also to notice here the uncertainty of their impulses, for they who said, "This is that Prophet;" they who were anxious to "take Him by force to make Him king" (Jn. 6:15), now when they have found Him take no such counsel, but having cast out their astonishment, they no longer admire Him for His former deeds. They sought Him, desiring again to enjoy a table like the first.

The Jews under the guidance of Moses passed over the Red Sea, but that case is widely different from this. He did all with prayer and as a servant, but Christ with absolute power. There when the south wind blew, the water yielded so as to make them pass over on dry land, but here the miracle was greater (Exod. 14:21). For the sea retaining its proper nature to bare its Lord upon its surface, thus testifying to the Scripture which says, "Who walks upon the sea as upon a pavement" (Job 9:8).

And with reason, when He was about to enter into stubborn and disobedient Capernaum, did He work the miracle of the loaves, as desiring not only by what took place within, but also by the miracles which were wrought without the city, to soften its disobedience. For was it not enough to soften even any stone, that such multitudes should come with great eagerness to that city? Yet they had no such feeling, but again desired food for the body, for which also they are reproached by Jesus.

Let us then, beloved, knowing these things, give thanks to God for things of sense, but much more for things spiritual; for such is His will. He gives the former because of the latter, leading in by these the more imperfect sort, and giving them previous teaching, because they are yet gaping upon the world...

"THE SHEWBREAD"

John of Damascus[64]

With bread and wine Melchizedek, the priest of the most high God, received Abraham on his return from the slaughter of the Gentiles. That table pre-imaged this mystical table, just as that priest was a type and image of Christ, the true high-priest, "for you are a priest for ever after the order of Melchizedek." (cf. Ps. 110:4) Of this bread the shewbread was an image. This surely is that pure and bloodless sacrifice which the Lord through the prophet said is offered to Him from the rising to the setting of the sun.

This bread is the first-fruits of the future bread which is...necessary for existence. For this.. .signifies either the future, that is Him Who is for a future age, or else Him of Whom we partake for the preservation of our essence. Whether then it is in this sense or that, it is fitting to speak so of the Lord's body. For the Lord's flesh is life-giving spirit because it was conceived of the life-giving Spirit. For what is born of the Spirit is spirit. But I do not say this to take away the nature of the body, but I wish to make clear its life-giving and divine power. But if some persons called the bread and the wine antitypes of the body and blood of the Lord, as did the divinely inspired Basil, they said so not after the consecration but before the consecration, so calling the offering itself.

"SEEK HIM FOR HIMSELF"

St. Augustine[65]

After the sacrament of the miracle, He introduces discourse, that, if possible, they who have been fed may be further fed, that lie may with discourse fill their minds, whose bellies He filled with the loaves, provided they take in. And if they do not, let that be taken up which they

---

[64] John of Damascus, *Concerning the Holy and Immaculate Mysteries of the Lord*, NPNF s. 2, v. 9, p. 233

[65] St. Augustine, Sermon 88 (on John 10:14), NPNF, s. 1, v. 7, pp. 1128-1136.

do not receive, that the fragments may not be lost. Wherefore let Him speak, and let us hear.

"Jesus answered them and said, 'Most assuredly, I say to you, you seek Me, not because you saw the signs, but because you ate of the loaves and were filled.' (Jn. 6:26) You seek Me for the sake of the flesh not for the sake of the Spirit."

How many seek Jesus for no other object but that He may bestow on them a temporal benefit?! One has a business on hand, he seeks the intercession of the clergy; another is oppressed by one more powerful than himself, he flies to the Church. Another desires intervention in his behalf with one with whom he has little influence. One in this way, one in that, the Church is daily filled with such people. Jesus is scarcely sought after for Jesus' sake.

"You seek Me, not because you saw the signs, but because you ate of the loaves and were filled. Do not labor for the food which perishes, but for the food which endures to everlasting life." (Jn. 6:26, 27)

You seek Me for something else, seek Me for My own sake." For He insinuates the truth, that Himself is that food: this shines out clearly in the sequel: "which the Son of Man will give you." (Jn. 6:27) You expect, I believe, again to eat bread, again to sit down, again to be satisfied. But He had said, "not the food which perishes, but for the food which endures to everlasting life."

"The Manna"

St. Augustine[66]

Let us turn to Him who did these things. He is Himself "The Bread which came down from heaven." But He is Bread which refreshes the failing, and does not fail; Bread which can be tasted, but cannot be wasted. The Manna also symbolized this Bread. Therefore it is said, "He gave them the Bread of heaven, man ate Angels' Bread." (cf. John 6:31) Who is the Bread of heaven, but Christ? But in order that man might eat Angels' Bread, the Lord of Angels was made Man. For if He had not been

---

[66] St. Augustine, Sermon 80 (on John 6:9), NPNF, s. 1, v. 6, pp. 1075-1079.

made Man, we should not have His Flesh; if we had not His Flesh, we should not eat the Bread of the Altar.

Let us hasten to the inheritance, seeing we have hereby received a great earnest of it. My brethren, let us long for the life of Christ, seeing we hold as an earnest the Death of Christ. How shall He not give us His good things, after he has suffered our evil things? In this earth of ours, in this evil world, what abounds, but to be born, to labor, and to die? Examine thoroughly man's estate, convict me if I lie: consider all men whether they are in this world for any other end than to be born, to labor, and to die? This is the merchandise of our country: these things here abound. To such merchandise did that Merchantman descend. And forasmuch as every merchant gives and receives; gives what he has, and receives what he has not; when he procures anything, he gives money, and receives what he buys: so Christ too in this His traffic gave and received. But what did He receive? That which abounds here, to be born, to labor, and to die, and what did He give? To be born again, to rise again, and to reign forever.

O Good Merchant, buy us. Why should I say buy us, when we should give You thanks because You have bought us? You deal out our Price to us, we drink Your Blood; so do You deal out to us our Price. And we read the gospel, our title deed. We are Your servants, we are Your creatures: You have made us, You have redeemed us. Any one can buy his servant, create him he cannot; but the Lord has both created and redeemed His servants; created them, that they might be; redeemed them, that they might not be captives ever. For we fell into the hands of the prince of this world, who seduced Adam, and made him his servant, and began to possess us as his slaves.

But the Redeemer came, and the seducer was overcome. And what did our Redeemer do to him who held us captive? For our ransom he held out His Cross as a trap; he placed His Blood in it as a bait. He indeed had power to shed His Blood, he did not attain to drink it. And in that he shed the Blood of Him who was no debtor, he was commanded to render up the debtors; he shed the Blood of the Innocent, he was commanded to withdraw from the guilty. He verily shed His Blood to this end, that He might wipe out our sins. That then whereby he held us fast was effaced by the Redeemer's Blood. For he only held us fast by the bonds of our own sins. They were the captive's chains. He came, He bound the strong one with the bonds of His Passion; He entered into his house—into the hearts—of those where he did dwell, and took away his vessels. We are his vessels. He had filled then with his own bitterness. This bitterness too he pledged to our Redeemer in the gall. He had filled us then as his vessels; but our Lord spoiling his vessels, and making them His Own, poured out the bitterness, filled them with sweetness.

Let us then love Him, for He is sweet: "Taste and see that the Lord is good." (Ps. 33:9) He is to be feared, but to be loved still more. He is Man and God; the One Christ is Man and God; as one man is soul and body: but God and Man are not two Persons. In Christ indeed there are two substances, God and Man; but one Person, that the Trinity may remain, and that there be not a Quaternary introduced by the addition of the human nature.

"Do Not Worry"

St. John Chrysostom[67]

He says something like this: "Do not care about this earthly food but for that spiritual food." But since some of those who desire to live in doing nothing have abused this speech, as though Christ would entirely abolish working, it is seasonable to say somewhat to them. For they slander, so to speak, all Christianity, and cause it to be ridiculed on the score of idleness. First however, we must mention that saying of Paul. What does he say? "Remember the Lord, how He said, 'It is more blessed to give than to receive.'" (Acts 20:35) Now how can it be possible for him to give who has not? How then does Jesus say to Martha, "You are concerned about many things, but one thing is needful, and Mary has chosen that good part?" (Lk. 10:41, 42) And again, "Do not worry about tomorrow." (Matt. 6:34) For it is necessary now to resolve all these questions, not only that we may check men if they would be idle, but also that the oracles of God may not appear to bring in what is contradictory.

Now Paul in another place says, "But we beseech you, brethren, that you increase more and more, that you study to be quiet, and to do your own business; that you may walk honestly toward them that are without;" (1 Thess. 4:10-12) and again, "Let him that stole, steal no more; but rather

[67] St. John Chrysostom, Homily 44 on John 6:26-27, NPNF, s. 1, v. 14, pp. 361-363.

let him labor, working with his own hands, that he may have to give to him that needs." (Eph. 4:28) Here the Apostle bids not simply "work," but to work so vigorously and laboriously, as to have thereby somewhat to give to others. And in another place the same says again; "These hands have ministered to my necessities, and to them that were with me." (Acts 20:34) And writing to the Corinthians he said, "What is my reward then? Verily, that when I preach the gospel, I may make the Gospel of Christ without charge." (1 Cor. 9:18) And when he was in that city, he abode with Aquila and Priscilla, "and wrought, for by their occupation they were tentmakers." (Acts 18:3)

These passages show a yet more decided opposition as to the letter; we must therefore now bring forward the solution. What then must be our reply? "Do not worry," does not mean "do not to work," but "not to be nailed to the things of this life." That is, do not care for tomorrow's worries, but consider it unnecessary. For a man may do no work, and yet lay up treasure for the morrow. But a man may work, yet care for nothing; for carefulness and work are not the same thing; it is not as trusting to his work that a man works, but, "that he may...give to him who has need." (Eph. 4:28) And that also which was said to Martha refers not to works and working, but to this, that it is our duty to know the right season, and not to spend on carnal things the time proper for listening.

Thus Christ spoke not the words as urging her to "idleness," but to rivet her to listening. "I came," He says, "to teach you needful things, but you are anxious about a meal. Do you desire to receive Me, and to provide for Me a costly table? Provide another sort of entertainment, by giving me a ready hearing, and by imitating your sister's longing for instruction." He said this not to forbid her hospitality, (away with the thought! how could that be?) but to show that she should not be busy about other matters during the time for listening. For to say, "Do not labor for the food that perishes," is not the expression of one implying that we should be idle (in fact, this most especially is "food that perishes," for idleness is wont to teach all wickedness); but that we should work and teach. This is food that never perishes; but if anyone is idle and gluttonous, and cares for luxury, that man works for "the food that perishes."

So too, if a man by his labor should feed Christ, and give Him drink, and clothe Him, who so senseless [could] react as to say that such an one labors for the meat that perishes, when there is for this the promise of the kingdom that is to come, and of those good things? This meat endures forever. But at that time, since the multitudes made no account of filth, nor sought to learn who it was that did these things, and by what power, but desired one thing only, to fill their bellies without working; Christ with good reason called such food, "meat that perishes." "I fed," He says, "your bodies, that after this you might seek that other food which endures, which nourishes the soul; but you again run after that which is earthy. Therefore you do not understand that I lead you not to this imperfect food, but to that which gives not temporal but eternal life, which nourishes not the body but the soul." Then when He had uttered such great words concerning Himself, and had said that He would give this food, in order that what was spoken might not stand in their way, to make His saying credible He attributes the supply to the Father.

For after saying, "Which the Son of Man shall give you;" He adds, "God the Father has sealed Him," that is, "has sent Him for this purpose, that He might bring the food to you." The saying also admits of another interpretation; for in another place Christ says, "He who hears My words, has set to his seal that God is true," (cf. Jn. 3:33) that is, has "showed forth undeniably." Which indeed the expression seems to me to hint at even in this place, for "the Father has sealed," is nothing else than "has declared," "has revealed by His testimony." He in fact declared Himself too, but since He was speaking to Jews, He brought forward the testimony of the Father...

Second Sunday

THE FIVE LOAVES

Meditations on the Second Sunday of the Blessed Month of Amshir

Gospel Reading of the Second Sunday

John 6:5-14

Then Jesus lifted up His eyes, and seeing a great multitude coming toward Him, He said to Philip, "Where shall we buy bread, that these may eat?" But this He said to test him, for He Himself knew what He would do. Philip answered Him, "Two hundred denarii worth of bread is not sufficient for them, that every one of them may have a little." One of His disciples, Andrew, Simon Peter's brother, said to Him, "There is a lad here who has five barley loaves and two small fish, but what are they among so many?" Then Jesus said, "Make the people sit down." Now there was much grass in the place. So the men sat down, in number about five thousand. And Jesus took the loaves, and when He had given thanks He distributed them to the disciples, and the disciples to those sitting down; and likewise of the fish, as much as they wanted. So when they were filled, He said to His disciples, "Gather up the fragments that remain, so that nothing is lost." Therefore they gathered them up, and filled twelve baskets with the fragments of the five barley loaves which were left over by those who had eaten. Then those men, when they had seen the sign that Jesus did, said, "This is truly the Prophet who is to come into the world."

"Five Loaves and Two Fish"

St. Cyril of Alexandria[68]

"Then Jesus lifted up His eyes, and seeing a great multitude coming toward Him, He said to Philip, 'Where shall we buy bread, that these may eat?' But this He said to test him, for He Himself knew what He would do." (Jn. 6:5, 6)

Again, Christ devised a most excellent lesson for His disciples, appropriate for most men, to persuading them in difficult times to overcome cowardice in respect of hospitality without any hesitation at all, rather with more zealous motions to attain this virtue. For what is there greater than this among those who know and will the things by which it befits to purchase unto themselves the friendship from above?

When a large crowd came to Him, and an innumerable multitude is poured out like waters on the parts, in which He had stopped, He immediately ordered (the disciples) to make preparations for feeding them. Truly, it was not unlikely that the zeal even of a very rich man would numb, by the multitude of those he saw startled into fear of not being able to be hospitable. But Christ shows that it is nothing at all great, when our brotherly love comes to a few, but wills that we should overcome with manful courage also things that surpass our expectation, firmly grounded by confidence in Him to boldness to all good things.

In regard then of the narrative, the significance of what is said, does not aim away from the mark. But when we view these things spiritually, and remove (our) gross impurities, we say more openly, that those who by good zeal and faith seek Him, God beholds from the mountain of His high and God-befitting foreknowledge, according to that which is said by Paul, "For whom He foreknew, He also predestined to be conformed to the Image of His Son." (Rom. 8:29) Christ then lifts up His eyes as showing that those who love Him are worthy of the Divine Gaze, even as it was said to Israel, "The Lord lift up His countenance upon you, and give you peace." (Num. 6:26)

But not by the mere looking on them is His grace toward them that honor Him bounded, but the blessed Evangelist adding something more, shows that the Lord was not unmindful of the multitudes, but well

[68] St. Cyril of Alexandria, *Commentary of the Gospel of St. John*, §24, Book 3, Ch. 4.

prepared for their food and refreshment. By this again you may understand that which is delivered us in Proverbs, "The Lord will not let the soul of the righteous man starve." (Prov. 10:3)

He sets before them Himself, as Bread from Heaven, Who will nourish the souls of those who fear Him and sufficiently prepares all things for their nourishment, as he says in the Psalms, "You give them their food in due season." (Ps. 103:27) And Christ Himself says, "He who comes to Me shall never hunger" (Jn. 6:35)—for He will give, as we said before, food from heaven, and will richly bestow the manifold grace of the Spirit. Moreover, He prepares to give food to them that come to Him, and does not even wait for their request. "For we do not know what we should pray for as we ought," (Rom. 8:26) but He comes to us in reaching out those things which preserve us unto eternal life.

He then says to Philip, "Where shall we buy bread?" We must see why He asks Philip, although the rest of the disciples were standing by and cleaving to Him. Philip then was a questioner and apt to learn, but not over quick in ready power of understanding the more Divine. You will learn this if you consider that he, after following the Savior for a long time, gathering many lessons concerning His Godhead, and receiving apprehension through both deeds and words, as though he had learned nothing.

But in the last times of the economy, he says to Jesus, "Lord, show us the Father, and it is sufficient for us." (Jn. 14:8) In his simplicity he was fitly reinstructed: "Have I been with you so long, and yet you have not known Me, Philip?" (Jn. 14:9), Christ says. Therefore as to one duller of understanding, and advancing more slowly than he should to the apprehension of things more Divine, He puts forth the question, exercising the disciple in faith. For this is one meaning of, "TO test him," in this passage, although as the blessed Evangelist affirmed, "He Himself knew what He would do." (Jn. 6:6)

But saying this, He demonstrates the inattention of money of those who were with Him, and their voluntary poverty for God's sake, for they did not even have any means to buy the necessary food. Together with this He works something, and orders it skillfully. For He says, not emptily, as to those who had taken no trouble to provide anything at all, but as to those who were accustomed to complete inattention for money. So excluding and most skillfully cutting short the expectation arising from money, He properly persuades them to go on to entreat the Lord, that He may, if He wills, create food for (the disciples) who have nothing to feed those that come to Him, by His unspeakable Power and God-befitting Might. For this was what yet remained, and He was calling them at length to see that their only remaining hopes were there, according to the Greek poets, the iron wound of necessity.

"Philip answered Him, 'Two hundred denarii worth of bread is not sufficient for them, that every one of them may have a little.'" (Jn. 6:7)

Again, Philip weakly answers, focusing not on the power of Jesus to do all things, but when hearing Him ask, "Where shall we buy," focuses only on the means of money without conceiving that they could accomplish this task in another way besides the common law and that practiced by all, that is to say, wasteful spending.

Therefore, due to the disciples' lack of care for money and their possessing nothing, and Philip's own apprehension, which still did not as with perfect clearness view the exceeding dignity of our Savior, kindness towards the multitudes is turned into an impossibility. But the will of the Savior was not so, and He conducts them to its completion. The impossible with men is possible with God, (cf. Mk. 10:27) and the Divine Power proves on all sides superior to the natural order of things with us, strong to accomplish all things wondrously, even what transcends our understanding.

"One of His disciples, Andrew, Simon Peter's brother, said to Him, 'There is a lad here who has five barley loaves and two small fish, but what are they among so many?'" (Jn. 6:8)

(Andrew) both thinks and reasons like Philip and is convicted of having a kindred apprehension of the Savior Christ. For neither considering the power, nor yet led by the greatness of the preceding works of Jesus' being able to do all things, and that most easily, he points out what the lad has. But Andrew is clearly weak in faith, for he says, "What are these among so many?"

But we must say, (Andrew) should have remembered those things which (Christ) had already miraculously done, and considered that it would not be strange or difficult for the One Who had transformed the water into wine (cf. Jn. 2:1-12) and healed the palsied man with one word, (cf. Matt. 9:1-8), to create food of that which had no being, and multiply Divinely the exceeding little that was found ready to hand. For wouldn't the Authority that worked in one also be able to work in the other?

Therefore the two disciples answered more feebly than was fitting. But we must consider this again. For those things which appear to have been little falls in the Saints, are oftentimes not without their share of profit, but have something wrapped up with them, helpful to the nature of that in regard to which is the charge of their apparent weakness. For the response of the two holy disciples mentioned above—that "two hundred dinarii of bread is not sufficient for them that every one may take a little," and that the five loaves and two little fish, "what are these among so many?"—raises the marvel to its height, and makes the Might of the Savior most obvious, indicating by their own words the multitude that but now was to be fed, and the strength of their unbelief is converted into good testimony to Christ. Because they confessed that so much money would not be enough for the multitude even by a small portion, by this very thing they crown the Ineffable Might of the Host, when He, while there was nothing (as Andrew says, what is the lad's food among so many?) very richly outdid His work of love towards the multitude.

Similarly, we find the same littleness of faith with the all-wise Moses in the wilderness. For the Israelites wept and sinfully lusted after the food of the Egyptians. By picturing unclean dishes of flesh and strangely craving onions, garlic, and other unseemly things, and disregarding the Divine good things, they attacked Moses, their mediator and leader (cf. Exod. 16"2-4). But God was not ignorant, for what the multitude were eagerly groaning, and promised to give them flesh. But since the promise of liberality was made in the wilderness, and the thing appeared hard of accomplishment, with regards to human understanding, Moses came to Him crying out, "The people I am among are six hundred thousand men on foot; yet You are saying, 'I will give them meat, so they may eat a whole month.' Shall sheep and oxen be slaughtered for them, to provide enough for them?" (Num. 11:21, 22) And what did God say to these things? "Is the Lord's hand unable to provide for them? Now you shall know whether or not My Word will overtake you." (Num. 11:23)

Therefore, one may well say to the words of Philip and Andrew also, "Is the Lord's arm unable to provide?" So let us also learn from this example and conclude that littleness of faith is the worst of sicknesses and surpasses all evil. So, if God works or promises to do so, be sure to received it with simple faith, and do not accuse God out of our inability to conceive how what is above us shall happen, by reason of our own powerlessness.

One who is good, sober-minded, and with sound reason will also consider how the bodily eye also does not see as far as one would like, but as far as it can and as the limit of our nature permits. For it cannot distinguish things that are set too high, but may only imagine them with difficulty, snatching even the slightest view of them.

So, too, you can imagine that the mind of man also attains and stretches out as far as the bounds given to it by its Maker allows, even if it is wholly purified. For it will see none of those things that are beyond, but will give way, even against its will, to what is above nature, fully unable to grasp them. The things then that are above us are received by faith, not by investigation. As he who believes is admired; he who doubts is by no means free from blame. The Savior Himself testifies of this, saying, "He who believes in Him is not condemned; but he who does not believe is condemned already." (Jn. 3:18)

Now having once taken up the discourse on the duty of not mistrusting God, come, let us again showing forth somewhat out of the sacred writings, put it forward, and display blazon the punishment of the unbelief for the profit of our readers.

Again, when the people were oppressed with intolerable thirst, Moses the Arch-prophet was once bidden in the wilderness to take Aaron and smite the rock with his rod that it might gush out fountains of water. But he, not wholly believing the words of Him Who commanded Him, but fainthearted by reason of human nature, says, "'Hear me, you disobedient ones. Must we bring water for you out of this rock?' Moses then lifted up his hand and struck the rock twice with his rod; and much water came out...But the Lord said to Moses and Aaron, 'Because you did not believe Me, to sanctify Me before the children of Israel, therefore you shall not bring this congregation into the land I am giving them'" (Num. 20:10-12).

Is it now clear to everyone how bitter the wages of unbelief are? If Moses, as great as he was, was reproved, whom shall God spare, and upon whom will He who thus does not respect persons, not inflict His wrath for their unbelief, since He would not spare even that Moses, to whom He had said, "I know you above all, and you have also found grace in My site" (Exod. 33:12).

"Then Jesus said, 'Make the people sit down.' Now there was much grass in the place. So the men sat down, in number about five thousand." (Jn. 6:10)

The Savior practiced His accustomed gentleness and takes away the sharpness of His reproaches. For He does not bitterly rebuke His disciples, although they were deeply slumbering in respect of their faintheartedness and littleness of faith in Him. Instead, He leads them by His Deeds to the apprehension of the things which as yet they did not believe.

The words, "Make them sit down" have no small significance, and clearly show Jesus speaking in this manner, "O slow to understand My Power, and to perceive Who it is Who speaks, make the people sit down so that you may see the people filled with the nothing that lies before you and marvel. Make the people sit down. For it is what is lacking to them. For two hundred denarii would not have sufficed to get means of life for the multitudes, but the lack of money such as men use, in respect of its being able to preserve life, My Power shall attain, which calls all things into being, and creates out of things which are not. Nor did Elijah the Prophet give the widow's cruse of oil unfailing, and make the barrel the source of unwasting food. But He, Who gave him the power, will He not be able to multiply nothing, and to give any mere chance supply a fount of His ineffable Bounty and the principle and root of unlocked for grace?"

It is not incredible that such were Christ's thoughts in what He said. The blessed Evangelist profitably mentions that there was much grass in the place, showing that the country was fit for the men to sit down in.

But observe how, whereas the multitude of those who were fed was random, and that women were there with their children, he numbered the men only, following I suppose the custom of the Law. For God commanded the hierophant Moses, saying, "Take a census of all the congregation of the children of Israel, and according to their families by their fathers' houses, and according to the number of names by their heads count, every male from twenty years old and above." (Num. 1:2-3)

The Prophet did as he was commanded, and collected a great list of names, and is seen to have completely passed over females and children, and enrolled the multitude that were of full age. Also honorable in the

Book of God is all that is manly and vigorous, and not what is infantile in purpose after good things. Therefore, He honored the custom of the Law also in this, and formed again some spiritual conception. For shall we not with reason say, "If we look to the whole context of the passage, Christ rightly turns away from and leaves the violent and vainglorious people of the Jews, but very graciously receives those who come to Him, and fills them with heavenly Food by preaching to them the Spiritual Bread which strengthens man's heart?"

For He does not feed them sadly, but joyously, freely and with much enjoyment in piety. For this is what the sitting of the multitudes on the grass signifies, so that now too it is fit that each one to whom such grace has been granted should say as in the Psalms, "The Lord is my Shepherd, and I shall not want; He makes me to lie down in green pastures." (Ps. 22:1) For in much enjoyment and delight through the gifts of the Spirit are the minds of the Saints fed, as it is said in the Song of Songs, "O friends, eat and drink, and O brother, drink abundantly." (Song of Sol. 5:1)

But while there were many, and they sitting down randomly, as we said before, he mentioned the men alone, passing over in silence the women and children profitably for the idea (conveyed by this). For He teaches us as in a riddle, that to those who quit them as men, that is, in good, the Savior will supply the food more fittingly and specially, and not to those who are effeminate to no good habit of life, nor yet to those who are infantile in understanding, so as to be by this unable to understand none of the things that are necessary to be known.

"And Jesus took the loaves, and when He had given thanks He distributed them to the disciples, and the disciples to those sitting down; and likewise of the fish, as much as they wanted." (Jn. 6:11)

He gives thanks, as an example to us and a pattern of the piety which should be in us, and attributes again as Man the Power of the miracle to the Divine Nature. This was His custom, both helping by an example of piety (as we just said) those to whom He was manifested as a most excellent Teacher, and, by an economy concealing His God-befitting Dignity until His Passion drew near. For it was His earnest care that it should be hid from the prince of this world. For this reason, He elsewhere also uses words befitting men, as a Man, and heals again the understanding of His hearers, sometimes making most-wise alluring as in the words, "Father, I thank You for You have heard Me." (Jn. 11:41)

See how humanlike His speech is, and well calculated (it is) to trouble the understanding of the more simple? But when He says this, as Man, then again He immediately unfolds the mode of the economy, and the object of His will to remain hidden, by most excellent arrangement fortifying the mind of the more simple which had received a shock.

"And I know that You always hear Me," He says. Why then do You say these things? "But because of the people who are standing by I said this, that they may believe that You sent Me," He says (Jn. 11:42). Then, isn't it clear that He sometimes speaks more lowly than He really is, to assist us and fulfill the secret economy with Flesh? Therefore, as in that passage, "I thank You," is taken economically, just as He blessed the bread here.

But we must observe that instead of gave thanks, you have said, blessed, but the edition of the saints will in no way differ. For Paul will show that they are both one, saying, "for every creature of God is good, and nothing is to be refused if it is received with thanksgiving; for it is sanctified by the word of God and prayer" (1 Tim. 4:4, 5). But that which is sanctified through the prayer in supplication, which we are accustomed to make over the table, is surely blessed.

But since it is fit that nothing profitable be left uninvestigated by us, come let us say a little of the five loaves which the lad had and of the two little fishes since both the species itself and the numbers are replete with mystery. For (some more studious person will say) why weren't the loaves rather five, and the fishes three? Why not five, and the fishes four? What occasion was there at all for recounting the number found, and why didn't he rather say more simply and absolutely that the innumerable multitude of them that followed Him were fed off exceeding few things? But the fact that the blessed Evangelist very diligently recounted these things also gives us something surely to think of, which we must search into.

He says then that there were five loves of barley, and two fishes, and with these Christ feeds them that love Him. I think (and let the lover of wisdom search for something better) that the five barley loaves signify the five-fold book of the all-wise Moses, -that is, the whole Law, bringing in as it were coarser food, that by the letter and history. For this the barley hints at.

But by the little fishes is signified the food obtained through the fishermen, that is, the more delicate books of the disciples of the Savior; and these two (he says), the apostolic and Evangelic preaching, shine forth among us. Both of these are the sketches and spiritual writings of the fishermen. Therefore, the Savior mingling the new with the old, by the Law and the teachings of the New Testament, nourishes the souls of them that believe on Him, unto life, plainly eternal life. That the disciples were of fishermen, is (I suppose) plain and clear. And though all were not so, yet since there are some such among them, our argument will not recede from truth in what has been said.

"So when they were filled, He said to His disciples, 'Gather up the fragments that remain, so that nothing is lost.' Therefore they gathered them up, and filled twelve baskets with the fragments of the five barley loaves which were left over by those who had eaten." (Jn. 6:12, 13)

To some, Christ may seem by the sparing of the fragments to have bidden His disciples to gather together. Yet (I think) every one will fitly imagine, that Christ would not endure to descend to such littleness. And why do I say Christ? Not even one of us would do so, for what would be the significance of the remnant of the five barley loaves? But the verse has a great economy, and makes the miracle evident to the hearers. For so great is the efficacy of God-befitting Authority in this matter, that not only was so great a multitude filled from five barley loaves and two little fishes, but twelve baskets full of fragments were gathered besides. Moreover the miracle repels, another (similar) suspicion, and by the finding of the fragments confirmed the belief of there having been really and truly an abundance of food, and not rather the appearance of a vision deceiving both the eye of the feaster and of those who minister to them.

But greater, more noteworthy, and of exceeding profit to us, is this: consider how by this miracle He makes us most zealous in our desire to exercise hospitality most gladly, nearly calling aloud to us by the things that were done, that the things of God shall not fail him that is ready to communicate, rejoices in habit of neighborly love, and readily fulfills what is written, "Share your bread with the hungry." (cf. Isa. 58:7) For we find that the disciples at the beginning were hampered by reluctance about giving, but seeing they were thus minded, the Savior gave them a rich gathering from the fragments; and teaches us also by this, that we, on expending a little for the glory of God, will receive richer grace according to the saying of Christ, "Good measure, pressed down, shaken together, and running over, will be put into your bosom." (Lk. 6:38)

Therefore, we must not be slothful to the communion of love to the brethren, but rather advance to good resoluteness, and put as far as possible from us the cowardice and fear that dispose us to inhospitality. Confirmed in hope through faith in the power of God to multiply little things, let us also open our hands to the needy, according to the appointment of the Law, for He says, "You shall surely open your hands to your brother, to your poor and needy in your land." (Deut. 15:11)

For when will you be found merciful, if you remain hard in this life? When will you fulfill the commandment, if you allow the time of being able to do it to slip by in idleness? Remember the Psalmist's saying, "For there is no remembrance of You in death; and in Hades who will give thanks to You?" (Ps. 6:6) For what fruit is there yet of the dead, or how shall one of them that have gone down into the pit remember God by fulfilling His commandments? For God closed upon him, as it is written. Therefore the most-wise Paul also instructed us, saying, "Therefore, as we have opportunity, let us do good to all." (Gal. 6:10)

And these things shall be said for profit from the narrative. But since, taking what has been said in a spiritual sense (for so we ought, and not otherwise), we said that by the five barley loaves the book of Moses was hinted at, and by the two little fishes, the wise writings of the holy Apostles, in the gathering together of the fragments too, I suppose we should perceive some mystical and spiritual conception, agreeing with the order of the account. The Savior then commanded the multitudes to sit down, and having blessed, He distributed the bread, and the fishes, i.e., through the ministry of the disciples.

But when they had eaten and were miraculously filled, He commands them to gather together the fragments, and twelve baskets are filled, one (it seems) for each of the disciples since there that many of them, too. What then shall we understand from this, except surely and truly that Christ is the President of those who believe in Him and nourishes those who come to Him with Divine and heavenly food. Doctrines plainly of the Law and Prophets, Evangelic and Apostolic.

But He does not allow Himself to entirely appear as the Worker of these things, but the disciples minister to us the grace from above—for as it is written, it is not they who speak, but the Spirit of the Father which speaks in them (cf. Matt. 10:20; Mk. 13:11). But the holy Apostles do not labor likewise without reward. For they having dispensed to us the spiritual food and ministered the good things of our Savior, will receive the richest reward and obtain the fullest grace of bounty from God. For this and nothing else, I think, is the meaning of the gathering together of a basketful by each at the commandment of Christ, after their toils and the service expended on the feasters. But there is no doubt, that after them the things typically signified will pass also to the rulers of the holy Churches.

"Then those men, when they had seen the sign that Jesus did, said, 'This is truly the Prophet who is to come into the world.'" (Jn. 6:14)

Those who marvelled at the sign were those who knew how to approve things God-befitting, and directed themselves by human reason rather than those diseased with unreason befitting the beasts, as were the blasphemous Jews, who, when they should have profited by the publicity of the miracles worked, lost even the power of right judgment. For they deemed that Jesus ought now to be stoned also, because He so often appeared as a worker of miracles. Superior then, and in no small degree, to the folly of those men, are those who marvelled, who were soberly persuaded by this one great miracle that it was surely He Whose coming into the world as a Prophet was foretold.

But observe, how great a difference appears here between the race of Israel, and those living outside of Judea. For the one, although they were spectators of many things, and those not unworthy of admiration, are not only hard of heart and inhuman, but also desire unjustly to slay Him Who was zealous to save them, driving Him with their wild folly from their city and country. While those who dwelt away from Jerusalem and signify the race of aliens, from one miracle alone glorify Him, and nobly determine that their conceptions of Him should be received with faith unhesitatingly. From all these things, was Israel shown to be self-condemned and self-invited to her final just rejection, and that it was fitting for the Gentiles to obtain at length their share of mercy from above and love through Christ.

"SITTING ON THE GRASS"

The Scholar Origen[69]

Perhaps by the five loaves they meant to make a veiled reference to the sensible words of the Scriptures, corresponding in number on this account to the five senses. The two fishes correspond either to the word expressed and the word conceived, which are a hint, so to speak, to the sensible things contained in the Scriptures—or to the word which had come to them about the Father and the Son. Therefore also after His Resurrection He ate of a broiled fish, having taken a part from the disciples, and having received that theology about the Father which they were in part able to declare to Him. Such is the contribution we have been able to give to the exposition of the word about the five loaves and the two fish; and probably those, who are better able than we to gather together the five loaves and the two fishes among themselves, would be able to give a fuller and better interpretation of their meaning.

It must be observed, however, that while in Matthew, Mark, and Luke, the disciples say that they have the five loaves and the two fishes, without indicating whether they were wheat or barley, John alone says, that the loaves were barley loaves. Therefore, perhaps, in the Gospel of John the disciples do not acknowledge that the loaves are with them. But in John, "There is a lad here who has five barley loaves and two small fish." (Jn. 6:9)

And so long as these five loaves and two fishes were not carried by the disciples of Jesus, they did not increase or multiply, nor were they able to nourish more; but, when the Savior took them, and in the first placed looked up to heaven, with the rays of His eyes, as it were, drawing down from it power which was to be mingled with the loaves and the fishes which were about to feed the five thousand. After this He blessed the five loaves and the two fishes, increasing and multiplying them by the word and the blessing.

Thirdly, after dividing and breaking, He gave to the disciples that they might set them before the multitudes. The loaves and the fishes were sufficient, so that all ate and were satisfied, and some portions of the loaves which had been blessed were unable to be eaten. For so much was left over

---

69 The Scholar Origen, *Commentary on St. Matthew,* Book 11, ANF v. 10, pp. 762-765.

from the multitudes, which was not according to the capacity of the multitudes but of the disciples who were able to take up that which remained of the broken pieces, and to place it in baskets filled with that which remained, which were in number so many as the tribes of Israel.

Concerning Joseph, then, it is written in the Psalms, "His hands served in the basket" (Ps. 80:7), but about the disciples of Jesus that they took up that which remained of the broken pieces twelve baskets, and twelve baskets, I take it, not half-full but filled. And there are, I think, up to the present time, and will be until the consummation of the age with the disciples of Jesus, who are superior to the multitudes, the twelve baskets, filled with the broken pieces of living bread which the multitudes cannot eat. Now those who ate of the five loaves which existed before the twelve baskets that remained were relatives in nature to the number five. For those who ate had reached the stage of sensible things, since also they were nourished by Him who looked up to heaven and blessed and brake them, and were not boys nor women, but men. For there are, I think, even in sensible foods differences, so that some of them belong to those who "have put away childish things" (1 Cor. 13:11), and some to those who are still babes and carnal in Christ...

And what is meant by the words, "Then He commanded the multitudes to sit down on the grass" (Matt. 14:19)? And what are we to understand in the passage worthy of the command of Jesus? Now, I think that He commanded the multitudes to sit down on the grass because of what is said in Isaiah, "All flesh is grass" (Isa. 40:6); that is to say, He commanded them to put the flesh under, and to keep in subjection "the mind of the flesh," so that one might be able to partake of the loaves which Jesus blesses. Since there are different orders of those who need the food which Jesus supplies and all are not nourished by equal words, on this account I think that Mark has written, "Then He commanded them to make them all sit down in groups on the green grass. So they sat down in ranks, in hundreds and in fifties" (Mk. 6:39); but Luke, "Then He said to His disciples, 'Make them sit down in groups of fifty'" (Lk. 9:14).

For it was necessary that those who were to find rest in the food of Jesus should either be in the order of the hundred—the sacred number—which is consecrated to God, because of the unit (in it), or in the order of the fifty— the number which signifies the remission of sins, in accordance with the mystery of the Jubilee which took place every fifty years, and of the feast at Pentecost.

And I think that the twelve baskets were in the possession of the disciples to whom it was said, "You will sit on twelve thrones, judging the twelve tribes of Israel" (Matt. 19:28, Lk. 22:30). And as the throne of him who judges the tribe of Reuben might be said to be a mystery, and the throne of him who judges the tribe of Simeon, and another of him who judges the tribe of Judah, and so on with the others; so there might be a basket of the food of Reuben, and another of Simeon, and another of Levi. But it is not in accordance with our present discourse now to digress so far from the subject in hand as to collect what is said about the twelve tribes, and separately what is said about each of them, and to say what each tribe of Israel may signify.

"Five and Two"

St. Augustine[70]

It was a great miracle that was worked, dearly beloved, for five thousand men to be filled from five loaves and two fish, and the remnants of the fragments to fill twelve baskets. A great miracle, but we shall not wonder much at what was done, if we give heed to Him Who did it. He multiplied the five loaves in the hands of those who broke them, who multiplies the seeds that grow in the earth, so as that a few grains are sown, and whole barns are filled. But, because he does this every year, no one marvels. Not the inconsiderableness of what is done, but its constancy takes away admiration of it. But when the Lord did these things, He spoke to those who had understanding—not by words only, but even by the miracles themselves.

The five loaves signified the five books of Moses' Law. The old Law is barley compared to the Gospel wheat. In those books are great mysteries concerning Christ contained. Hence He says, "If you believed Moses, you would believe Me; for he wrote of Me." (Jn. 5:46) But as in barley the marrow is hid under the chaff, so in the veil of the mysteries of the Law is Christ hidden. And as those mysteries of the Law are developed and

[70] St. Augustine, *Sermon 80* (on John 6:9), NPNF, s. 1, v. 6, p. 1075.

unfolded, so too those loaves increased when they were broken. And in this that I have explained to you, I have broken bread to you.

The five thousand men signify the people ordered under the five books of the Law. The twelve baskets are the twelve Apostles, who themselves were also filled with the fragments of the Law. The two fishes are either the two precepts of the love of God and our neighbor, or the two people of the circumcision and uncircumcision, or those two sacred personages of the king and the priest. As these things are explained, they are broken; when they are understood, they are eaten.

"The Number Five"

St. Irenaeus of Lyons[71]

But that this point is true, that that number which is called five, which agrees in no respect with their argument, and does not harmonize with their system, nor is suitable for a typical manifestation of the things in the Pleroma, (yet has a wide prevalence,) will be proved as follows from the Scriptures. Σοτηρ *(soteer,* Greek for Savior) is a name of five letters; πατηρ *(pateer,* Greek for father) also contains five letters; Αγαπε *(agape,* Greek for love) also consists of five letters. Our Lord, after blessing the five loaves, fed five thousand men with them.

Five virgins were called wise by the Lord, and five called foolish.

Again, five men are said to have been with the Lord when He obtained testimony from the Father—namely, Peter, and James, and John, and Moses, and Elijah. The Lord also, as the fifth person, entered into the apartment of the dead maiden, and raised her up again. For, the Scripture says, "He permitted no one to go in except Peter, James, and John, and the father and mother of the girl" (Lk. 8:51).

The rich man in hell declared that he had five brothers, to whom he desired that one rising from the dead should go.

The pool from which the Lord commanded the paralytic man to go into his house, had five porches.

---

[71] St. Irenaeus of Lyons, *Against the Heresies*, Book 2, ANF v. 1, pp. 817-818.

The very form of the cross, too, has five extremities, two in length, two in breadth, and one in the middle, on which the (last) person rests who is fixed by the nails.

Each of our hands has five fingers; we have also five senses; our internal organs may also be reckoned as five, that is, the heart, the liver, the lungs, the spleen, and the kidneys. Moreover, even the whole person may be divided into this number (of parts)—the head, the breast, the belly, the thighs, and the feet.

The human race passes through five ages: first infancy, then boyhood, then youth, then maturity, and then old age. Moses delivered the law to the people in five books. Each table which he received from God contained five commandments. The veil covering the holy of holies had five pillars. The altar of burnt-offering was also five cubits in breadth. Five priests were chosen in the wilderness—namely, Aaron, Nadab, Abiud, Eleazar, and Ithamar. The ephod and the breastplate, and other priestly vestments, were formed out of five materials, for they combined in themselves gold, blue, purple, scarlet, and fine linen.

And there were five kings of the Amorites, whom Joshua the son of Nun shut up in a cave, and directed the people to trample on their heads. Any one, in fact, might collect many thousand other things of the same kind, both with respect to this number and any other he chose to fix upon, either from the Scriptures, or from the works of nature lying under his observation. But although such is the case, we do not therefore affirm that there are five Aeons above the Demiurge. Nor do we consecrate the Peptad, as if it were some divine thing; nor do we strive to establish things that are untenable, nor ravings (such as they indulge in), by means of that vain kind of labor. Nor do we perversely force a creation well adapted by God (for the ends intended to be served), to change itself into types of things which have no real existence. Nor do we seek to bring forward impious and abominable doctrines, the detection and overthrow of which are easy to all possessed of intelligence.

"The Five Thousand"

The Scholar Origen[72]

We have spoken these things because of the words, "Now those who had eaten were about five thousand men, besides women and children" (Matt. 14:21), which is an ambiguous expression. For either those who ate were five thousand men, and among those who ate there was no childor woman, or the men only were five thousand, and the children and the women not being considered. Some, then, as we have said by anticipation, have so understood the passage that neither children nor women were present, when the increase and multiplication of the five loaves and the two fishes took place.

But someone might say that, while many ate and according to their worthiness and capacity participated in the loaves of blessing, some worthy to be numbered, corresponding to the men of twenty years old who are numbered in the Book of Numbers, were Israelites, but others who were not worthy of such account and numbering were children and women. Moreover, interpret with me allegorically the children in accordance with the passage, "And I, brethren, could not speak to you as to spiritual people but as to carnal, as to babes in Christ" (1 Cor. 3:1), and the women in accordance with the saying, "that I may present you as a chaste virgin to Christ" (2 Cor. 11:2), and the men according to the saying, "But when I became a man, I put away childish things" (1 Cor. 13:11).

"Christ Was Testing Them"

St. John Chrysostom[73]

"Then Jesus lifted up His eyes, and seeing a great multitude..." (Jn. 6:5)

This shows that He did not sit idly at anytime with the disciples, but perhaps carefully conversing with them, and making them attend and turn towards Him, a thing which peculiarly marks His tender care, and the humility and condescension of His demeanor towards them. For they sat with Him, perhaps looking at one another; then having lifted up

[72] Origen, *Commentary on the Gospel according to St. Matthew*, Book 11, ANF v. 10, p. 763-764.

[73] St. John Chrysostom, *Commentary on Gospel of St. John*, NPNF, s. 1, v. 14, pp. 348-352.

His eyes, He beheld the multitudes coming to Him. Now the other Evangelists say, that the disciples came and asked and besought Him that He would not send them away fasting, while St. John says, that the question was put to Philip by Christ. Both occurrences seem to me to be truly reported, but not to have taken place at the same time, the former account being prior to the other, so that the two are entirely different.

Why then does He ask Philip? He knew which of His disciples needed most instruction. For Philip is the who later said, "Show us the Father, and it is sufficient for us" (Jn. 14:8), and on this account Jesus was beforehand bringing him into a proper state. For if the miracle was simply performed, the wonder would not have been so great, but now He beforehand constrains him to confess the existing want, that knowing the state of matters he might be the more exactly acquainted with the magnitude of the miracle about to take place.

Therefore He asks, "Where shall we buy bread, that these may eat?" (Jn. 6:5) As He spoke to Moses in the Old Testament, for He did not work the sign until He had asked him, "What is in your hand?" (Exod. 4:2) Because things coming to pass unexpectedly and all at once, tend to throw us into forgetfulness of things previous, therefore He first involved him in a confession of present circumstances, that when the astonishment should come on him, he might be unable afterwards to drive away the remembrance of what he had confessed, and thus might learn by comparison the greatness of the miracle, which in fact takes place in this instance. And Philip being asked, replied,

"But this He said to test him, for He Himself knew what He would do. Philip answered Him, 'Two hundred denarii worth of bread is not sufficient for them, that every one of them may have a little.'" (Jn.6:6, 7)

What does it mean to "test him"? Did He not know what would be said by him? We cannot assert that. What then is the meaning of the expression? We may discover it from the Old Testament. For there too it is said, "And it came to pass after these things that God tested Abraham, and said to him, 'Take now your beloved son, Issac, whom you love'" (Gen. 22:1-2). Yet it does not appear in that place either, that when He said this He waited to see the end of the trial, whether Abraham would obey or not. How could He, Who knows all things before they come into existence? But the words in both cases are spoken from a human understanding. For as when the Psalmist says that He "searches the hearts of men" (cf. Ps. 7:10), he does not mean a search of ignorance but of exact knowledge. Similarly, when the Evangelist says that He "tested" Philip, he means only that He understood him completely.

One might also say that by bringing him by this question to an exact knowledge of the miracle He was adding to Philip's merit, as He once made Abraham more approved. The Evangelist therefore, that you may not stop at the feebleness of the expression, and so form an improper opinion of what was said, adds, "For He Himself knew what He would do."

Moreover we must observe this, that when there is any wrong suspicion, the writer immediately corrects it very carefully. As then in this place that the hearers might not form any such suspicion, he adds the corrective, saying, "For He Himself knew what He would do." So also in another place, when He says, that "the Jews sought all the more to kill Him, because He not only broken the Sabbath, but also said that God was His Father, making Himself equal with God" (Jn. 5:18), if there was not the assertion of Christ Himself confirmed by His works, he would there also have added this correction. For if even in the words which Christ speaks the Evangelist is careful that none should have suspicions, much more in the cases when others were speaking of Him would he have looked closely, had he perceived that an improper opinion prevailed concerning Him. But he did not make any corrections or additions, for he knew that this was His meaning, and an immovable decree. Therefore after saying, "making Himself equal with God," he did not use any such correction. For the matter spoken of was not an erroneous fancy of theirs, but His own assertion ratified by His works.

"Andrew, Simon's brother, said, 'There is a lad here, who has five barley loaves and two small fishes, but what are they among so many?'" (Jn. 6:8, 9)

Andrew is higher minded than Philip, yet had not he attained to everything. Yet I do not think that he spoke without a reason, but as having heard of the miracles of the Prophets, and how Elisha worked a sign with the loaves (cf. 2 Kgs. 4:43), on this account he mounted to a certain height, but could not attain to the very top. Let us learn then, we who give ourselves to luxury, what was the fare of those great and admirable men; and in quality and quantity let us behold and imitate the thriftiness of their table.

What follows also expresses great weakness. For after saying, "who has five barley loaves," he adds, "but what are they among so many?" He supposed that the Worker of the miracle would make less out of less, and more out of more. But this was not the case, for it was alike easy to Him to cause bread to spring out from more and from less, since He needed no subject-matter. But in order that the creation might not seem foreign to His Wisdom, as afterwards slanderers and those affected with the disease of Marcion said, He used the creation itself as a groundwork for His marvels.

When both the disciples had lost hope, then He worked the miracle. They profited the more from the miracle by having first confessed the difficulty of the matter, that when it should come to pass, they might understand the power of God. And because a miracle was about to be worked, which had also been performed by the Prophets, although not in an equal degree, and because He would do it after first giving thanks, lest they should fall into any suspicion of weakness on His part, observe how by the very manner of His working He entirely raises their thoughts of it and shows them the difference between Himself and others. For when the loaves had not yet appeared, that you may learn, that things that are not existent are to Him as though they were—as Paul says, "who calls those things which do not exist as though they did." (Rom. 4:17) He commanded the multitude as though the table were prepared and ready, immediately to sit down, rousing by this the minds of His disciples. And because they had profited by the questioning, they immediately obeyed, and were not confounded, nor said, "How is this, why do You ask us sit down when there is nothing before us?" The same people, who at first disbelieved so much as to say, "From where shall we buy bread?" began so far as to believe even before they saw the miracle, that they readily made the multitudes to sit down.

But why when He was about to restore the paralytic did He not pray, nor when He was raising the dead, or bridling the sea, while He does so here over the loaves? It was to show that when we begin our meals, we should give thanks to God. Moreover, He does it especially in a lesser matter, that you may learn that He does it not as having any need; for were this the case, much more would He have done so in greater things. But when He did them by His own authority, it is clear that it was through condescension that He acted as He did in the case of the lesser. Besides, a great multitude was present, and it was necessary that they should be persuaded that He had come according to the will of God. Therefore, when He does miracles in the absence of witnesses, He exhibits nothing of the kind, but when He does them in the presence of many, to persuade them that He is no enemy of God, no adversary of Him Who has begotten Him, He removes the suspicion by thanksgiving.

"And He gave to them that were set down, and they were filled." (cf. Jn. 6:11)

Do you see how great is the difference between the servants and the Master? They having grace by measure, worked their miracles accordingly, but God, who acts with free power, did all most abundantly.

"And He said to His disciples, 'Gather up the fragments that remain, so that nothing is lost. Therefore they gathered them up, and filled twelve baskets." (Jn. 6:12)

This was not a superfluous show, but in order that the matter might not be deemed a mere illusion, and for this reason He creates from matter already subsisting. "But why did He not give the bread to the multitudes to carry off, but only to His disciples?" Because He was most desirous to instruct these who would teach of the world. The multitude would not as yet reap any great fruit from the miracles, (at least they immediately forgot this one and asked for another,) while these would gain no common profit. And what took place was moreover no ordinary condemnation of Judas, who bore a basket. And that these things were done for their instruction is plain from what is said afterwards, when He reminded them, saying, "Do you not yet understand, or remember the five loaves of the five thousand and how many baskets you took up?" (Matt. 16:9) And for the same reason it was that the baskets of fragments were equal in number to the disciples; afterwards, when they were instructed, they took not up so many, but only seven baskets (cf. Matt. 15:37).

And I marvel not only at the quantity of loaves created, but besides the quantity, at the exactness of the surplus, that He caused the superabundance to be neither more nor less than just so much as He willed, foreseeing how much they would consume—a thing which demonstrated unspeakable power. The fragments then confirmed the matter, showing both these points: that what had taken place was no illusion, and that these were from the loaves by which the people had been fed. As to the fishes, they at this time were produced from those already subsisting, but at a later period, after the Resurrection, they were not made from subsisting matter. "Why?" That you may understand that even now He employed matter, not from necessity, nor as needing any base to work on, but to stop the mouths of heretics.

"Then those men...said, 'This is truly the Prophet who is to come into the world.'" (Jn. 6:14)

O, excess of gluttony! He had done ten thousand things more admirable than this, but nowhere did they make this confession, except when they had been filled. Yet here it is evident that they expected some remarkable prophet; for those others had said to John, "Are you the Prophet?" while these say, "This is the Prophet."

Third Sunday

THE BREAD OF LIFE

Meditations on the Third Sunday of the Blessed Month of Amshir

GOSPEL READING OF THE THIRD SUNDAY

JOHN 6:27-46

Now great multitudes went with Him. And He turned and said to them, "If anyone comes to Me and does not hate his father and mother, wife and children, brothers and sisters, yes, and his own life also, he cannot be My disciple.

"And whoever does not bear his cross and come after Me cannot be My disciple. For which of you, intending to build a tower, does not sit down first and count the cost, whether he has enough to finish it—lest, after he has laid the foundation, and is not able to finish, all who see it begin to mock him, saying, 'This man began to build and was not able to finish.'

"Or what king, going to make war against another king, does not sit down first and consider whether he is able with ten thousand to meet him who comes against him with twenty thousand? Or else, while the other is still a great way off, he sends a delegation and asks conditions of peace.

"So likewise, whoever of you does not forsake all that he has cannot be My disciple. Salt is good; but if the salt has lost its flavor, how shall it be seasoned? It is neither fit for the land nor for the dunghill, but men throw it out.

"He who has ears to hear, let him hear!"

"Let Us eat of that Eternal Food"

St. Cyril of Alexandria[74]

"Do not labor for the food which perishes, but for the food which endures to everlasting life" (Jn. 6:27).

Let us then, as the Savior says, "not labor not for the food which perishes." For when (the food) passes into the belly and for a very little while deludes the mind with the pettiest pleasure, it goes out into the draught and is carried out again from the belly. But the spiritual food which strengthens the heart, satisfies man unto everlasting life, which Christ also promises to give us, saying, "which the Son of Man will give you." (Jn. 6:25) Immediately, He unites the Human with the Divine and connects the whole mystery of the Economy with Flesh in its order. But He hints, I suppose, at the Mystic and more Spiritual Food, by which we live in Him, sanctified in body and soul. But we shall see Him speaking more openly of this after this. This discourse then must be kept for its proper time and place.

"Therefore they said to Him, "What sign will You perform then, that we may see it and believe You? What work will You do? Our fathers ate the manna in the desert; as it is written, 'He gave them bread from heaven to eat.'" (Jn. 6:30, 31)

He was not ignorant, as God, of the charges that would result from Jewish foolishness, nor of the reasons why they were often foolishly enraged. He knew that they would reason in themselves, looking to the flesh alone, and not conceiving of God the Logos therein, Who is This Who seizes upon God-befitting words? For who can give to people food that keeps them to everlasting life? For this is completely foreign to human nature, and it belongs to Him alone Who is fully God.

Therefore, the Savior defends Himself beforehand with suitable arguments, and rebukes their shameless talk. For He says that the Son of Man will give them the Food which nourishes them to everlasting life, and immediately affirmed that He is sealed by the Father. Sealed again is either put for anointed (for he who is anointed is sealed), or as showing that He has been by Nature formed unto the Father. Just as if He had said, "I am not unable to give you food, which endures and brings up unto everlasting

[74] St. Cyril of Alexandria, *Commentary of John*, Book 3, Ch. 5, §25

life and delight. For though I seem as one of you, that is Man with flesh, yet I was anointed and sealed by God the Father unto an exact Likeness with Him. For you shall see (He says) that He is in Me, and I again in Him Naturally, even though for your sakes I was born Man of a woman, according to the ineffable order of the Economy. For I can do all things in God-befitting authority and do not in any way come short of the Might inherent in My Father. And though God the Father gives you the Spiritual Food, which lasts to everlasting life, it is clear that the Son too will give It, even though made in Flesh, since He is His exact Image; the Likeness in everything being conceived, not after the characteristics of flesh, nor yet conceived of in bodily form, but in God-befitting glory and equal power and royal authority."

But we must observe again, that when He says that Son of Man will give the things God-befitting and that He has been sealed to the Image of God the Father, He does not allow the division of him that separates the Temple of the Virgin from the true Sonship, but defines Himself and wills to be conceived of again as one. For Christ is one in truth over us, bearing as it were the royal purple His Own, I mean His Human Body, or His Temple—of Soul and Body; since Christ is also One of both.

Most excellent sir, realize how the one opposing Christ will twist the verse and claim a false truth saying, "Behold, this clearly proves that the Son is not of the Essence of the Father, but rather a copy of His Essence." The opposers of Christ also say suppose some such thing as we say: a seal or signet impressed on wax, for example, or any other matter fit to receive it, and engraving a likeness only of itself, is taken away again by him who pressed it on, having lost no part of itself. So also the Father, having imposed and imprinted Himself completely on the Son in some way by a most accurate Likeness, from Himself He has surely no part of His Essence, nor is conceived of as from It but a mere image and accurate likeness.

Realize that our opponent is darting on us like a serpent, and raises his head full of venom, but He Who shatters the head of the Dragon, will also shatter it, and will give us power to escape his manifold stubbornness. Then let him tell us, who was just shouting at us with dreadful words, "Does not the seal or signet, which is made of wood, iron or gold, certainly seal with some impress those things on which it comes, and will it not be and be conceived of as a seal apart from the impress?"

"THE MANNA IS CHRIST"

St. Cyril of Alexandria[75]

"Then they said to Him, 'What shall we do, that we may work the works of God?'" (Jn. 6:28)

This inquiry was not out of good intentions. Although it seems that this question proceeds from their desire of knowledge, but it is rather the result of exceeding arrogance. For as if they would humble themselves to learn anything beyond what they knew already, they almost say something like this: "Good sir, the writings of Moses are enough for us. We know as much as we need to about the things which he who is skillful in the works of God should aim at. So then, what new thing will you supply in addition to those things which were given at that time? What strange thing you will teach, which was not shown to us before by the Divine words?"

Thus, the inquiry is rather of foolishness, than really of a studious will. Something like this also appears in the gospel of the blessed Matthew. For a certain young man, overflowing with not the most easily obtained abundance of wealth, was hinting that he would enter on the due service of God. When he came to Jesus, he eagerly inquired what he should do that he might inherit eternal life. To whom the Lord says, "You know the commandments, 'You shall not murder,' 'You shall not commit adultery,' 'You shall not steal,' 'You shall not bear false witness,' 'Honor your father and your mother,' and, 'You shall love your neighbor as yourself'" (Matt. 19:18, 19; Mk. 10:19; Lk. 18:20).

But he, as lacking none of these things, or even not accepting an exposition of teaching which fell far short of his existing practice, says, "All these things have I kept from my youth up. What do I still lack?" (Matt. 19:20) So, he mixed mixing pride and ignorance in his question, "What do I still lack?" These (Israelites) do the same through their great arrogance alike and self-conceit, saying, "What shall we do, that we might work the works of God?"

Therefore, modesty is a good work. It is the work of a noble soul to commit to her teachers the thorough knowledge of what is profitable, and

[75] St. Cyril of Alexandria, *Commentary of John*, Book 3, Ch. 6, §26.

to yield to their lessons, which they think it proper to instill, seeing they are superior in knowledge. For how shall they be accepted at all as teachers, if they do not have the superiority of understanding above what the mind of their pupils have, since their advance will scarcely end at the measure of their masters' knowledge, according to the word of the Savior, "The disciple is not above his teacher, nor a servant above his master. It is enough for the disciple that he be as his teacher, and a servant like his master" (Matt. 10:24, 25)

"Jesus answered and said to them, 'This is the work of God, that you believe in Him Whom He sent.'" (Jn. 6:29).

Most severely does the Lord, even though secretly and obscurely, attack the foolishness of the questioners. For one would suppose, looking merely at the simple meaning of the words, that Jesus was commanding them nothing else except to believe on Him.

But on examining the intent of the words, one will see that they refer to something else. For on purpose does He arrange His discourse suitably to the foolishness of the questioners. For they, as though they sufficiently learned through the Law how to work what was well-pleasing to God, blasphemously neglect the teaching of our Savior, saying, "What shall we do, that we might work the works of God?" But it was necessary that He should show them, that they were still very far removed from the worship most pleasing to God, and that they knew not at all of the true good things, who cleaving to the letter of the law, have their mind full of mere types and forms.

Therefore, He says with great emphasis, opposing the fruit of faith to the worship of the Law, "This is the work of God that you believe on Him whom He sent." That is, "It is not what you supposed," He says, "looking to the types alone. But you know, even though you will not learn it, that the Lawgiver takes no pleasure in your sacrifices of oxen, nor do you need to sacrifice sheep, as though God willed and required this. For what is frankincense, though it curl the air in fragrant steam, what will the male goat profit, and the costly offerings of cinnamon? God does not eats the flesh of bulls, nor drinks the blood of goats. He knows all the birds of heaven, and the wild beasts of the field are with Him. But He has hated and despised your feasts. He will not smell in your solemn assemblies, as Himself says (cf. Isa. 1:14), nor will He speak to your fathers concerning whole burnt offerings or sacrifices. Therefore this is not the work of God, but rather that you should believe on Him whom He sent. For truly much better than the legal and typical worship is the salvation through faith and the grace that justifies than the commandment that condemns.

The work then of the pious soul is faith to Christ, and far more excellent is the zeal to become wise in the knowledge of Him than the cleaving to the typical shadows. Besides this you will also marvel at how while Christ was accustomed to take no notice of those who questioned Him, tempting Him, He answered this question for the present economically (even though He knew that they would not receive any profit from it) to their own condemnation, as He says elsewhere also, "If I had not come and spoken to them, they would have no sin; but now they have no excuse for their sin" (Jn. 15:22).

"Therefore they said to Him, 'What sign will you perform then, that we may see it and believe You? What work you will do? Our fathers ate the manna in the desert; as it is written, "He gave them bread from heaven to eat."' (Jn. 6:30, 31)

The character of the Jews reveals itself by little and little, although hidden and buried in obscure reasoning. For they were saying in their foolishness, "What shall we do that we might work the works of God?" As if, as we said before, they held the commandment through Moses sufficient to conduct them to all wisdom, by which they might know how to perform what was well-pleasing to God.

But their aim being such was concealed, but is now being revealed, and little by little it comes out more plainly. "For nothing is secret," as the Savior says, "that will not be revealed." (Lk. 8:17) Thus, they say, "So then, what sign will You show us? The blessed Moses was honored (he says) and with great reason, he was set out as a mediator between God and man. Yes, and he also gave a sufficient sign, for all those who were with him ate the manna in the wilderness. But do You at length, since You come to us in a position greater than his, and do not shrink from adding to the things decreed of old, with what signs you will give us a warrant, or what of wondrous works do You showing us, introduce Yourself as the author of more novel doctrines to us?"

By this also, our Savior's word proves to be true. For they are convicted by their own words of thinking that they should seek Him, not to admire Him for those things which He had in God-befitting manner done, but because they ate of the loaves and were filled (cf. Jn. 6:26). For they demand a sign of Him, not any random one, but one like (they thought) Moses did. For he fed the people who came out of Egypt in the wilderness, not for one day, but for forty whole years, with the supply of manna. For, knowing nothing at all (it seems) of the Mysteries in the Divine Scriptures, they did not consider that it was fit to attribute the marvelous working of this to the Divine power which worked it, but very foolishly crown the head of Moses for this.

Therefore, they ask of Christ a sign equal to that, giving no wonder at all to the sign which had been shown to them for a day, even though it were great, but saying that the gift of food should be extended to them for a long time, so that even so hardly would He shame them into confessing and agreeing that most glorious was the Power of the Savior, and His Doctrine therefore to be received. Manifest then is it even though they do not say it in plain terms, that they wholly disregard signs, and under pretext of marveling at them, are zealous to serve the impure pleasure of the belly.

"Then Jesus said to them, 'Most assuredly, I say to you, Moses did not give you the bread from heaven.'" (Jn. 6:32)

Now the Savior severely convicts them of being without understanding and exceedingly ignorant of what is in the Mosaic writings. For they should have known quite clearly that Moses was providing the things of God to the people, and again those of the children of Israel to God, and was himself the worker in none of the miracles, but a minister rather than a bestower of those things which the Giver of all good things willed to do for them for the benefit of those who had been called out of bondage.

Thus, Christ removes away that which they were sinfully imagining. For they foolishly and sinfully attributed the things which befit and are due to the Divine Nature alone, to the honor of men. Thus, He deprived the hierophant Moses of the miracle, and withdrew it out of his hand, and instead attributes the glory of it to Himself, together with the Father, even though He abstained from speaking more openly because of the ignorance of His listeners. For it is expected that they would rage and be kindled to extreme anger, as if Moses were insulted by such words—never inquiring what the truth was, nor recognizing the dignity of the Speaker, but heedlessly honoring only Moses, and not reasonably as it happened, when he was compared with what excelled him.

Let us learn then, with more judgment and reason, to practice respect towards our holy fathers, and to render, as it is written, fear to whom fear, honor to whom honor (cf. Rom. 13:7). For we shall in no way injure, if we render what fittingly belongs to each, since the spirits of the Prophets are subject to the Prophets, but when any discourse about our Savior Christ is entered into, then we must say, "Who in the clouds can be equaled to the Lord? Or who among the sons of the mighty shall be likened to the Lord?"

"But My Father gives you the true bread from heaven. For the bread of God is He Who comes down from heaven and gives life to the world." (Jn. 6:32, 33)

He needed to remove Moses from God-befitting authority (according to their conception) to show that Moses was a minister of that miraculous working, rather than the bestower of it; and to lessen the wonder though miraculously done, showing that it was nothing at all in comparison with the greater. For imagine Christ telling them something like this: "You are comparing, sirs, the great things, with the little and insignificant, and the beneficence of the Lord of all you have dispensed with most petty limits. For you greatly err to assume that the manna is the Bread from heaven, for it only fed the race of the Jews in the wilderness, while there are numerous other nations throughout the world. And you assumed that God desired to show such limited loving-kindness as to give food to one people only (for these were types of universalities, and in the pier partial was an illustration of His general Kindness, as it were in pledge, to those who first received it). But when the time of the Truth was at our doors, My Father gives you the Bread from heaven, which the gift of manna was only a shadow of from ancient times. Do not think that this was the true Bread which came from heaven, but rather let him give his judgment in favor of That which is clearly able to feed the whole earth, and to give in full life to the world."

Therefore, He accuses the Jew of cleaving to the typical observances and refusing to examine into the beauty of the Truth. For that was not the manna, properly speaking, but the Only Begotten Word of God Himself, who from the Essence of the Father, since He is by Nature Life, and gives life to all things. For since He sprang of the Living Father, He also is by Nature Life, and since the work of that which is by Nature Life is to give life, Christ gives life to all things. For as our earthly bread which is made of the earth does not let the frail nature of flesh to waste away, so too He, through the operation of the Spirit, gives life to our spirit, and also holds together our very body unto incorruption.

But since our meditations have got on the subject of manna, it will not be amiss (I think) for us to consider and say a little on it also, taking out of the Mosaic books themselves several the things written in them. For thus having made the statement of the matter most clear, we shall rightly discern each of the things which are signified by them. But we will show through them all, that the very Manna is Christ Himself, understood as given under the type of manna to them of old by God the Father.

The beginning of the oracles about the manna speaks in this manner: "On the fifteenth day of the second month after they departed from the land of Egypt. Then the whole congregation of the children of Israel complained against Moses and Aaron in the wilderness. The children of Israel said to them, 'Oh, that we had died, smitten by the LORD in the land of Egypt, when we sat by the pots of meat and when we ate bread to the full! For you brought us out into this wilderness to kill this whole assembly with hunger.'" (Exod. 16:1-3)

This matter of history is clear and very plain, and I do not think it needs any words to test the obvious meaning. But we will speak of it, looking only to the spiritual meaning. So, the children of Israel, while still in the country of the Egyptians, by Divine command were keeping typically their feast to Christ, and having taken their supper of the lamb, did the children of Israel hardly escape the tyranny of Pharaoh's rule and shake off the intolerable yoke of bondage. After having miraculously crossed the Red Sea, they went into the wilderness. Starving there, they craved flesh to eat and were dragged down to the habitual desire for food. So they began murmuring against Moses and fell into repenting of their free gift from God when they should have given no small thanks for it.

Thus, Egypt will be darkness and will signify the condition of the present life and the worldly state, in which we are enrolled as in some state. There, (the Jews) served in bitter slavery—not working for God at all, but doing works that greatly pleased the Devil. They submitted to the pleasures of the impure flesh, like clay or stinking mud, and endured miserable toil, without pay or profit, and pursued a shameful (so to say) love of pleasure.

But when the Law of God speaks to our soul and we fully realize the bitter bondage of these things, then we, thirsting to free ourselves from all evil, come to Christ Himself, as to the beginning and door of freedom. Supplied with the security and grace that come through His Precious Blood, we leave the carnal condition of this life—as it were a turbulent and stormy sea—and out of all the tumult of the world, we at length reach a more spiritual and purer state, as it were sojourning in the wilderness.

But since the one following the Law is not untrained to virtue, but through the Law is trained in it, when we find that we are at length in this case, then we falling into the temptations which try us, are sometimes devoured by the memory of carnal lusts, and then, when the lust inflames us mightily, we often times cry out of recklessness. And although the Divine Law has called us to liberty, hungering for our old habitual pleasures and making slight account of our toils after restraint, we look on the bondage of the world as no longer evil. Truly, the will of the flesh is sufficient to draw the mind to all faintheartedness after goodness.

"And the Lord said to Moses, 'Behold I will rain bread out of heaven for you'" (Exod. 16:4).

"In these words you may very clearly see that which is sung in the Psalms, "He rained manna for them to eat, and gave them the bread of heaven. Man ate the bread of angels; He sent them food in abundance" (Ps. 77:24, 25).

I suppose that it is evident to all that of the reasonable Powers in heaven, none other is the Bread and Food, except the Only Begotten of God the Father. He, then, is the true Manna, the Bread from heaven, given to the whole rational creation by God the Father.

But entering into the order of our subject we say this: Observe how the Divine grace from above draws to itself the nature of man even though at times sick after its accustomed things, and saves it in diverse ways. For the lust of the flesh like a stone that falls on the mind, thrusts it down, and forces it to its own will like a dictator. But Christ brings us round again as with a harness to make us long for better things, and recovers them that are diseased to God-loving habits of mind. Behold, He promises to those who are sinking down into carnal pleasures to give Food from Heaven, the consolation, that is, through the Spirit, the Spiritual Manna. Through this, we are strengthened to all endurance and manliness and obtain that we fall not through infirmity into those things we should not. Therefore, the Spiritual Manna, that is, Christ, was previously also strengthening us to holiness.

But since we have once, by reason of need, digressed, I think it well not to leave the subject uninvestigated, since it is very conducive to our profit. Someone then may reasonably ask, "Why is God who is so Loving to man and so loves when it behoved Him to come before their request, is tardy in respect of His Promise. And why did He in no way punish those men who were so perverse, although He punished them afterwards, when they were sick with the same lusting, and pictured to themselves bread to the fullest, and fleshpots, and admitted longing for the most abundant vegetation (cf. Num. 11:5)? For we shall find in Numbers, that both were punished, and the place, in which they were then encamping, was called the graves of lust, for there they buried the people that lusted (cf. Num. 11:34). With respect then to the first question, we say that it assuredly behoved Him to wait for the desire, and so at length to reveal Himself in due season the Giver. For most welcome is the gift to those in good case, when certain pleasures appear before it and precede it, inciting to thirst after what is not yet come. But the soul of man will be devoid of a more grateful sensation, if it does not first stretch after and labor for the pleasures of being well off. But perhaps you will say that there had been no way of entreaty from them, but murmuring rather than repentance and outcry, for this would indeed be speaking more truly. To this we say, that entreaty through prayer will befit those who are of a perfect habit. And perhaps the murmuring of the more feeble from depression or whatever cause, will partake of the Savior of all, who being loving to man is not altogether angry at it. For as in those who are yet babes, crying will sometimes avail to the asking of their needs, and the mother is often called by it to find out what will please the child. So, too, those who were yet babes, and had not yet advanced to understanding, the cry of weariness so to say, has the force of petition before God. For this reason (as seems to me) He does not punish in the beginning, even though He see them defeated by earthly lusts, but only after a later time. They who were but newly come out of Egypt, not having yet received the manna, nor having the Bread from heaven, which strengthens man's heart, fall as might be expected into carnal lusts, and therefore are pardoned. But they who had already delighted in the Lord, as it is written, on preferring carnal delights to the spiritual good things, have to give most righteous satisfaction, and over and above their suffering have assigned them a notable memorial of their fate. For the graves of lust is the name of the place of their punishment.

"And the people shall go out and gather a certain quota every day." (Exod. 16:4)

We will consider the sensible manna a type of the spiritual manna; and the spiritual manna signifies Christ Himself, but the sensible manna represents the uncultivated teaching of the Law. With reason is the gathering daily, and the lawgiver forbids keeping it till the following day, darkly hinting to them of old, that when the time of salvation at length shines forth, in which the Only Begotten appeared in the world with Flesh, the legal types should be wholly abolished, and the gathering food from there in vain, while the Truth Itself lies before us for our pleasure and enjoyment.

"So it shall be on the sixth day, they shall prepare what they bring in, and it shall be twice as much as they gather daily." (Exod. 16:5)

Observe again, that you may understand, that He does not allow them to gather on the seventh day the sensible manna, but commands that which is already provided and gathered to be prepared for their food beforehand. For the seventh day signifies the time of the Advent of our Savior, in which we rest in holiness, ceasing from the works of sin, and receiving for food, both the fulfillment of our faith, and the knowledge already arranged in us through the Law, no longer gathering as of necessity, since more excellent food is now before us, and we have the Bread from heaven. The manna is collected in double measure before the holy sabbath; and you will understand from this, that the Law being concluded in respect of its temporal close, and the holy sabbath, that is, Christ's coming, already beginning, the getting of the heavenly goods will be after some sort in double measure, and the grace twofold, bringing in addition to the advantages from the Law, the Gospel instruction also. The Lord Himself, too, may be conceived to teach this when He says, as in the form of a parable, "Therefore every scribe instructed concerning the kingdom of heaven is like a householder who brings out of his treasure things new and old" (Matt. 13:52); the old are the things of the Law, the new are those through Christ.

"Then Moses and Aaron said to all the congregations of the children of Israel, At evening you shall know that the Lord has brought you out of the land of Egypt. In the morning you shall see the Lord's glory... The Lord's glory shall be seen when He gives you meat to eat in the evening, and in the morning bread to the full."" (Exod. 16:6-8)

Moses promises to the Israelites that quails shall be given to them by God in the evening, and declares that by this they shall know surely that the Lord brought them up out of Egypt.

"And in the morning you shall see the Lord's glory," he says, "the Lord's glory shall be seen when He shall give you bread to the full." I ask you to consider the difference between each of these. For the quail signifies the Law (for this bird always flies low and about the earth). Thus will you see those also who are instructed through the Law to a more earthly holiness through types—I mean such as relate to sacrifice and purifications and Jewish washing.

For these birds are lifted a little above the earth, and seem to rise above it, but are nevertheless in it and about it. For not in the Law is that which is perfectly good and lofty to understanding. Moreover, it is given in the evening; the evening signifies the obscurity of the letter, or the darksome condition of the world, when it did not yet have the Very Light, that is, Christ, who when He was Incarnate said, "I have come as a Light into the world." (Jn. 12:46). But He says the children of Israel shall know that the Lord brought them out of Egypt. For knowledge only of the salvation generally through Christ is seen in the Mosaic book, while grace was not yet present in every person. This very thing He hinted at, when He added, "In the morning you shall see the glory of the Lord, in that He gives you bread to the full." For when the mist of the Law, as it were night, has been dispersed, and the spiritual Sun has risen upon us all, behold as in a glass the glory of the Lord now present, receiving the Bread from heaven to the full, I mean Christ Himself.

"So it was that quails came up at evening and covered the camp, and in the morning the dew lay all around the camp. But when the layer of dew lifted, there, on the surface of the wilderness, was a small round substance, white like coriander seed, like frost on the ground." (Exod. 16:13-14)

Look at the arrangement of the things to be considered. He says about the quails that they covered the camp; about the manna that in the morning when the dew was lifted, it lay on the surface of the wilderness all around the camp. For the instruction through the Law, I mean that in types and figures, which we have compared to the appearance of quails, covers the synagogue of the Jews. For, as Paul says, "the veil lies on their heart" (2 Cor. 3:15), and hardness in part. But when it was morning, that is, when Christ had now risen, and shined on all the world, and when the dew was gone up, that is, the uncultivated and mist-like introduction of legal ordinances (for Christ is the end of the Law and the Prophets); then surely the true and heavenly manna will come down to us, I mean the Gospel teaching, not on the congregation of the Israelites, but all around the camp, that is, to all the nations, and on the surface of the wilderness, that is the Church of the Gentiles, of which it is said that more are the children of the desolate than of the married wife (cf. Isa. 54:1). For over the whole world is dispersed with the grace of the spiritual manna, which is also compared to the coriander seed, and is called small. For the power of the Divine Word being of a truth subtle, and cooling the beat of the passions, lulls the fire of carnal motions within us, and enters into the deep of the heart. For they say that the effect of this herb, I mean the coriander, is most cooling.

"So when the children of Israel saw it, they said one to another, 'What is this?'" (Exod. 16:15)

They did not know what it was because they were not used to miraculous works and were not able to say from experience what it was. So they asked one to another, "What is this?" But this very thing which is questioned, they make the name of the thing, and call it in the Syrian tongue, Manna, that is, "What is this?" And you will then see how Christ would be unknown among the Jews. For that which prevailed in the type, proved that it had also force in the truth.

Moses then said, 'Let no one leave any of it till morning.' Notwithstanding, they did not heed Moses. But some of them left part of it until morning, and it bred worms and stank. So Moses was angry with them." (Exod. 16:19, 20) The morning, here, signifies the bright and most glorious time of the coming of our Savior, when the shadow of the Law and the mist of the Devil among the nations, being in some sort undone, the Only-Begotten rose upon us like light, and spiritual dawn appeared.

The blessed Moses, then, commanded that they do not leave the typical manna until morning; for when the aforementioned time has risen upon us, the shadows of the Law are unnecessary and completely out of place because of the present truth. Paul showed that the righteousness of the Law is truly useless when Christ has shined forth, saying that for His sake Him (he has) "suffered the loss of all things," and that glorying in the Law "I count them as rubbish, that I may gain Christ and be found in Him, not having my own righteousness which is from the Law, but that which is through the faith in Christ." (Phil. 3:8, 9)

See then, how as a wise man he took care not to leave of it till the morning? Those who kept it until the morning are a type of the Jewish multitude which should not believe, whose eager desire to keep the law in the letter, would become corrupted with worms. Do you hear how the Lawgiver is greatly exasperated against them?

"Moses then said to Aaron, "Take a golden pot and put one full omer of manna in it, and lay it up before God to be kept for your generations" (Exod. 16:33).

We may truly marvel at this and say, "Oh, the depth of the riches both of the wisdom and knowledge of God!" (Rom. 11:33) For truly incomprehensible is the wisdom hidden in the God-inspired Scriptures, and deep their depth, as it is written, who can find it out? Do you see then how our last comment fitted these things? For since Christ Himself was shown to be our Very Manna, declared in type by way of image to them of old, needs does he teach in this place, of Whom and of what virtue and glory will he be full, who treasures up in himself the spiritual Manna, and brings Jesus into the inmost recesses of his heart, through right faith in Him and perfect love.

For you hear how the omer full of manna was put in a golden pot, and by the hand of Aaron laid up before the Lord to be kept. For the holy and truly pious soul, which strives for the Word of God perfectly in herself, and receives entire the heavenly treasure will be a precious vessel, like as of gold, and will be offered by the High Priest of all to God the Father, and will be brought into the Presence of Him Who holds all things together and preserves them to be kept, not allowing that which is of its own nature perishable to perish.

Thus, the righteous man is described as having the spiritual Manna in a golden vessel, that is Christ, attaining to incorruption, as in the Sight of

God, and remaining to be kept, that is, to long-enduring and endless life. Therefore, Christ has reason to convict the Jews of no slight madness, in supposing that the manna was given by the all-wise Moses to them of old, and in focusing on this point in their discourse and considering nothing at all of the things that presignified the manna, He says, "Most assuredly, I say to you, Moses did not give you the manna." (Jn. 6:32) For they should have considered this and perceived that Moses had brought in the service of mediation merely; but that the gift was no invention of human hand, but the work of Divine Grace, outlining the spiritual in the coarser, and signifying to us the Bread from Heaven, Which gives Life to the whole world, and does not feed the one race of Israel as it were by preference.

"Then they said to Him, 'Lord, give us this bread always.'" (Jn. 6:34)

By this, the aim of the Jews is clearly revealed, although they greatly desired to hide it. We may see from this that it is not possible for the Truth to lie, Who said that they eagerly followed Him not because they "saw the miracles but because (they) ate of the loaves and were filled." (Jn. 6:26) Thus, they were justly condemned for their great dullness. I suppose one should truly say to them, "Behold, a foolish people and without heart, they have eyes and see not, they have ears and hear not." (cf. Jer. 5:21)

For while our Savior Christ by many words, as one may see, is drawing them away from carnal imaginations and by His all-wise teachings is lifting them to spiritual contemplation, they do not attain above the profit of the flesh. Hearing of the Bread which gives life to the world, they still picture the earth, having their belly as their god, as it is written (cf. Phil. 3:19), and overcome by the evils of the belly, that they may justly hear, "whose glory is in their shame." (Phil. 3:19)

You will find such language very similar to that of the Samaritan Woman. For when our Savior Christ spent a long time speaking with her, telling her about the spiritual waters, and saying clearly, "Whoever drinks of this water will thirst again, but whoever drinks of the water that I will give him shall never thirst, but the water that I shall give him shall be in him a well of water springing up into everlasting life" (Jn. 4:13-14), she understood this through the dullness that was in her. She let the spiritual fountain go and did not think about it at all, but sunk down to the gift of sensible wells and said, "Lord, give me this water, that I may not thirst nor come here to draw." (Jn. 4:15) Therefore her language is similar to the

Jews. For as she was weakly by nature, in the same way (I think) these too had nothing masculine or manly in their understanding, but were effeminate to the unmanly lusts of the belly, and prove what is truly written about them, "For the foolish man will utter folly, and his heart will imagine vain things."

The remainder of this sermon is included in part five of this series, the Holy Fifty Days, Chapter 5.

"Christ: The True Vine and The Bread of Life"

The Scholar Origen[76]

To what we have said must be added how the Son is the true vine. Those will have no difficulty in apprehending this who understand, in a manner worthy of the prophetic grace, the saying: "Wine makes glad the heart of man." (Ps. 103:15) For if the heart is the intellectual part, and what rejoices it is the Word most pleasant of all to drink which takes us off human things, makes us feel ourselves inspired, and intoxicates us with an intoxication which is not irrational but divine. This, I believe, is the wine with which Joseph made his brethren merry. Thus, it is very clear how He Who brings wine thus to rejoice the heart of man is the true Vine.

He is the true Vine, because the grapes He bears are the truth, the disciples are His branches, and they also bring out the truth as their fruit. It is somewhat difficult to show the difference between the vine and bread, for He says, not only that He is the Vine, but that He is the Bread of life. It may be that as bread nourishes and makes strong, and is said to strengthen the heart of man, but wine, on the contrary, pleases and rejoices and melts him, so ethical studies, bringing life to him who learns them and reduces them to practice, are the bread of life, but cannot properly be called the fruit of the vine, while secret and mystical speculations, rejoicing the heart and causing those to feel inspired who take them in, delighting in the Lord, and who desire not only to be nourished but to be made happy, are called the juice of the true Vine, because they flow from it.

---

[76] Origen, *Epistle to Gregory*, ANF v. 10, pp. 532-533.

"I Desire Bread And Death"

St. Ignatius of Antioch[77]

The prince of this world wants to carry me away and corrupt my disposition towards God. Therefore, let none of you who are (in Rome) help him. Rather, be on my side, that is, on the side of God. Do not speak of Jesus Christ and yet set your desires on the world. Do not let envy find a dwelling-place among you; nor even should I, when present with you, exhort you to it, be persuaded to listen to me, but rather give credit to those things which I now write to you. For though I am alive while I write to you, yet I am eager to die. My love has been crucified, and there is no fire in me desiring to be fed; but there is within me a water that lives and speaks, saying to me inwardly, "Come to the Father." I have no delight in corruptible food or in the pleasures of this life. I desire the bread of God, the heavenly bread, the bread of life, which is the flesh of Jesus Christ, the Son of God, who became afterwards of the seed of David and Abraham; and I desire the drink of God, namely His Blood, which is incorruptible love and eternal life.

"Our Daily Bread"

St. Cyprian of Carthage[78]

The prayer, "Give us this day our daily bread," may be understood both spiritually and literally, because either way of understanding it is rich in divine usefulness to our salvation. For Christ is the bread of life; and this bread does not belong to all men, but it is ours. Just as we say, "Our Father" because He is the Father of those who understand and believe, we also call it "our bread," because Christ is the Bread of those who are in union with His body. And we ask that this bread should be given to us daily, that we who are in Christ, and daily receive the Eucharist for the food of salvation, may not, by the interference of some heinous sin, by being prevented, as withheld and not communicating, from partaking of the heavenly bread, be separated from Christ's Body, as He Himself predicts, and warns, "I am the living bread which came down from heaven.

---

[77] St. Ignatius, *Epistle to the Romans*, ANF v. 1, pp. 157-158.

[78] St. Cyprian, *Treatise VI: On the Lord's Prayer*, ANF v. 5, pp. 972-973.

If anyone eats of this bread, he will live forever; and the bread that I shall give is My flesh, which I shall give for the life of the world" (Jn. 6:51).

When, therefore, He says, that whoever shall eat of His bread shall live forever, it is manifest that those who partake of His body and receive the Eucharist by the right of communion are living. So, on the other hand, we must fear and pray lest anyone who, being withheld from communion, is separate from Christ's body should remain at a distance from salvation, as He Himself threatens, and says, "Unless you eat the flesh of the Son of Man and drink His blood, you have no life in you." (Jn. 6:53) And therefore we ask that our bread—that is, Christ—may be given to us daily, that we who abide and live in Christ may not depart from His sanctification and body.

"Our Daily Bread"

The Scholar Tertullian[79]

But how gracefully has the Divine Wisdom arranged the order of the prayer; so that after things heavenly—that is, after the "Name" of God, the "Will" of God, and the "Kingdom" of God—it should give earthly necessities also room for a petition! For the Lord had in addition issued His edict, "Seek first the kingdom and His righteousness, and all these things these shall be added to you" (Matt. 6:33); however, we may rather understand, "Give us this day our daily bread," spiritually. For Christ is our Bread, because Christ is Life, and bread is life. "I am," He said, "the Bread of Life" (Jn 6:35), and, a little above, "The Bread is the Word of the living God, who came down from the heavens." Then we find, too, that His body is reckoned in bread: "This is my body." And so, in petitioning for "daily bread," we ask for perpetuity in Christ, and indivisibility from His body. But, because that word is admissible in a carnal sense too, it cannot be so used without the religious remembrance in addition to spiritual Discipline. For (the Lord) commands that bread be prayed for, which is the only food necessary for believers, "for after all (other) things the Gentiles seek" (Matt. 6:33).

This lesson He both teaches by examples and repeatedly handles in parables, when He says, "Does a father take away bread from his children

[79] The Scholar Tertullian, *On Prayer*, Ch. 5, ANF v. 3, pp. 1280-1281

and give it to dogs?" (cf. Matt. 15:26), and again, "Does a father give his son a stone when he asks for bread?" (cf. Matt. 7:9). For He thus shows what it is that sons expect from their father. No, even that nocturnal knocker knocked for "bread." (cf. Lk. 11:6-8) Moreover, He justly added, "Give us this day," seeing He had previously said, "Do not worry about tomorrow, saying, 'What you shall we eat.'" (Matt. 6:31) To which subject He also adapted the parable of the man who pondered on an enlargement of his barns for his up coming fruits, and on seasons of prolonged security, but that very night he dies (cf. Lk. 16:1-8).

"WISDOM'S BANQUET"

The Scholar Origen[80]

Those who receive the interpretation of Scripture according to the understanding of the apostles, entertain the hope that the saints will eat. Yes, they will eat the Bread of life which nourishes the soul with the food of truth and wisdom, and enlightens the mind, causing it to drink from the cup of divine wisdom, according to the declaration of holy Scripture: "Wisdom has prepared her table, she has slaughtered her meat, she has mixed her wine in her cup, and she cries with a loud voice, 'Come to me, eat the bread which I have prepared for you, and drink the wine which I have mixed.'" (Prov. 9:1, 2, 5)

By this Food of wisdom, the understanding, being nourished to an entire and perfect condition like that in which man was made at the beginning, is restored to the image and likeness of God; so that, although an individual may depart from this life less perfectly instructed, but who has done works that are approved, he will be capable of receiving instruction in that Jerusalem, the city of the saints, that is, he will be educated and molded, and made a living stone, a stone elect and precious, because he has undergone with firmness and constancy the struggles of life and the trials of piety. And there he will come to a truer and clearer knowledge of that which here has been already predicted, that is, that "Man shall not live by bread alone, but by every word that proceeds from the mouth of God" (Deut. 8:3; Matt. 4:4).

[80] Origen, *On the First Principles*, ANF v. 4, p. 618

"Bread From Heaven"

St. Augustine[81]

There are three views as to what the daily bread signifies. First, the daily bread can refer to those things which meet the needs of this life—in reference to which He says in His teaching, "Do not worry about tomorrow." (Matt: 6:34) This is why it is added, "Give us this day." Second, the bread can refer to the sacrament of the body of Christ, which we daily receive. Third, it can mean the spiritual food, of which the same Lord says, "Do not labor for the food which perishes" (Jn. 6:27), and again, "I am the bread of life which came down from heaven." (Jn. 6: 41)

But which of these three views is the more probable? For perhaps someone may wonder why we should pray that we may obtain the things which are necessary for this life—such, for instance, as food and clothing—when the Lord Himself says, "Do not about what you will eat... or what you will put on." (Matt: 6:25) Can anyone not worry about something for which he prays that he may obtain, given that prayer is to be offered with such great zealousness of mind, that to this refers all that has been said about shutting our closets (cf. Matt: 6:6) and also the command, "Seek first the kingdom of God and His righteousness, and all these things shall be added to you"? Certainly He does not say, "Seek first the kingdom of God, and then seek those other things," but "all these things," he says, "shall be added to you," that is to say, even though you are not seeking them. But I do not know whether it can be found out, how one is rightly said not to seek what he most earnestly pleads with God that he may receive.

But with respect to the sacrament of the Lord's body in order that they may not start a question, who, the most of them being in Eastern parts, do not partake of the Lord's supper daily, while this bread is called daily bread, in order, therefore, that they may be silent, and not defend their way of thinking about this matter even by the very authority of the Church, because they do such things without scandal, and are not prevented from doing them by those who preside over their churches, and when they do not obey are not condemned. From this it is proved that this is not understood as daily Bread in these parts. For, if this were the case,

---

[81] St. Augustine, *Sermon on the Mount*, NPNF, s. 1, v. 6, pp. 93-94.

they would be charged with the commission of a great sin, who do not on that account receive It daily. But, as has been said, not to argue at all to any extent from the case of such parties, this consideration at least should occur to those who reflect, that we have received a rule for prayer from the Lord, which we should not to transgress, either by adding or omitting anything. And since this is the case, who is there who would venture to say that we should only once use the Lord's Prayer, or at least that, even if we have used it a second or a third time before the hour at which we partake of the Lord's body, that afterwards we are assuredly not to pray it during the remaining hours of the day? For we shall no longer be able to say, "Give us this day," concerning what we have already received; or else everyone will be able to compel us to celebrate that sacrament at the very last hour of the day.

It remains, therefore, that we should understand the daily bread as spiritual, that is to say, divine precepts, which we should daily meditate on and labor after. For with respect to these the Lord says, "Do not labor for the food which perishes." That food, moreover, is called daily food at present, so long as this temporal life is measured by means of days that depart and return. And, in truth, so long as the desire of the soul is directed by turns, now to what is higher, now to what is lower, that is to say, now to spiritual things, now to carnal, as is the case with him who at one time is nourished with food, at another time suffers hunger. Bread is daily necessary, in order that the hungry man may be sustained and he who is falling down may be raised up. As, therefore, our body in this life, that is to say, before that great change, is sustained with food, because it feels loss;, 1 so may the soul also be reinvigorated by the food of the precepts, since by means of temporal desires the soul sustains as it were a loss in its striving after God.

Moreover, it is said, "Give us this day," as long as it is called today, that is, in this temporal life. For we will be so abundantly provided with spiritual food after this life to eternity, that it will not then be called daily bread because there the flight of time, which causes days to succeed days, from where it may be called today, will not exist. But as it is said, "Today, if you will hear His voice" (Ps. 94:7), which the apostle interprets in the Epistle to the Hebrews, as long as it is called today (Heb. 4:6-8); so here also the expression is to be understood, "Give us this day." But if anyone wishes to understand the sentence before us as also about food necessary for the body or about the sacrament of the Lord's Body, we must take all three meanings conjointly; that is to say, that we are to ask for all at once as daily bread, both the bread necessary for the body, and the visible hallowed Bread, and the invisible bread of the Word of God.

"The Bread of Saints and Sinners"

St. Athanasius the Apostolic[82]

The righteous man, although he appears dying to the world, uses boldness of speech, saying, "I shall not die, but live, and tell of the Lord's works" (Ps. 117:17). For God is not ashamed to be called their God (cf. Heb. 11:16) by those who truly mortify their members which are on the earth (cf. Col. 3:5), but live in Christ; for He is the God of the living, not of the dead (cf. Matt. 22:32). And He by His living Word makes alive all men, and gives Himself to be Food and Life to the saints, as the Lord declares, "I am the bread of life" (Jn. 6:48). The Jews, because they were weak in perception, and had not exercised the senses of the soul in virtue, and did not comprehend this discourse about bread, murmured against Him, because He said, "I am the bread which came down from heaven and gives life to men." (Jn. 6:51)

For sin has her own special bread of death, and calling to those who are lovers of pleasure and lack understanding, she says, "Grasp with pleasure the secret bread and the sweet waters of theft." (Prov. 9:20) For he who merely touches them does not know that that which is born from the earth perishes with her. For even when the sinner thinks to find pleasure, the end of that food is not pleasant, as the Wisdom of God says again, "Bread of deceit is pleasant to a man; but afterwards his mouth shall be filled with gravel." (Prov. 20:17) And, "For honey drips from the lips of a prostitute, or for a season she is pleasing to your taste; afterward, however, you will find her more bitter than gall and sharper than a two-edged sword." (Prov. 5:3, 4) Thus then he eats and rejoices for a little time, afterwards he rejects it when he has removed his soul afar. For the fool does not know that those who depart far from God shall perish. Besides, there is the restraint of the prophetic admonition which says, "What concern of yours is the road to Egypt, to drinking the water of the Nile?

[82] St. Athanasius the Apostolic, *Festal Letter* 7, NPNF, s. 2, v. 4.

Why concern yourself about the road to Assyria, or drinking the waters of the rivers?" (Jer. 2:18)

And the Wisdom of God which loves mankind forbids these things, crying, "But hurry off, do not continue in the place, neither set your eye toward her; for so you shall pass through strange water and cross beyond a strange river." (Prov. 9:22, 23) She also calls them to herself, "For wisdom built her house, and she supported it with seven pillars. She offered her sacrifices; she mixed her wine in a bowl and prepared her table. She sent her servants, inviting people to the bowl with a lofty proclamation, and saying, 'He who is without discernment, let him turn aside to me'; and to those in need of discernment, she says, 'Come, eat my bread and drink the wine I mixed for you.'" (Prov. 9:1-5)

And what hope is there instead of these things? "Forsake lack of discernment, and you may shall live; seek discernment so you may live." (Prov. 9:6) For the bread of Wisdom is living fruit, as the Lord said: "I am the living bread which came down from heaven. If anyone eats of this bread, he will live forever." (Jn. 6:51) For when Israel ate of the manna, which was indeed pleasant and wonderful, yet they still died, and they who ate it did not in consequence live forever, but all that multitude died in the wilderness. The Lord teaches, saying, "I am the bread of life. Your fathers ate the manna in the wilderness, and are dead. This is the bread which comes down from heaven. If anyones eats of this breatd, he will live forever." (Jn. 6:48-51)

Now wicked men hunger for bread like this, for effeminate souls will hunger; but the righteous alone, being prepared, shall be satisfied, saying, "As for me, in righteousness I shall behold Your face; I shall be satisfied when Your glory is revealed." (Ps. 16:15) For he who partakes of divine bread always hungers with desire; and he who thus hungers has a never-failing gift, as Wisdom promises, saying, "The Lord will not let the soul of a righteous man starve." (Prov. 10:3) He promises also in the Psalms, "Blessing, I shall bless her provision; I shall satisfy her poor with bread." (Ps. 131:15) We may also hear our Savior saying, "Blessed are those who hunger and thirst after righteousness, for they shall be filled." (Matt. 5: 6)

Well then do the saints and those who love the life which is in Christ raise themselves to a longing after this Food. And one earnestly implores, saying, "As the deer pants for the springs of waters, so my soul longs for

You, O God! My soul thirsts for the living God; when shall I come and appear before the face of God?" (Ps. 41:1, 2), and another, "O God, my God, I rise early to be with You; my soul thirsts for You. How often my flesh thirsts for You in a dessolate, impassable, and waterless land. So in the holy place I appear before You, to see Your power and Your glory." (Ps. 62:1-3)

Since these things are so, my brethren, let us mortify our members which are on the earth, and be nourished with living Bread, by faith and love to God, knowing that without faith it is impossible to be partakers of such Bread as this. For our Savior, when He called all people to Himself, and said, "If any man thirsts, let him come to Me and drink" (Jn. 7:37), He immediately spoke of the faith without which a man cannot receive such Food, for "He who believes in Me, as the Scripture has said, out of his heart will flow rivers of living water." (Jn. 7:38) To this end He continually nourished His believing disciples with His words, and gave them life by the nearness of His divinity.

But He did not even reply to the Canaanite woman because she was not yet a believer, although she stood greatly in need of food from Him. He did not do this out of contempt—for the Lord is loving to all people and good, and on that account He went into the coasts of Tyre and Sidon. But He did this because of her unbelief and because she was of those who had not the word of faith. He did it righteously, my brethren, for there would have been nothing gained by her offering her supplication before believing, but by her faith she would support her petition. "For He who comes to God must believe that He is, and that He is a rewarder of those who diligently seek Him," and that "without faith it is impossible to please Him." (Heb. 11:6), this Paul teaches. That she was up till now an unbeliever, one of the profane, He shows by saying, "It is not good to take the children's bread and throw it to the little dogs." (Matt. 15:26) She then, being convinced by the power of the Word, and having changed her ways, also gained faith. For the Lord no longer spoke to her as a dog, but conversed with her as a human being, saying, "O woman, great is your faith!" (Matt. 15:28) As therefore she believed, He granted her the fruit of faith, and said, "'Let it be to you as you desire.' And her daughter was healed from that very hour".

For the righteous man, being nurtured in faith and knowledge, and the observance of divine precepts, has his soul always in health. Therefore it is commanded to "receive one who is weak in the faith" and to nourish him, even if he is not yet able to eat bread, but herbs, for "he who is weak eats only vegetables." (cf. Rom. 14:1, 2)

Even the Corinthians were not able to partake of such bread, being still babes, and like babes they drank milk (cf. 1 Cor. 3:1). "For everyone who partakes only of milk is unskilled in the word of righteousness" according to the words of St. Paul (Heb. 5:13). The Apostle Paul exhorts his beloved son Timothy, in his first Epistle, to be "nourished in the words of faith and of the good doctrine which you have carefully followed." (1 Tim. 4:6) And in the second, "Hold fast the pattern of sound words which you have heard from me, in faith and love which are in Christ Jesus." (2 Tim. 1:13)

And not only here, my brethren, is this Bread the food of the righteous, neither are the saints on earth alone nourished by such Bread and such Blood, but we also eat them in heaven, for the Lord is the Food even of the exalted spirits, and the angels, and He is the joy of all the heavenly host. And to all He is everything, and He has pity on all according to His loving-kindness.

Already has the Lord given us the food of angels (cf. Ps. 77:25), and He promises to those who continue with Him in His trials, saying: "And I bestow upon you a kingdom, just as My Father bestowed one upon Me, that you may eat and drink at My table in My kingdom, and sit on thrones judging the twelve tribes of Israel." (Lk. 22:29, 30)

O what a banquet is this, my brethren, and how great is the harmony and gladness of those who eat at this heavenly table! For they delight themselves not with that food which is cast out, but with that which produces life everlasting. Who then shall be deemed worthy of that assembly? Who is so blessed as to be called, and accounted worthy of that divine feast? Truly, "blessed is he who shall eat bread in the Kingdom of God!" (Lk. 14:15).

"The Creed"

St. Athanasius the Apostolic[83]

We believe, conformably to the evangelical and Apostolic Tradition, in One God, the Father Almighty, the Framer, and Maker, and Provider of the Universe, from whom are all things.

And in one Lord Jesus Christ, His Son, Only-Begotten God (Jn. 1:18), by Whom are all things, Who was begotten before all ages from the Father, God from God, whole from whole, sole from sole, perfect from perfect, King from King, Lord from Lord, Living Word, Living Wisdom, true Light, Way, Truth, Resurrection, Shepherd, Door, both unalterable and unchangeable. Exact Image of the Godhead, Essence, Will, Power and Glory of the Father; the First-born of every creature, Who was in the beginning with God, God the Word, as it is written in the Gospel, "and the Word was God." (Jn. 1:1) By Whom all things were made, and in whom all things consist, Who in the last days descended from above, and was born of a Virgin according to the Scriptures, and was made Man, Mediator between God and man, and Apostle of our Faith, and Prince of Life, as He says, "I came down from heaven, not to do My own will, but the will of Him Who sent Me." (Jn. 6:38) Who suffered for us and rose again on the third day, and ascended into heaven, and sat down on the right hand of the Father, and is coming again with glory and power, to judge the living and dead.

And in the Holy Spirit, who is given to those who believe for comfort, and sanctification, and initiation, as also our Lord Jesus Christ commanded His disciples, saying, "Go therefore and make disciples of all the nations, baptizing them in the Name of the Father and of the Son and of the Holy Spirit" (Matt. 28:19)—namely of a Father Who is truly Father, and a Son Who is truly Son, and of the Holy Spirit Who is truly Holy Spirit, the names not being given without meaning or effect, but denoting accurately the peculiar subsistence, rank, and glory of each that is named, so that They are three in subsistence, and in agreement one.

Holding then this faith, and holding it in the presence of God and Christ, from beginning to end, we anathematize every heretical deviation.

---

[83] St. Athanasius the Apostolic, "History of Arian Opinions," *De Sententia Dionysii*, NPNF s. 2, v. 4, pp. 1114-1115.

And if anyone teaches, beside the sound and right faith of the Scriptures, that time, or season, or age, either is or has been before the generation of the Son, he is anathema. Or if anyone says, that the Son is a creature as one of the creatures, or an offspring as one of the offspring, or a work as one of the works, and not the aforesaid articles one after another, as the divine Scriptures have delivered, or if he teaches or preaches beside what we received, he is anathema. For all that has been delivered in the divine Scriptures, whether by prophets or apostles, do we truly and reverentially both believe and follow.

"And it Happened One Day"

St. Shenoute of Atripe[84]

These words (of mine) vex the blasphemer who says, "How are bread and wine the Body and Blood of the Lord?" There are some among us who have said this, as their heart is stricken by the words of Origen. But I myself give answer to their foolishness, "Is the One Who made earth into a human being not able to cause bread and wine to become Body and Blood?" Or, when He says, "This is My Body; this is My Blood" (cf. Matt. 26:26, 27), for your part who are you? Who, among those who read the Scriptures well, does not know that the human being whom God created was himself adorned with all his bodily members, but he did not experience any movement at all? However, when the Lord God Almighty breathed into his face a breath of life, he (the human being) became a living being (cf. Gen. 2:7) and he moved all of himself, he spoke, he walked, he stretched his hands to (do) their work, and he blessed with his tongue the One Who fashioned him. In this way also, the bread and the wine, while they lie on the holy table of the Lord and while they rest on it, they are called bread and wine, but when that fearful Eucharistic Blessing is recited over them, and when the Lord sends on them His Holy Spirit from heaven, from this moment on it is no longer bread or wine, but the Body and Blood of the Lord. All of these things of God are matters of faith. If you have faith, then you have the fullness of the Sacrament; if you

---

84 St. Shenoute, "And It Happened One Day" (c. 455) ed. L.T. Lefort, "Catéchèse christologique de Chenoute," *Zeitschrift für ägyptische Sprache und Altertumskunde* 80 (1955), 40-5. trans. Stephen Davis, *Coptic Christology in Practice* (New York: Oxford university Press, 2008), 286-8. Used with permission.

do not have faith, then you do not have hope in the Sacrament and in the Lord of the Sacrament.

Again, we have written many words on account of the Sacrament but it is (useful) that we say a little bit more as well. For the beginning (of these words) is sure, and their end is a testimony first and foremost for those who do not believe. As for us, we believe that it is His Body and His Blood, and we will not doubt that it is the true Bread Which came down from heaven. Bread, along with water, is life for human bodies, but the Body and Blood of the Lord are spiritual life....because His body is true food and His Blood true drink.

Fourth Sunday

ZACCHAEUS

Meditations on the Fourth Sunday of the Blessed Month of Amshir

GOSPEL READING OF THE FOURTH SUNDAY[85]

LUKE 19:1-10

Then Jesus entered and passed through Jericho. Now behold, there was a man named Zacchaeus who was a chief tax collector, and he was rich. And he should see who Jesus was, but could not because of the crowd, for he was of short stature. So he ran ahead and climbed up into a sycamore tree to see Him, for He was going to pass that way. And when Jesus came to the place, He looked up and saw him, and said to him, "Zacchaeus, make haste and come down, for today I must stay at your house." So he made haste and came down, and received Him joyfully. But when they saw it, they all complained, saying, "He has gone to be a guest with a man who is a sinner." Then Zacchaeus stood and said to the Lord, "Look, Lord, I give half of my goods to the poor; and if I have taken anything from anyone by false accusation, I restore fourfold." And Jesus said to him, "Today salvation has come to this house, because he also is a son of Abraham; for the Son of Man has come to seek and to save that which was lost."

[85] See also Third Sunday of Tute in Volume I*a* of this series.

"How to Endure Wrongs from Others Without Wronging Others"

St. John Chrysostom[86]

Always give thanks; for this is a mark of a philosophic soul. Have you suffered any evil? If you wish, it is no evil. Give thanks to God, and the evil is changed into good. Say as Job said, "Blessed be the name of the Lord forever." (Job 1:21)

Tell me, what great thing have you suffered? Has disease befallen you? Yet it is nothing strange. For our body is mortal, and liable to suffer. Has a want of possessions overtaken you? But these also are things to be acquired, and again to be lost, and that remain here. But is it plots and false accusations of enemies? But it is not we who are injured by these, but they who are the authors of them. "For the soul," He says, "who sins, he shall die." (Ezek. 18:4) And he who suffers the evil has not sinned, but he who has done the evil.

On him therefore who is dead you should not take revenge, but pray for him that you may deliver him from death. Do you not see how the bee dies upon stinging someone? By that animal God instructs us not to grieve our neighbors. For we ourselves receive death first. For by striking them perhaps we have pained them for a little time, but we ourselves will not live any longer, even as that animal will not. And yet the Scripture commends the bee, saying that it is a worker, whose work kings and private men make use of for their health (cf. Wis. Sol. 11:3). But this virtue does not preserve it from dying, but it must perish. And if its other excellence does not deliver it when it does injury, much less will it us.

For indeed it is the part of the fiercest beasts, when no one has injured you, to begin the injury, or rather not even of beasts. For they, if you permit them to feed in the wilderness, and do not reduce them to necessity by force, they will never harm you, nor come near you, nor bite you, but will go their own way.

But you being a rational man, honored with so much rule and honor and glory, do not even imitate the beasts in your conduct to your fellow creature, but you injure your brother, and devour him. And how you will

---

[86] St. John Chrysostom, *Homily 10 on 1 Thessalonians*, NPNF, s. 1, v. 13.

be able to excuse yourself? Do you not hear Paul saying, "Why do you not rather accept wrong? Why do you not rather let yourselves be cheated? No, you yourselves do wrong and cheat, and you do these things to your brethren!" (1 Cor. 6: 7, 8). Do you see that suffering wrong consists in doing wrong, but that to suffer wrongfully is to receive a benefit?

Tell me, if any one were to revile his rulers, or if he were to insult those in power, whom does he injure, himself or them? Clearly himself. So then the one who insults a ruler insults not him, but himself—and the one who insults a Christian does he not through him insult Christ? By no means, you say. What do you say? He who casts a stone at the images of the king or the Emperor, at whom does he cast a stone? Is it not at himself? If he who casts a stone at the image of an earthly king, cast a stone at himself, does not the one who insults the image of God (for man is the image of God) injure himself?

How long shall we love riches? For I will not cease exclaiming against riches, for they are the cause of everything. How long do we not get our fill of this insatiable desire? What is the good of gold? I am astonished at the thing! There is some enchantment in the business, that gold and silver should be so highly valued among us. For our own souls indeed we have no regard, but those lifeless images engross much attention.

How is it that this disease has invaded the world? Who shall be able to cause its destruction? What reason can cut off this evil beast, and destroy it with utter destruction? The desire is deeply sown in the minds of men, even of those who seem to be religious. Let us be put to shame by the commands of the Gospel. Words only lie there in Scripture, they are nowhere shown by works.

And what is the deceptive plea of the many? "I have children," one says, "and I am afraid lest I myself be reduced to the extremity of hunger and want, lest I should stand in need of others. I am ashamed to beg." For that reason, therefore, do you cause others to beg? "I cannot," you say, "endure hunger." For that reason do you expose others to hunger? Do you know what a dreadful thing it is to beg, how dreadful it is to perish by hunger? Spare also your brethren! Are you ashamed, tell me, to be hungry, and are you not ashamed to rob? Are you afraid to perish by hunger, and not afraid to destroy others? And yet to be hungry is neither a disgrace nor a crime, but to cast others into such a state brings not only disgrace, but extreme punishment.

All these are pretenses, words, and trifles. Those who indeed have no children, nor will have any, but who yet toil and harass themselves and are busy in acquiring wealth, as much as if they had innumerable children to leave it to, testify to the fact that it is not on account of your children that you act like this. It is not the care for one's children that makes a person covetous, but a disease of the soul. On this account many, even of those who have no children, are mad about riches; and others living with a great number of children even despise what they have. They will accuse you in that Day. For if the necessities of children compelled people to accumulate riches, they also must necessarily have the same longing, the same lust. And if they have not, it is not from the number of children that we are thus mad, but from the love of money.

"And who are they," you say, "who having children, yet despise riches?" Many, and in many places. And if you will allow me, I will speak also of instances among the ancients. Did not Jacob have twelve children? Did he not lead the life of a hireling? Was he not wronged by his kinsman? Did he not often disappoint him? Did his number of children ever compel him to seek any dishonest counsel? What about Abraham? With Isaac, did he not also have many other children? What then? Did he not possess all he had for the benefit of strangers? Do you see, how he not only did not do wrong, but even gave up his possessions, not only doing good, but choosing to be wronged by his nephew?

For to endure being robbed for the sake of God is a much greater thing than to do good. Why? Because the former is the fruit of the soul and of free choice, and for this reason it is also easily performed, but the latter is injurious treatment and violence. And a man will more easily throw away ten thousand talents voluntarily, and will not think that he has suffered any harm, than he will bear meekly being robbed of three pence against his will. So that this rather is philosophy of soul. And this, we see, happened in the case of Abraham. "For Lot," it is said, "lifted his eyes and saw all the plain of Jordan, that it was well watered everywhere, like the garden of God... and he chose (it)." (Gen. 13:10, 11) And Abraham said nothing against it. Do you see that he not only did not wrong him, but he was even wronged by him?

Why, O man, do you accuse your own children? God did not give us children for this end, that we should seize the possessions of others. Take care, lest in saying this you provoke God. For if you say that your children are the causes of your grasping and your avarice, I fear lest you be deprived of them, as injuring and ensnaring you. God has given you children that they may support your old age and that they may learn virtue from you.

For God on this account has willed that mankind should thus be held together, providing for two most important objects: on the one hand, appointing fathers to be teachers, and on the other, implanting great love. For if everyone were merely to come into being, no one would have any relation towards any other. For if even now, when there are the relations of fathers, children, and grandchildren, many do not regard many, much more would it then be the case. On this account God has given you children. Do not therefore accuse the children.

But if those who have children have no excuse, what can they say for themselves, who having no children wear themselves out about the acquisition of riches? They have a saying for themselves, which is destitute of all excuse. And what is this? That, instead of children we may have our riches as a memorial. This is truly ridiculous. "Instead of children," one says, "my house becomes the immortal memorial of my glory." Not of your glory, O man, will it be the memorial, but of your covetousness.

Do you not see how many now as they pass the magnificent houses say one to another, "What frauds, what robberies such a one committed, that he might build this house, and now he is become dust and ashes, and his house has passed into the inheritance of others!" It is not of your glory then that you leave a memorial, but of your covetousness. And your body indeed is concealed in the earth, but do not permit the memorial of your covetousness to be concealed, as it might have been by the length of time, but cause it to be turned up and unearthed through your house. For as long as this stands, bearing your name, and called such a one's, certainly the mouths of all too must be opened against you. Do you see that it is better to have nothing than to sustain such an accusation?

And these things are indeed here. But what shall we do there? Tell me, having so much at our disposal here, if we have imparted to no one of our possessions, or at least very little, how shall we put off our dishonest gains? For he who wishes to put off covetous gain, does not give a little out of a great deal, but many times more than he has robbed, and he ceases from robbing.

Hear what Zacchaeus says, "And if I have taken anything from anyone by false accusation, I restore fourfold." (Lk. 19:8) But you, taking wrongfully ten thousand talents, if you give a few drachmas, think you have restored the whole, and are affected as if you had given more. And even this grudgingly. Why? Because you should have both restored these, and to have added other out of your own private possessions. For as the thief is not excused when he gives back only what he has stolen, but often he has added even his life; and often he compounds upon restoring many times as much, so also should the covetous man. For the covetous man also is a thief and a robber, far worse than the other, by how much he is also more tyrannical.

He, indeed, by being concealed, and by making his attack in the night, cuts off much of the audacity of the attempt, as if he were ashamed and feared to sin. But the other having no sense of shame, with open face in the middle of the marketplace steals the property of all, being at once a thief and a tyrant. He does not break through walls, nor extinguishes the lamp, nor opens a chest, nor tears off seals. But what? He does things more insolent than these, in the sight of those who are injured by carrying things out by the door, opening everything with confidence, and compelling them to expose all their possessions themselves. Such is the excess of his violence.

This man is more wicked than those, in that he is more shameless and tyrannical. For he that has suffered by fraud is indeed grieved, but he has no small consolation, that he who injured him was afraid of him. But he who together with the injury he suffers is also despised, will not be able to endure the violence. For the ridicule is greater. Tell me, if one committed adultery with a woman in secret, and another committed it in the sight of her husband, who grieved him the most, and was most likely to wound him. The latter, for he indeed, together with the wrong he has done, treated him also with contempt. But the former, if he did nothing else, showed at least that he feared him whom he injured. So also in the case of money. He who takes it secretly, does him honor in this respect, that he does it secretly; but he who robs publicly and openly, together with the loss adds also the shame.

Let us therefore, both poor and rich, cease from taking the property of others. For my present discourse is not only to the rich, but to the poor also. For they too rob those who are poorer than themselves. And artisans who are better off, and more powerful, outsell the poorer and more distressed, tradesmen outsell tradesmen, and so all who are engaged in the marketplace. So that I wish from every side to take away injustice. For the injury consists not in the measure of the things plundered and stolen, but in the purpose of him who steals. And that these are more thieves and defrauders, who do not despise little gains, I know and remember that I have before told you, if you also remember it. But let us not be over exact. Let them be equally bad with the rich. Let us instruct our mind not to covet greater things, not to aim at more than we have. And in heavenly things let our desire of more never be satiated, but let each be ever coveting more. But on earth let everyone be for what is needful and sufficient, and seek nothing more, that so he may be able to obtain the real goods, by the grace and loving kindness of our Lord Jesus Christ, with whom to the Father, together with the Holy Spirit, be glory, strength, honor, now and always, and world without end. Amen.

Ⲇⲟⲝⲁⲥⲓ ⲟ̀Ⲑⲉⲟⲥ ⲏ̀ⲙⲱⲛ

APPENDIX OF SOURCES AND CHURCH FATHERS

St. Ambrose of Milan (340-397AD)

He was born in Trier, Arles or Lyons, from a Roman Christian family. His father, Ambrosius, was a prefect of Gallia Narbonensis (which included France, Britain and Spain). He was the youngest of three children: his sister, Marcellina became a nun and his brother, Satyrus, became a prefect. With his classical and legal education he was assigned to a government post in Milan around 370. In 373-374 he was baptized and ordained as bishop by popular demand after a child cried out, "Bishop Ambrose," and the crowd responded, apparently against Ambrose's will. St. Ambrose greatly influenced St. Augustine, guided him back to the true faith, and baptized him. His major work on the New Testament was a commentary on the Gospel according to Luke. He also wrote treatises such as *To the New Emperor Gratian,* and *On the Holy Spirit* (381), which is taken largely from St. Basil the Great's treatise on the same subject. He mastered the Greek language and literature. Upon his departure Paulinus wrote his biography.

St. Athanasius the Apostolic (ca. 295-373 AD)

This great saint is called "Apostolic" by the Coptic Orthodox Church because he is considered a successor to the Apostles due to his erudite theological and biblical teaching. We know little about his childhood, except for an incident in which he was baptizing children by the sea and was discovered by Pope Alexander, who later began to teach the young Athanasius. He spent three years in the desert under the guidance of St.

Antony the Great along with St. Serapion. He spent six years as a reader in Alexandria, was later ordained as a deacon by Pope Alexander, and helped at the Council of Nicaea in 325. According to the Coptic Encomium, he was 33 when he was ordained as pope and patriarch in 328. As the twentieth pope of Alexandria, he fought diligently against Arius and his teachings. He was exiled five times and spent 16 of his 46 years as pope in exile. Among his writings are *On the Incarnation*, the *Orations against the Arians, The Life of Antony, Against Apollinarius,* and various epistles to monks and bishops. We commemorate his departure on 7 Bashans, and the miracle of his return to Alexandria on 30 Tout.

St. Augustine of Hippo (354-430AD)

He was a prolific father of the Church born in Tagasta, North Africa to Patritius, his pagan father and Roman official, and St. Monica, his faithful Christian mother. At the age of 16, he went to Carthage to study law, literature, and philosophy. He became a teacher of rhetoric in Tagaste, Carthage, and Rome, taught in Rome and Milan, and lived a sinful life. His famous prayer in resisting God, was "Give me chastity and continence, but not yet." Due to the prayers of his mother, the intellect and competence of St. Ambrose of Milan, St. Athanasius' amazing biography of St. Antony, and the impact of Romans 13:13, he was finally baptized at the age of 33 (in 387). In the same year, St. Monica departed. He returned to Italy, established a monastery there, was ordained a priest, and later a bishop of Hippo. He would have attended the Council of Nicaea, but he departed when Barbarians were attacking his diocese in Hippo. His extant writings include the *Confessions, The City of God,* his Commentaries on the Old and New Testaments, *On the Trinity, On Rebuke and Grace, Against the Manicheans, On Christian Doctrine,* and *The Predestination of the Saints,* his last major work. Despite many of his wonderful writings, prayers, and contemplations, he is also attributed with being the source of many problematic teachings such as the *Filioque,* the doctrine of original sin and grace, predestination, purgatory, and other such beliefs. Many claim this was due to his lack of Greek, and thus his lack of knowledge of the Eastern fathers.

St. Clement of Alexandria (ca. 150-211 AD)

Clement, officially called Titus Flavius Clemens, is praised by some as the first systematic teacher of Christian doctrine. He was the famous teacher at the catechetical school in Alexandria, where he became renowned for his Christian theology, strongly influenced by Greek philosophy. There, he was succeeded by the great scholar, Origen on whom he had a great influence. Clement's best-known work is a set of three treatises entitled *Protrepticus,* an "Exhortation" to the Greeks contrasting pagan religions with the Gospel of Christ; *Paedagogus,* which focused on Christ as the true "Instructor" of Christial life and moral living; and *Stromata,* the "Patchwork" of many theological subjects. During the persecutions at Alexandria in 202 Clement felt obliged to withdraw from the School, and remains for some time in Caesarea with Alexander, his friend and former student.

St. Cyril of Alexandria (ca. 380-444AD)

Also known as "The Pillar of Faith" in the Coptic tradition, this father is the twenty-fourth Patriarch of the See of St. Mark. St. Cyril was the son of the sister of Pope Theophilus (23rd patriarch), who trained him in Theology and Philosophy at the School of Alexandria, then sent him to the monastery of St. Macarius in the wilderness. There he studied the Church books and sayings of the fathers for five years under a righteous monk named Sarabamon. Later he was sent to the honorable bishop Abba Serapion, and he increased in wisdom and knowledge. After St. Cyril returned to Alexandria, Pope Theophilus ordained him a deacon, appointed him a preacher in the cathedral, and made St. Cyril his scribe. When his uncle departed in 412, St. Cyril was enthroned as 24th patriarch of Alexandria on 20 Babeh, 128 AM (October 17, 412). He is famous for his exceptional biblical exegesis and Christological formulas, which he used to defend the faith while presiding over the Council of Ephesus against Nestorius. He remained a pope for 31 years. He is one of the greatest fathers of the ancient Church, whose life and teachings have been decisive in shaping the Orthodox tradition. We commemorate his departure on 3 Abib.

St. Cyril of Jerusalem (d. 386 AD)

Not much is known about his early life, but he was ordained a priest at Jerusalem before 343. Around 348, he was appointed bishop of Jerusalem, despite the attacks from leaders of other sects, and being exiled three separate times. He is most famous for his Catechetical Lectures, which were written for those desiring to join the Christian faith (although a few scholars have attributed this to his successor, John of Jerusalem). His messages focused on the importance of the death and Resurrection of our Lord Jesus Christ. He was exiled by Acacius after selling church vessels to support the needy during a famine in Palestine, but returned to his see in 356 AD. We commemorate his departure on 22 Baramhat.

St. Ephrem the Syrian (ca. 306-379AD)

One of the early fathers of the Church from Syria. He was baptized by St. James bishop of Nissibis. He was among those who attended the Council of Nicaea. He is famous for his poetical hymns, especially those relating to the Annunciation, Nativity, and Holy Theotokos. He wrote a famous commentary on Tatian's Diatessaron, the Book of Daniel, and the Pauline Epistles. Often he quoted the Peshitta translation, which is among the earliest manuscripts of the Old Testament today. His writings well represent the Syrian patristic tradition. He is also known for his famous visit to St. Pishoy in Egypt, in what is now El-Sourian (The Syrian) Monastery. He also witnessed the departure of St. Basil the Great. We commemorate his departure on 15 Abib.

Eusebius of Caesarea (ca. 263-339)

A student under Pamphlilius (ca. 240-309), Eusebius was a Christian scholar and priest in the church of Caesarea who was influenced by the Origenist tradition. His most famous work was the *History of the Church*, which preserves many quotations of the fathers that have been otherwise lost. Many scholars note that since Caesarea lay half way between Antioch and Alexandria, Eusebius' approach to scripture lies in between these two "schools" of exegesis.

St. Gregory of Nazianzus, "the Theologian" (ca. 330-389AD)

This father was born at the country estate belonging to his father called Arianzus, near Nazianzus—a place quite unknown to early writers. His parents were rich Christian landowners and his father was bishop of Nazianzus. Gregory studied in the major centers of learning before being baptized in 358. His father forced him to accept ordination as a priest in 361. In 371, his friend Basil unsuccessfully attempted to persuade him to accept being ordained as a bishop. However, eight years later, St. Gregory finally agreed to accept the responsibility of being the bishop of Constantinople in 379, where he served for two years before resigning. His poetry and theological writings earned him the title of "the Theologian." He is included among the Cappadocian Fathers, with St. Basil the Great and St. Gregory of Nyssa. We commemorate his departure on 21 Tubah.

St. Gregory of Nyssa (ca. 330-ca. 396 AD)

He was born in Cappadocia, in the year 330 AD and was ordained bishop by his brother, St. Basil the Great, in the year 372 AD He was exiled during the reign of Emperor Valens, then returned in the year 378 AD, by the order of Emperor Theodosius the Great. He wrote many church books and departed in peace around the year 396 AD.

St. Gregory the Wonder-Worker, "Thaumaturgus" (210-260)

He was the enthusiastic disciple of Origen, and the apostle of Pontus; was born in Neo-Caesarea in Pontus, and destined for some kind of civil career, but happened to come to Caesarea in Palestine, where Origen had settled down shortly before (in 231), and remained there, studying under his tutorship, for eight years. Before he returned home he wrote his panegyrics on his great teacher, and shortly after his arrival home he was consecrated bishop of his native city by Phaedimus of Amisus. He found seventeen Christians in Neo-Caesarea when he entered his office: there were only seventeen Pagans left when he died (about 270). Testimonies of the energy he developed and the influence he exercised are not only the legends which cluster around his name, but also the writings he left —his so-called canonical letter on discipline—one of the most interesting documents of ancient Christianity, the confession he used for the catechumens of his church, and his paraphrase of Ecclesiastes.

St. Hilary of Poitiers (ca. 315-367)

He was born in Gaul (France) and ordained the bishop of Poitiers in 350. He is known as the "Athanasius of the West" because of his success in converting the neo-Arians to the Nicene point of view, and his exile to the east by an Arian council. His exegetical writings include commentary on the Gospel according to Gospel according to St. Matthew, the Psalms, Hosea, and Job. He is most famous for his dogmatic writings against the Arians, including *On Mysteries, On the Trinity, On the Synods,* and his three books against Constantinus in defense of St. Athanasius. He returned to Gaul in 360, and reestablished orthodoxy there.

St. Ignatius of Antioch (d. 107 AD)

One of the most famous disciples of St. John the Beloved, St. Ignatius was consecrated bishop over the city of Antioch. He is famous for his seven pastoral letters—the Ephesians, Magnesians, Romans, Philadelphians, Smyrna, Tralles, and Polycarp—that were written between 100-107 AD. Although he does not quote from the Old testament, he had a strong focus on eschatology as well as church unity. The theology of his writings foreshadows the later definitions of the Ecumenical Councils.

St. Irenaeus of Lyons (d. 202AD)

This saint was born at Smyrna in Asia Minor, where he studied under St. Polycarp, the disciple of St. John the Beloved. After living at Rome for a time, he settled in Lyons in 177, where he was consecrated as bishop of a Greek-speaking community. He mastered the Greek and Latin languages, and served in France and Rome against the Gnostic movement. His most famous work, *Against the Heresies,* describes and refutes the teachings of the Gnostics, while explaining about the gospels, the sacraments, the apostolic tradition, and the hierarchy of the Church.

St. Jerome (350-420AD)

He was born as Sophronius Eusebius Hieronymous and soon showed immense potential as a scholar. He lived for a while in Jerusalem, then was summoned by Pope Damasus of Rome in 382 to revise the Latin translation of the Holy Scriptures, called the Vulgate. He completed his revision of the gospels in 383 or 384, but seems to have largely abandoned the work to devote his energies to the Hebrew Old Testament. He died in 419 or 420. Besides his translations (which include patristic works as well as the Vulgate), he left a number of letters and assorted commentaries plus biographies of "Famous Men." Interestingly, the text used by Jerome in his commentaries often differs from that in the Vulgate.

John Cassian (ca. 360 - 433)

A faithful writer honored in the East and West for his mystical writings. He is known both as one of the "Scythian monks" and as one of the "Desert Fathers." He was born around 360 possibly in the Eastern Roman Empire. At one time, it was widely believed that he was a Scythian by birth, but recent scholarship has called that tradition into doubt. Probably this came from the fact that he originated from the Roman province of Scythia Minor, where the "Scythian Monks" community existed. As a young adult, he and a friend traveled to Palestine, where they entered a hermitage near Bethlehem. After a while there, they journeyed to Egypt and visited a number of monastic foundations. He wrote much about this journey in his Institutes and Conferences, making him one of the earliest references to the prayer and life of the Egyptian monks. Later, John Cassian went to Constantinople, where he became a disciple and friend of St. John Chrysostom, the patriarch there. When St. John Chrysostom ran into theological trouble, John Cassian was sent to Rome to plead his cause before the Pope. It was possibly when he was in Rome that he accepted the invitation to found an Egyptian style monastery in southern Gaul, near Marseilles. He is one of the founders of Latin monasticism, and his writings profoundly influenced Benedict of Nursia (ca. 480-ca. 550 AD), whose rule ordered the regular reading of Cassian's works and is followed by Benedictine, Cistercian, and Trappist monks in the West.

St. John Chrysostom (ca. 347-407 AD)

St. John Chrysostom was born in Antioch between 347 and 349. His father was a soldier in Syria and his mother was a faithful Christian. After his father died when he was very young, he was raised by his mother, Anthusa. He was so gifted that she arranged for him to study Philosophy, Rhetoric, and Greek. He agreed with two of his classmates, Evagrius and Basil (most probably not Basil the Great), to seek the monastic life, but because of the tears of his mother he agreed to continue his education as an advocate (lawyer) instead. At the age of 18, he studied under Patriarch Meletius, who encouraged him to stay with him. At 21, he was baptized, and three years later, he was ordained a reader and composed Against the Jews and many pamphlets. After deceiving his friend, Basil, into ordination, John defended himself with the treatise *On the Priesthood.* Upon the death of his mother, he gave all his goods to the poor, chose one of the poorest monasteries, and meditated on the Scriptures and wrote three treatises on the monastic life. He was later ordained as a deacon, and wrote many more treatises. The Patriarch Flavian ordained him as priest. Some called him "the mouth of Christ," others "a second Paul," and others the "golden-mouthed (Chrysostom)." This last name was given to him by a woman during one of his sermons. He was ordained the bishop of Constantinople by force in 398. His sermons led the city through many crises, but his enemies eventually exiled him three times. He spent his last days of his earthly life in exile. We commemorate his departure on 17 Hatour.

John of Damascus (673-749)

He is considered on of the great fathers of the Eastern Orthodox church. He was born in Damascus to a wealthy family. For a time, he represented Christians in the court of the caliphs. A few years later, he became a monk, living in Jerusalem. His most famous work is *The Fountain of Knowledge* is a three section treatise against the heretical sects of the fifth and sixth centuries. Because he lived and wrote after the Council of Chalcedon, he is not officially recognized as a saint in the Coptic Orthodox Church. His writings contain several references from the Church Fathers. He wrote strongly against monothelitism (one will of Christ) Eutychian monophysitism (one nature of Christ), as well as Islam.

St. Justin Martyr (b. 100-110; d. 163-167AD)

He was born into a pagan family in Samaria between 100 and 110 AD. After practicing Stoic, Peripatetic, and Pythagorean philosophies, he finally converted to Christianity most probably in Ephesus. Due to his philosophical background, he is the first Christian thinker to seek to reconcile the claims of faith and reason. Among his many works, he is most famous for his Apology (ca. 155 AD), addressed to Emperor Antoninus Pius and his colleagues; as well as his *Dialogue with Trypho,* a discussion with a Jew named Trypho about the differences in the two faiths. These, among his other works, make him one of the most important of the apologists of the second century and one of the noblest personalities of early Christian literature. Clothed in the palladium, a cloak worn by Greek philosophers, he traveled about as an itinerant teacher. He arrived in Rome during the reign of Antoninus Pius (138-161 A.D) and founded a school there. One of his pupils was Tatian, destined later to become an apologist. St. Justin suffered martyrdom in Rome between 163 and 167 AD.

The Scholar Origen (185-254AD)

He was born into a Christian family: his father Leonides was a righteous scholar who was martyred during the persecution of Septimius Severus in 202 AD. At an early age, Origen dedicated his life to reading and scholarly endeavors. St. Jerome praised his love of reading and said that Origen read while eating, walking, resting, etc. When Pope Demetrius, the twelfth Patriarch of Alexandria, heard of his fame, he appointed him dean of the School of Alexandria. He increased its fame and thinking and became a teacher of many bishops and priests, as well as many men, women, young and old. He was famous for his allegorical interpretation, such as his famous interpretation of the Song of Songs. He was imprisoned and tortured for his Christian faith. He was courageous, ascetic and a man of fasting and prayer. He exaggerated in his asceticism by castrating himself (defending his action by saying that he was protecting his chastity). He was such a prolific writer that some of his admirers said, "There is no human mind that can absorb all what he wrote." St. Epiphanius (315-403 AD) stated that Origen had 6,000 manuscripts, including his famous *Hexapla,* a 28-year study comparing six manuscripts of the Old Testament and their translations. Pope Demetrius excommunicated Origen for theological mistakes, as well as being ordained in Palestine, outside of his diocese. He spent the rest of his time there, where he established a famous theological school. He is one of the most controversial as well as influential ancient writers.

The Scholar Tertullian (c.160-225AD)

He was a scholar born to a pagan family in Carthage, North Africa. His father was a Roman centurion. He received a good education in Literature and Rhetoric, practiced law in Rome, and visited Athens and Rome in his youth. He was converted to Christianity before 197 AD and returned to his native city as a Christian shortly before the turn of the third century. He wrote extensively against the various enemies of the Church. But, like many converts, the fixed life of the official church was not sufficient for him. He wanted a return to prophecy. After some years of trying and failing to restore the spiritual nature of the Church in the West, he became a Montanist (ca. 207). St. Jerome reported that this happened in his "middle age." According to St. Jerome, he became a priest, but there are other indications that he remained a layman. Shortly after 220, Tertullian seems to have tried to form an independent congregation before his death. He was the author of a long list of apologetic, theological, and ascetic works. No list of Tertullian's works is extant, but historians have identified at least 43 titles, of which all or part 31 survive. Some of these, however, were written after he left the Church. Among his apologetic writings he addressed a work *To the Heathen (Ad Nations,* two books), in which he protested against the laws condemning Christians without examining their behavior. Nevertheless, St. Cyprian called him "the master," and made it a policy to read from his works every day. Tertullian's text is rather unique, as he wrote in Latin but apparently used primarily Greek texts which he translated himself. One historian says, "He touched almost nothing which he did not exaggerate."

INDEX OF SUNDAY AND HOLY PASCHA GOSPEL READINGS

Index of Notations

Tute 2	*Tute Second Sunday Gospel Reading*
Great Lent 7	*Great Lent Seventh Sunday Gospel Reading*
Holy Pascha Mon. Eve, 1st H	*Eve of Holy Pascha Monday, First Hour Reading*
Great Fri. Eve., 3rd H-3	*Eve of Great Friday, Third Hour, Third Reading*

Matthew		Mark		Luke		John	
2:1-12	Nativity Feast	2:1-12	Babeh 1	1:1-25	Kiahk 1	1:18-34	Tubah 2
2:13-23	Tubah 1	3:22-35	Mesori 3	1:26-38	Kiahk 2	2:13-17	Holy Pascha Mon. 6th H
4:1-10	Great Lent 3	8:27-33	Holy Pascha Mon. Eve 9th H	1:39-56	Kiahk 3	3:22-36	Tubah 3
6:1-8	Great Lent 1	10:17-31	Hatour 4	1:57-80	Kiahk 4	4:1-42	Great Lent, 5; Holy Fifty 3
6:24-34	Great Lent 2	10:32-34	Holy Pascha Mon. Eve 6th H	2:1-20	Paramon of Nativity	5:1-18	Great Lent 6
12:22-28	Babeh 3	11:1-11	Palm Sunday	4:1-13	Bashans 4	5:19-29	Palm Sunday Funeral
12:22-37	Baona 3	11:11-19	Holy Pascha Mon. 3rd H	5:17-26	Baona 2	6:22-27	Amshir 1
13:1-9	Hatour 2	11:12-24	Holy Pascha Mon. 1st H	5:27-39	Mesori 2	6:5-14	Amshir 2
17:19-23	Holy Pascha Mon. Eve, 11th H	13:3-31	Mesori-4	5:1-11	Babeh 2	6:27-46	Amshir 3

Matthew		Mark		Luke		John	
18:1-9	Abib 2	13:32-14:2	Holy Pascha Wednesday Eve, 11th H	6:27-38	Amshir 5; Baona 4	6:35-45	Holy Fifty 2
20:20-28	Palm Sunday 11th H	14:3-11	Holy Pascha Thurs. Eve, 3rd H	7:11-17	Babeh 4	8:12-20	Holy Pascha Wednesday 6th H
21:1-16	Palm Sunday	14:12-16	Holy Pascha Thurs., 6th H	7:28-35	Tute 1	8:21-29	Holy Pascha Wednesday 1st H
21:10-17	Palm Sun, 9th H	14:26-31	Holy Pascha Good Fri. Eve, 3rd H-2	7:37-50	Tute 4	8:51-59	Holy Pascha Mon., 11th H
21:23-27	Holy Pascha Mon. 9th H	14:32-41	Holy Pascha Good Fri. Eve, 6th H-2	8:4-15	Hatour 1	9:1-38	Tubah 4
22:1-14	Holy Pascha Wednesday Eve 1st H	14:43-54	Holy Pascha Good Fri. Eve, 9th H-2	9:10-17	Abib 3	9:1-41	Great Lent 7
23:29-36	Holy Pascha Wednesday Eve 9th H	14:55-72	Holy Pascha Good Fri. Eve, 11th H-2	9:18-22	Holy Pascha Mon. Eve, 3rd H	10:17-21	Holy Pascha Thurs. Eve, 1st H
23:37-24:2	Holy Pascha Wednesday, 3rd H	15:1-5	Holy Pascha Good Fri., 1st H-2	10:1-20	Abib 1	10:29-38	Holy Pascha Thurs. Eve, 9th H
24:3-35	Holy Pascha Wednesday, 9th H	15:6-25	Holy Pascha Good Fri., 3rd H-2	Lk.10:21-28	Tute 2	11:1-44	Lazarus Saturday
24:3-25	Nasie (Mesori 5)	15:26-33	Holy Pascha Good Fri., 6th H-2	10:25-37	Bashans 3	11:1-45	Abib 4
24:36-51	Holy Pascha Wednesday Eve 3rd H	15:34-37	Holy Pascha Good Fri., 9th H-2	11:1-13	Baona 1	11:46-57	Holy Pascha Wednesday, 1st H
25:1-13	Holy Pascha Wednesday	15:38-41	Holy Pascha Good Fri.,	11:37-52	Holy Pascha Wednesday Eve, 9th H	11:55-57	H Wed. Eve, 11th H

Matthew		Mark		Luke		John	
	Eve 6th H		11th H-2				
26:3-16	Holy Pascha Wednesday, 9th H	15:42-16:1	Holy Pascha Good Fri., 12th H-2	13:23-30	Holy Pascha Wednesday Eve, 1st H	12:1-8	Holy Pascha Wednesday, 6th H
26:17-19	Holy Pascha Thurs., 3rd H, 9th H			13:31-35	Holy Pascha Wednesday Eve, 3rd H	12:12-19	Palm Sunday 4
26:20-29	Holy Pascha Thurs. Lit. Gospel			14:25-35	Hatour 3	12:20-36	Eve Holy Pascha Mon. 1st H
26:30-35	Holy Pascha Good Fri. Eve, 3rd H-1			15:11-32	Great Lent 4	12:27-36	Holy Pascha Wednesday, 11th H
26:36-46	Holy Pascha Good Fri. Eve, 6th H-1			19:1-10	Tute 3; Amshir 4	12:35-50	Holy Fifty 4
26:47-58	Holy Pascha Good Fri. Eve, 9th H-1			19:29-40	Palm Sunday	12:36-43	Holy Pascha Thurs. Eve, 6th H
26:59-75	Holy Pascha Good Fri. Eve, 11th H-1			20:9-19	Mesori 1	12:44-50	Holy Pascha Thurs. Eve, 11th H
27:1-14	Holy Pascha Good Fri., 1st H-1			21:34-38	Holy Pascha Wednesday Eve 6th H	13:21-30	Holy Pascha Thurs., 11th H
27:15-26	Holy Pascha Good Fri., 3rd H-1			22:1-6	Holy Pascha Wednesday, 3rd	13:33-17:26	Holy Pascha Good Fri. Eve, 1st H
27:27-45	Holy Pascha Good Fri., 6th H-1			22:7-13	Holy Pascha Thurs., 1st H	14:1-11	Holy Fifty 5
27:46-50	Holy Pascha Good Fri., 9th H-1			22:31-39	Holy Pascha Good Fri. Eve, 3rd H-3	15:26-16:15	Holy Fifty 7 (Pent.)

Matthew		Mark		Luke		John	
27:51-56	Holy Pascha Good Fri., 11th H-1			22:40-46	Holy Pascha Good Fri. Eve, 6th H-3	16:23-33	Holy Fifty 6
				22:47-55	Holy Pascha Good Fri. Eve, 9th H-3	18:1,2	Holy Pascha Good Fri. Eve, 3rd H-4
				22:56-65	Holy Pascha Good Fri. Eve, 11th H-3	18:3-9	Holy Pascha Good Fri. Eve, 6th H-4
				22:66-23:12	Holy Pascha Good Fri., 1st H-3	18:10-14	Holy Pascha Good Fri. Eve, 9th H-4
				23:13-25	Holy Pascha Good Fri., 3rd H-3	18:15-27	Holy Pascha Good Fri. Eve, 11th H-4
				23:26-44	Holy Pascha Good Fri., 6th H-3	18:28-40	Holy Pascha Good Fri., 1st H-4
				23:45-46	Holy Pascha Good Fri., 9th H-3	19:1-12	Holy Pascha Good Fri., 3rd H-4
				23:47-49	Holy Pascha Good Fri., 11th H-3	19:13-27	Holy Pascha Good Fri., 6th H-4
				23:50-56	Holy Pascha Good Fri., 12th H-3	19:28-30	Holy Pascha Good Fri., 9th H-4
				24:36-53	Ascension	19:31-37	Holy Pascha Good Fri., 11th H-4
						19:38-42	Holy Pascha Good Fri., 12th H-4
						20:19-31	Holy Fifty 1
						25:14-26:2	Holy Pascha Wednesday, 11th H

Made in the USA
Coppell, TX
18 October 2022